IMAGES
of America

CAMPTON

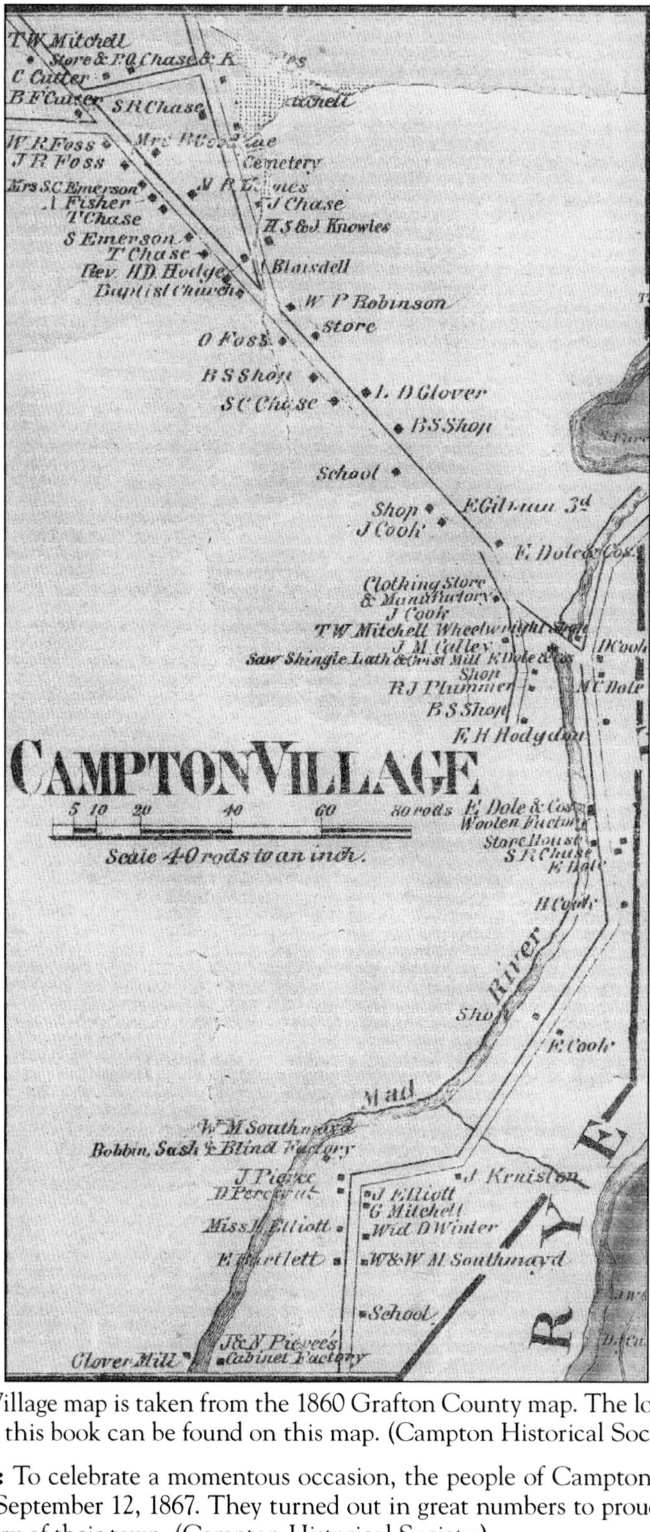

The Campton Village map is taken from the 1860 Grafton County map. The location of several of the images in this book can be found on this map. (Campton Historical Society.)

On the Cover: To celebrate a momentous occasion, the people of Campton gathered at the town house on September 12, 1867. They turned out in great numbers to proudly celebrate the 100th anniversary of their town. (Campton Historical Society.)

IMAGES
of America

CAMPTON

Campton Historical Society

ARCADIA
PUBLISHING

ISBN 978-1-4671-2593-2

Published by Arcadia Publishing
Charleston, South Carolina

Printed in the United States of America

Library of Congress Control Number: 2016957628

For all general information, please contact Arcadia Publishing:
Telephone 843-853-2070
Fax 843-853-0044
E-mail sales@arcadiapublishing.com
For customer service and orders:
Toll-Free 1-888-313-2665

Visit us on the Internet at www.arcadiapublishing.com

This pictorial history is dedicated to Robert Mardin who, as the historian and assistant curator of Campton Historical Society, quietly gets things done! Thank you, Bob, for your hard work, unfailing support, and dedication to this project.

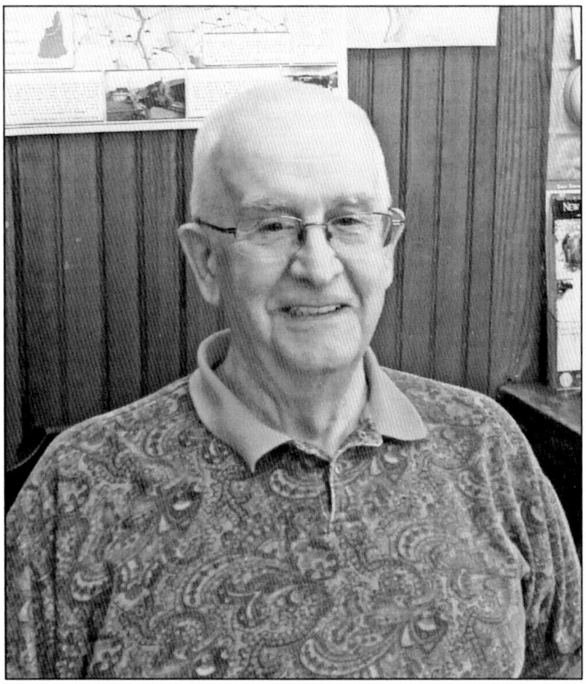

Contents

ACKNOWLEDGMENTS

The Campton Historical Society would like to thank the family of Marjorie McCoy Broad for sharing their mother's wonderfully researched books on Campton schools and on Campton hotels and guesthouses. The society would also like to thank Dwight Newcomb, great-grandson of F. Schuyler Mathews, for generously sharing family photographs and watercolors done by his great-grandfather. Appreciation also goes to Ann Morgan, from the Lancaster Historical Society, for her orientation to the publishing process, to the Campton Selectmen for their strong support, and to local historian Bob Pulsifer for filling in the blanks and setting us straight on many occasions. And finally, the society wishes to thank all those who selflessly gave of their time and talents to make this book a reality as well as those individuals who, over the years, donated countless photographs to the society, creating the archives that were invaluable in preparing this publication.

Unless otherwise noted, all images appear courtesy of the Campton Historical Society.

Introduction

Nestled among the forests and valleys of the Pemigewasset, Beebe, and Mad Rivers is the Grafton County town of Campton. The Pemigewasset, or Great River, runs through the town to meet the Winnepesaukee River in the town of Franklin, where they form the Merrimack River. The Pemi, as it is called today, has enriched the lives of the area's inhabitants as far back as the Abenakis. The town is said to have gotten its name from King George III's early surveyors who camped along the river. Over time, Camptown was shortened to Campton.

The Great River had many smaller streams and rivers flowing into it, making it a major source of waterpower for the early mills in town and a natural resource for lumbering and fishing. The game and fish were plentiful in the region, and this was of great importance to the early settlers. Salmon was especially abundant in the early days. Fishing continues to be enjoyed in the area, along with kayaking and canoeing. The Pemi divides the town into east and west, and before bridges were built in the 1800s, the sections of town were isolated from each other in the spring when the water was high.

Moose and deer were also common. A story is told about the hunting skills of Hobart Spencer, one of the town's earliest settlers. Reportedly, he was a man of great strength, and on one occasion he is said to have gone up to the foot of Mount Moosehillock (today known as Moosilauke) where moose were plentiful and brought home, upon his back, his own weight in moose meat.

The charter for the town of Campton was granted to Gen. Jabez Spencer, of East Haddam, Connecticut, in 1761. However, he died before all was settled, and the title became invalid. In 1767, the heirs of General Spencer and other interested parties obtained a new charter. The area was originally home to the Abenaki Indians; the first white settlers in town came between 1762 and 1773. These early settlers included General Spencer's sons, Joseph and Hobart Spencer; Issac and Winthrop Fox; Enoch Taylor; Abel Willey; Samuel Holmes; and John Southmayd. Most of the early inhabitants came from Connecticut by journeying to Worcester, then to Nashua, and up the Merrimack; from parts of Massachusetts near the mouth of the Merrimack River; and from southern New Hampshire communities, also along the Merrimack River.

The first settlers traveled on the Indian Trail that ran along the west side of the Pemigewasset. Parts of this trail later became the first road along the river and the first road to the White Mountains. In October 1769, Darius Willey was appointed to a committee charged with laying out the land, setting town boundaries, and planning the roads. He was one of the town's first highway surveyors, and according to town reports, he held this position for many years.

Campton sent 10 soldiers to the Revolutionary War, five of whom died in service to their new country. The town was well represented in the Civil War as well. Young men left their farms to fight to preserve the Union. Many of these young men never returned to Campton, having died on the battlefields, succumbed to disease, or moved West for what they saw as broader opportunities.

The need for a house of worship was felt early in the history of the town. The Campton Congregational Church was the first church, organized on June 1, 1774. Services were held in private homes until the town purchased the home of Joseph Pulsifer for a church and a town house. In 1802, a church was constructed at the top of Wishman's Hill. This church was later sold to the Town of Plymouth for $150. It was moved and served as a town hall for many years. In 1824, the present Campton Congregational Church was built on the west side of the Pemi and later moved across the river to its present location, on New Hampshire Route 175, near the current Campton Historical Society.

The Campton Baptist Church was organized in 1811, and the present brick building was constructed in 1826. The parsonage was built later, some distance from the road at the request of the minister, who did not want his congregation to hear his wife scolding him! In the early days, there were two other churches in town—the Freewill Baptist, on Ellsworth Hill, and Blair Chapel, on the west side of the Pemigewasset River near the Blair Covered Bridge.

The first school was held in the home of Col. Moses Baker (believed to be the current Colonel Spencer Inn). In 1780, school was taught by a young tutor named Mr. Rawson, who was hired to teach Colonel Baker's sons. Later, other children were invited to the school. In the 19th century as the population grew, school districts were developed throughout town and one-room schoolhouses were built to provide education for all. The Blair School was built on property given to the town in 1802 by Col. Moses Baker with the condition that the land be used only for a schoolhouse.

Campton has always valued literacy and education, so it is no surprise that a social library was established early in the town. It was started by individuals loaning books from their private libraries and minimally supplemented by town taxes. At times, this library boasted 300 volumes, including histories, biographies, travel books, and books on New England theology. It was not unheard of for young people to determine to read every volume in the library.

The 19th century brought the first tourists to Campton and the surrounding mountains. The early tourists came by stagecoach, but a major change was brought to the town with the advent of the railroad in 1850. At one time, Campton had four railroad stations serving neighborhoods throughout the town: Campton Village, Beebe River, Blair, and Rocky Falls (Livermore). The railroad made it much faster and easier for tourists to travel to Campton from cities to the south. The railroad also hastened the construction of larger hotels and guesthouses to lodge these summer tourists, eager to leave the city for a few weeks, or even months, of clean air and recreation. Tourism became an important business in Campton in the 19th century and has continued as such into the 21st century.

Life was not easy for our ancestors, but they were strong and resilient. They learned to adapt. They persevered because the land offered them new opportunities and a sense of ownership. These same characteristics are evident in our town today. Our way of life has changed dramatically; our old businesses are gone, but we continue to move forward, adapting to the changing times yet holding on to those values we hold dear.

All towns carry some of their past into the present. Local architecture, road names, churches, cemeteries, schools, even rivers and mountains, serve as testimony to the past. Campton is no different. We would like readers to see, through this pictorial narrative, that while many markers of the town's history have been lost, many more have withstood the test of time and remain not only as living reminders of Campton's rich past but also as integral parts of its present.

One

All About Town

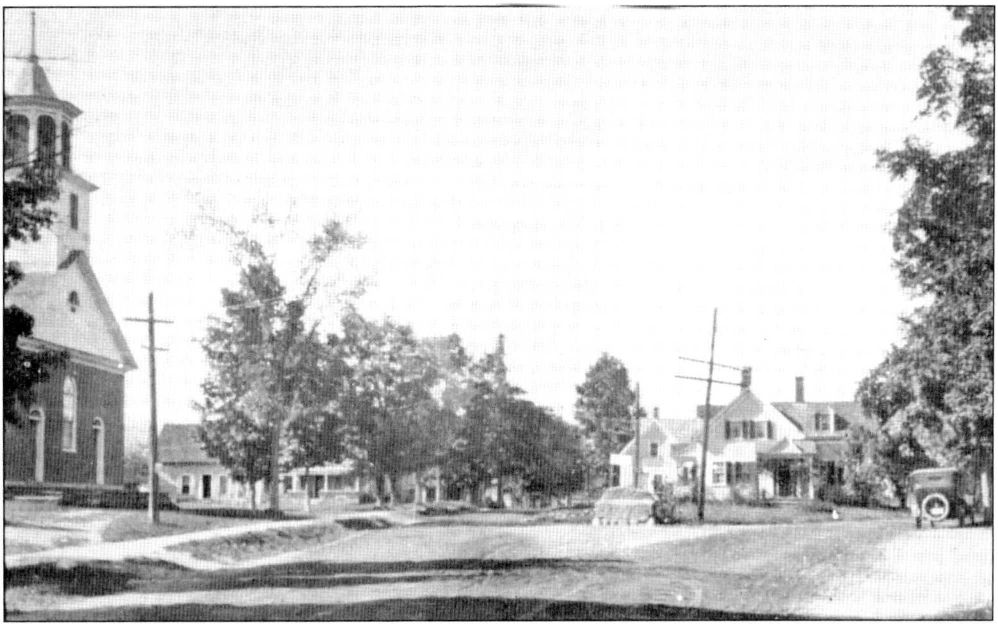

The house that was the Damon Tavern in the 1880s is in the fork where Mad River Road and Route 175 come together in the Upper Village. Notice the granite watering trough for animals at the intersection.

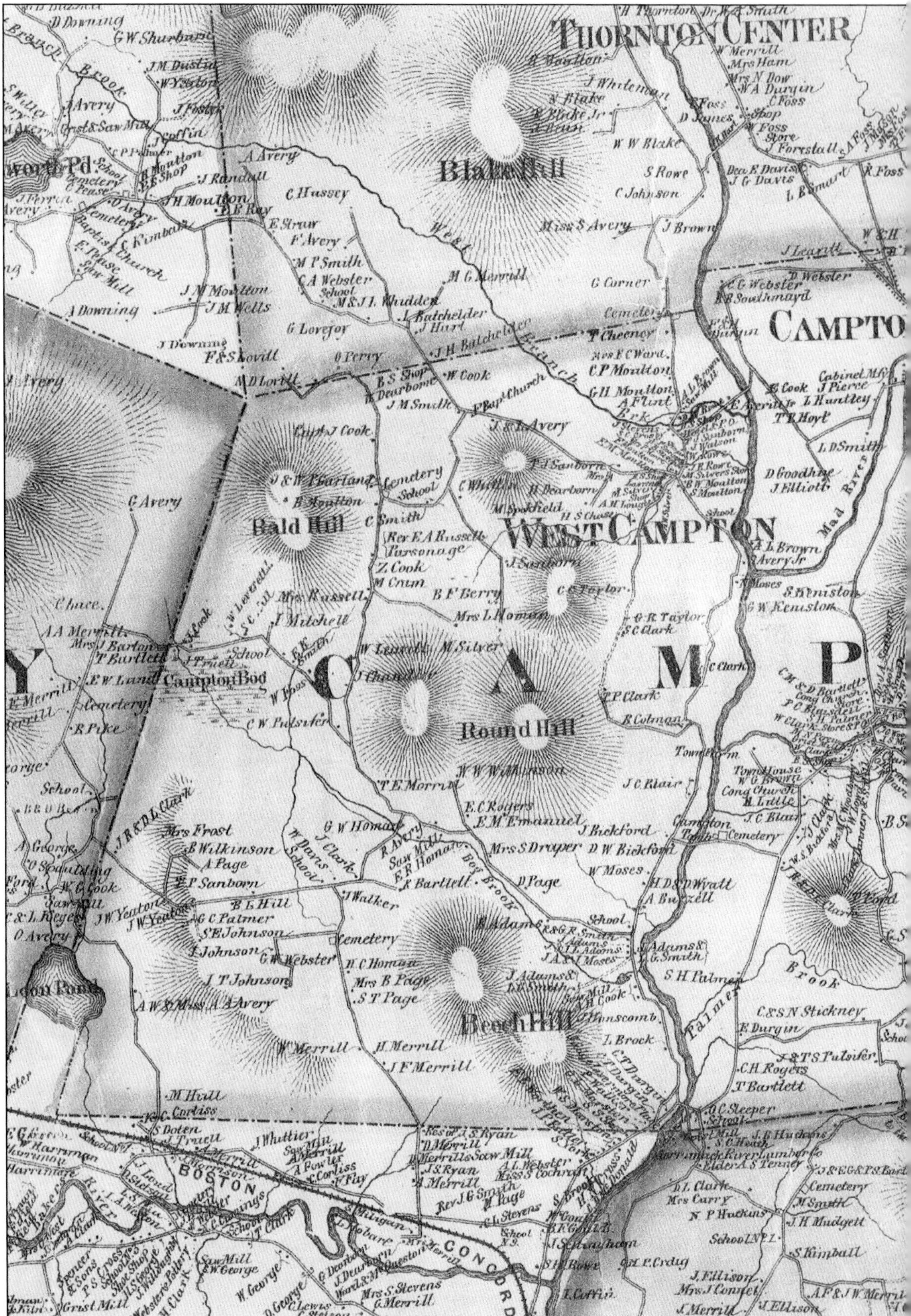
THORNTON CENTER
CAMPTO
WEST CAMPTON
C A M P
Blake Hill
Bald Hill
Round Hill
Beech Hill
Campton Bog
Campton Town
BOSTON
CONCORD
Mad River
Brook
Bog Brook
Palmer Brook
West Branch
D Downing
G W Shurburne
J M Dustin
J Avery
Grist & Saw Mill
J Foster
A Avery
J Randall
J H Moulton
C Hussey
E Straw
F Avery
M P Smith
C A Webster
School
M G Merrill
J M Moulton
J M Wells
A Downing
G Lovejoy
J Hart
L Batchelder
J H Batchelder
F & S Kovill
O Perry
W Cook
J M Smith
F Bapt Church
J & L Avery
Capt J Cook
J & W P Garland
Cemetery
C Smith
B Moulton
Rev E A Russell
Parsonage
Z Cook
M Crum
B F Berry
Mrs L Homans
Mrs Russell
J Mitchell
C Avery
A A Merrill
Mrs J Barton
T Bartlett
E W Land
R Pike
C W Pulsifer
W Leavitt
M Silver
J Chandler
T E Morrill
W W Wilkinson
E C Rogers
E M Emanuel
J Bickford
D W Bickford
Mrs S Draper
W Moses
H D & S D Wyatt
A Buzzell
J C Blair
Town Farm
Town House
Cong Church
Mrs Frost
B Wilkinson
A Page
J R & D L Clark
G W Homans
R Avery
Saw Mill
E R Homans
R Bartlett
D Page
J Walker
B L Hill
J W Yeaton
G C Palmer
S E Johnson
I Johnson
G W Webster
H C Homans
Mrs B Page
S T Page
J T Johnson
A W & Miss A A Avery
W Merrill
H Merrill
J F Merrill
Adams & G Smith
S H Palmer
C & S N Stickney
E Durgin
J & T S Pulsifer
C H Rogers
T Bartlett
L Brock
C Hanscomb
M Hall
S Doten
J Truell
J Whittier
A Fowler
Saw Mill
D Merrill
Merrills Saw Mill
J S Ryan
A Merrill
A L Webster
Rev J G Smith
W Page
J L Stevens
S H Rowe
J Coffin
J Ellison
Mrs J Connel
J Merrill
N P Hutkins
D L Clark
Mrs Carry
School
J H Mudgett
S Kimball
M Smith
Cemetery
Elder A S Tenney
J R Hutchins
Merrimack River Lumber Co
Mrs S Stevens
G Merrill
W George
D George
C Lewis
C Stetson
Saw Mill
S W George
Spencer & Sons
P S Cross
H Clark
W W Blake
S Rowe
C Johnson
Miss S Avery
J Brown
J Learitt
G Corner
D Webster
C G Webster
B B Southmayd
T Cheeney
Mrs E C Ward
C P Moulton
G H Moulton
A Flint
E Cook
J Pierce
Cabinet Mfy
L Huntley
T B Hoyt
L D Smith
D Goodhue
J Elliott
A L Brown
Avery Jr
N Moses
S Keniston
G W Keniston
G R Taylor
S C Clark
C C Taylor
J Sanborn
H Dearborn
M Spafford
P P Clark
R Colman
C Clark
J Whiteman
N Blake
D James
C Foss
W Foss
J Forstall
R Foss
Dea E Davis
J G Davis
W Merrill
Mrs Ham
Mrs N Dow
W A Durgin

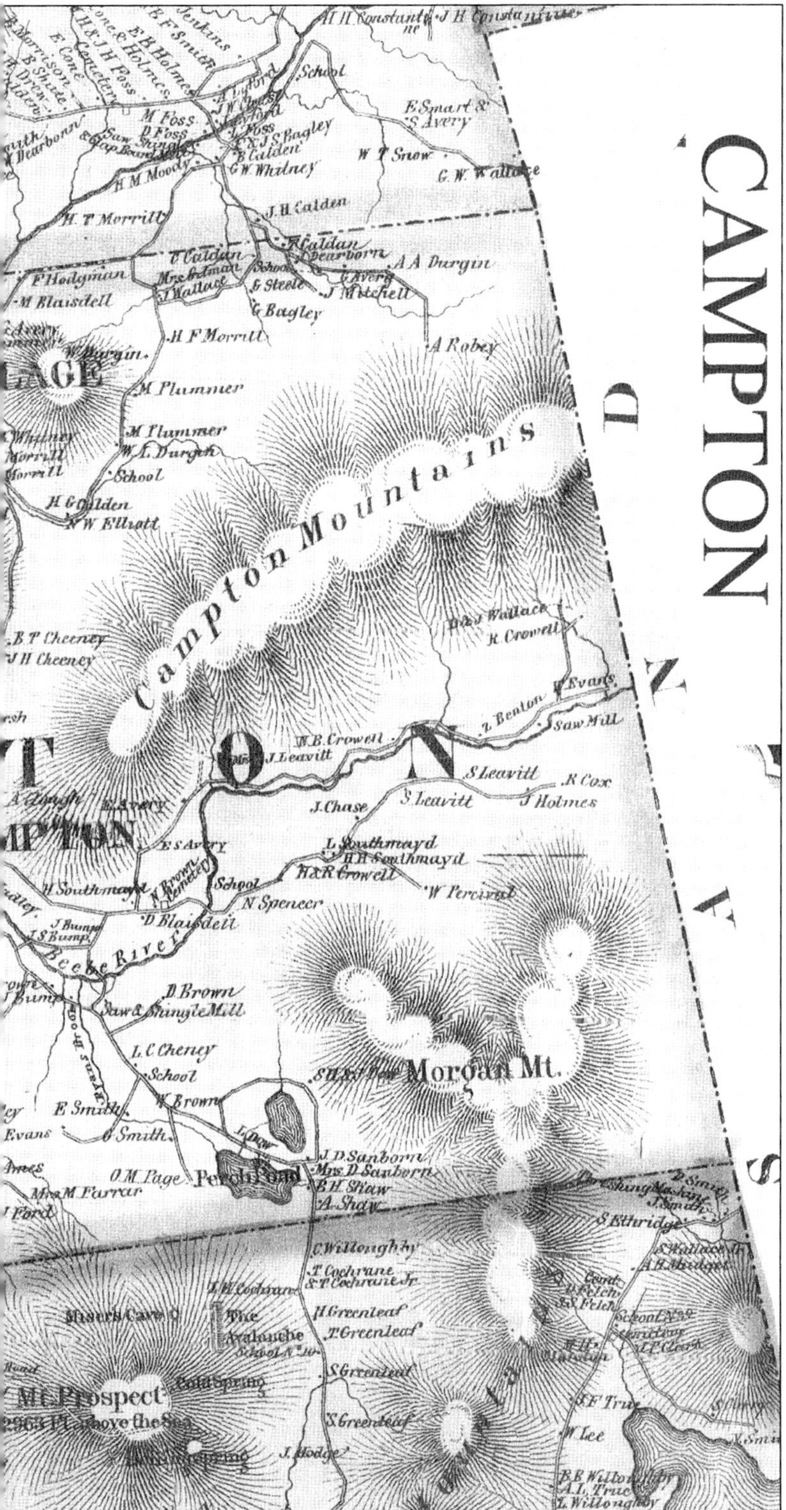

This map of Campton was taken from the 1860 Grafton County map. Both the Campton Historical Society Building and the Campton Town Clerk's Office display originals of this county map.

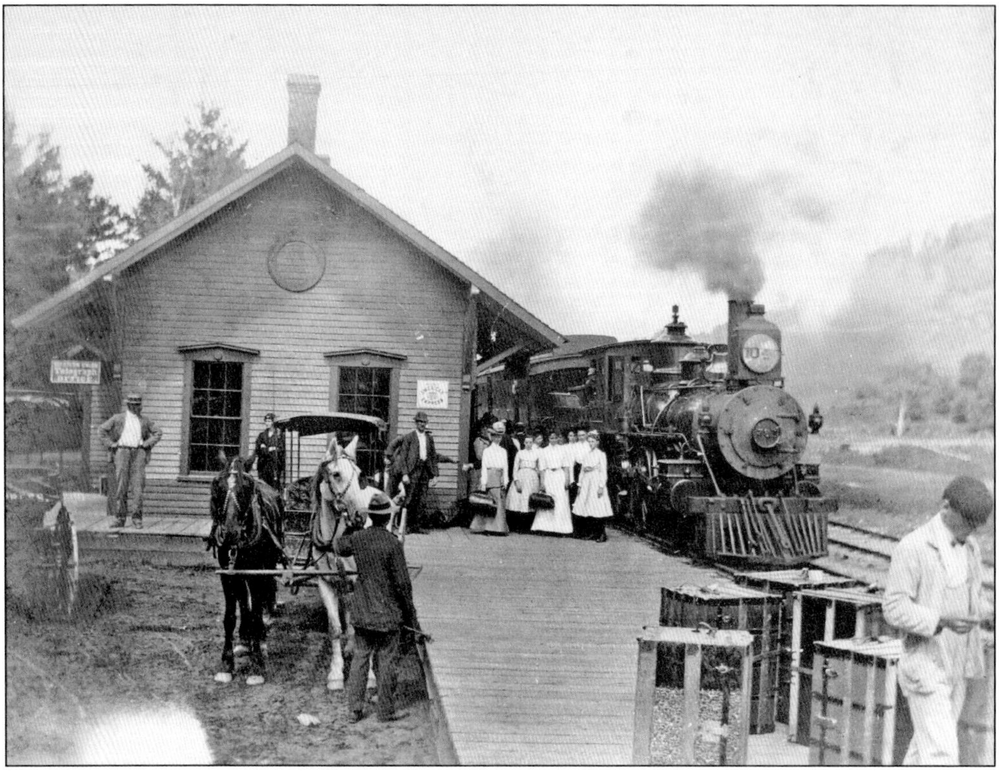

The Campton Railroad Station (seen around 1890) was located on Owl Street, just north of where Hoyt's Log Yard is today. Campton Station was the farthest north of the town's four stations on the Pemigewasset Valley Branch of the Concord & Montreal Railroad.

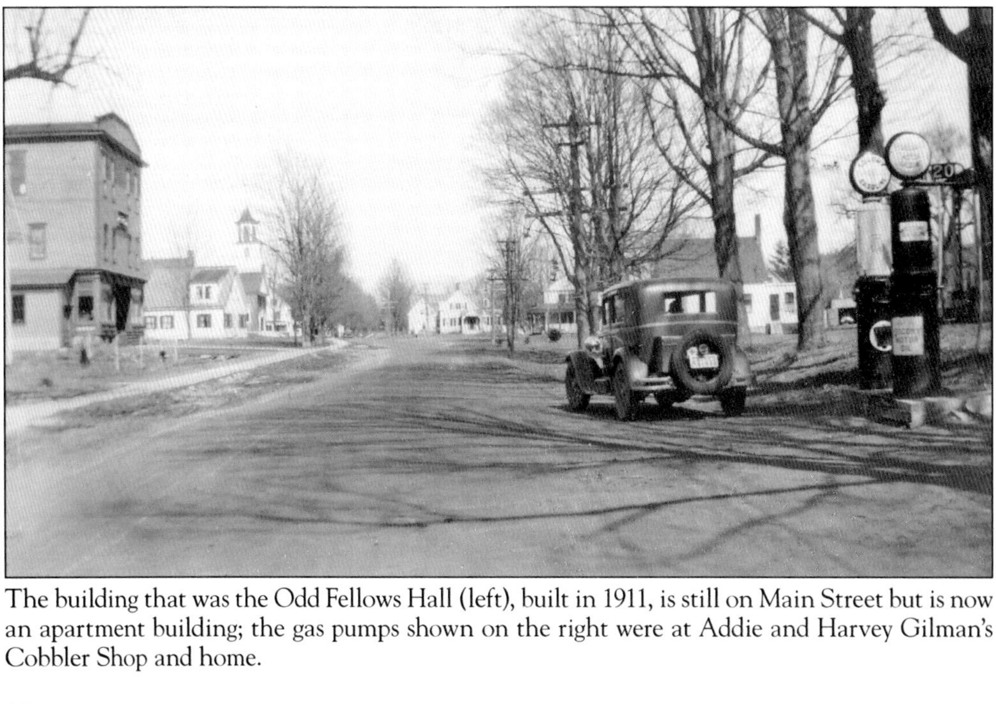

The building that was the Odd Fellows Hall (left), built in 1911, is still on Main Street but is now an apartment building; the gas pumps shown on the right were at Addie and Harvey Gilman's Cobbler Shop and home.

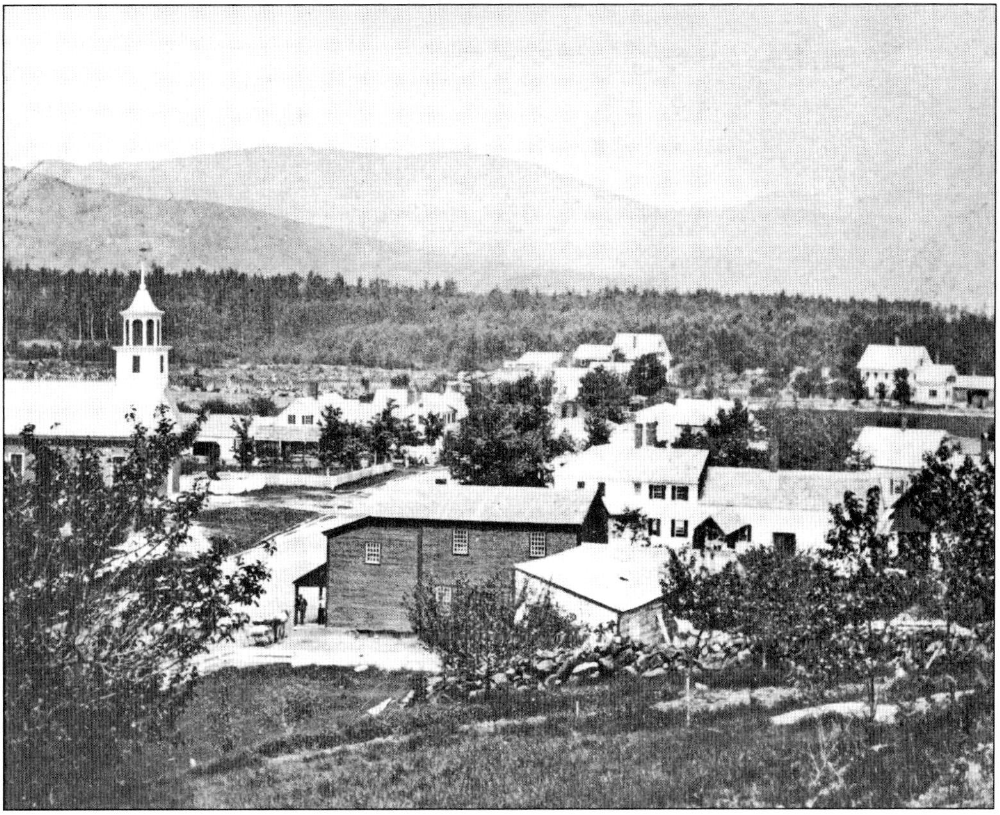

In 1867, the Campton Baptist Church (left) and Fifield's General Store (right) dominated upper Main Street. Many of the buildings shown still exist today but are primarily private homes that have been modified somewhat over the years. The photograph was taken from Fifield's field, which is across the street from the current Campton Cupboard, formerly Morrison's General Store.

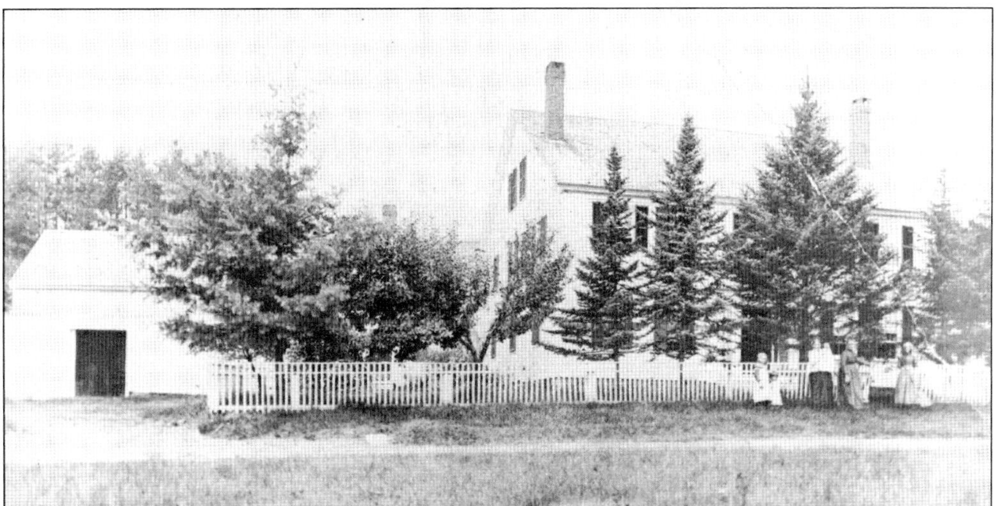

The Cook-Adams House is at the intersection of Routes 49 and 175, near the Campton Dam. In the mid to late 20th century, it was the home of Jane and Burt Pierce, and today it houses Woodpecker's Restaurant.

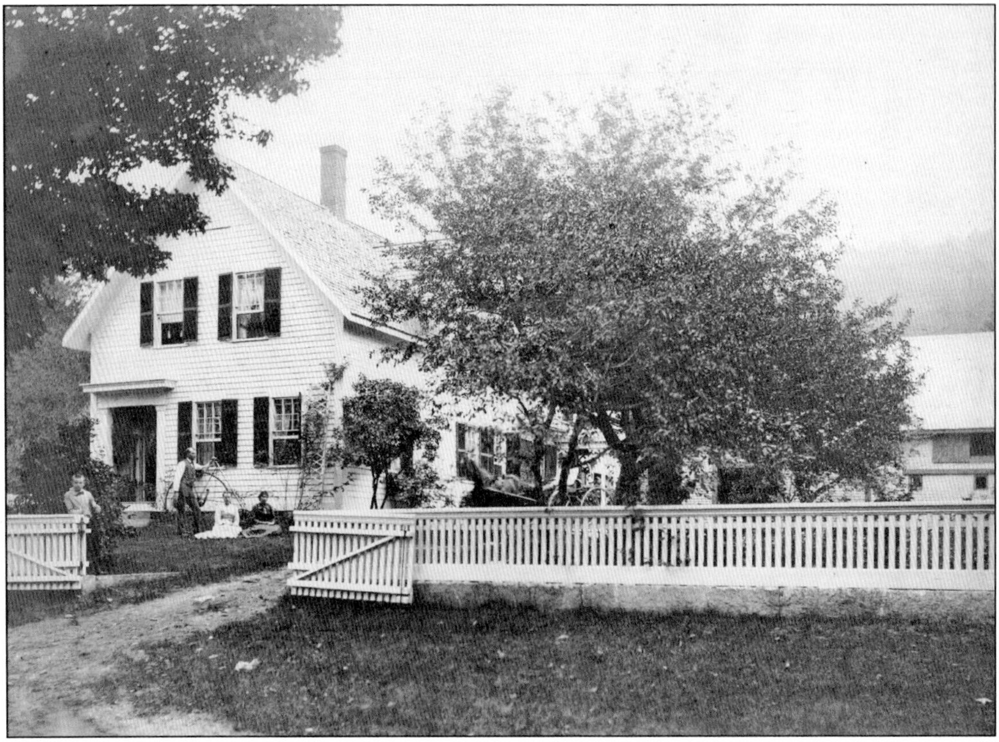

The Moody Dole House is located in the Lower Village, across the street from the Dole Mill. The house was built in the mid-19th century by the Dole family. Shown are Allan Wilde, by the gate; Herbert Dole, with the bicycle; Frances Galdon, in the white dress; Lillian (Mrs. Moody) Dole, in the dark dress; and Moody Dole, in the buggy.

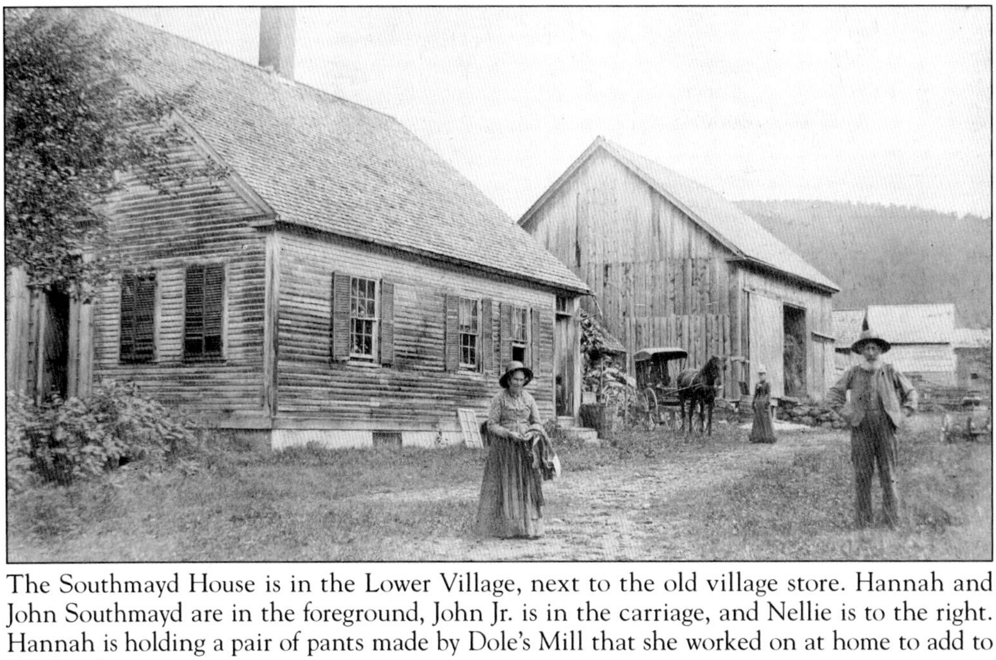

The Southmayd House is in the Lower Village, next to the old village store. Hannah and John Southmayd are in the foreground, John Jr. is in the carriage, and Nellie is to the right. Hannah is holding a pair of pants made by Dole's Mill that she worked on at home to add to the family income.

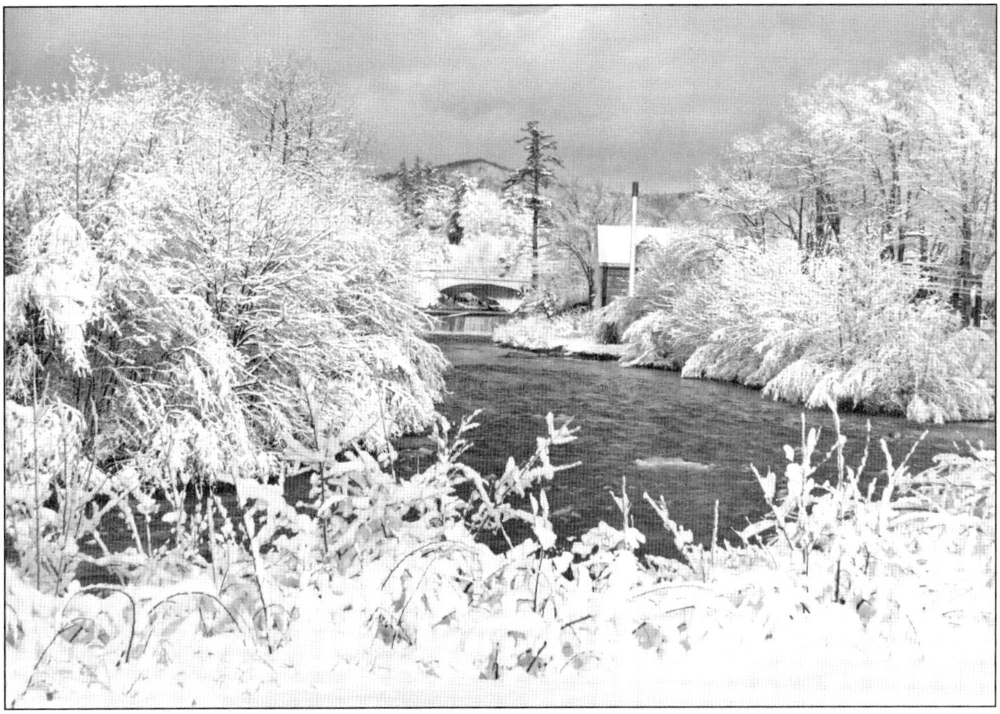

This was the scene of the Mad River Bridge, the wooden dam, and Dole's Mill as seen from the Lower Village in the winter of 1940. The cement bridge was built in the 1930s, during the Great Depression, by the Civilian Conservation Corps. The United States was propelled into World War II, and Dole's Mill lost some of its workforce to the military in 1941, causing the management to hire more women to meet the demands for woolen clothing to support the war effort.

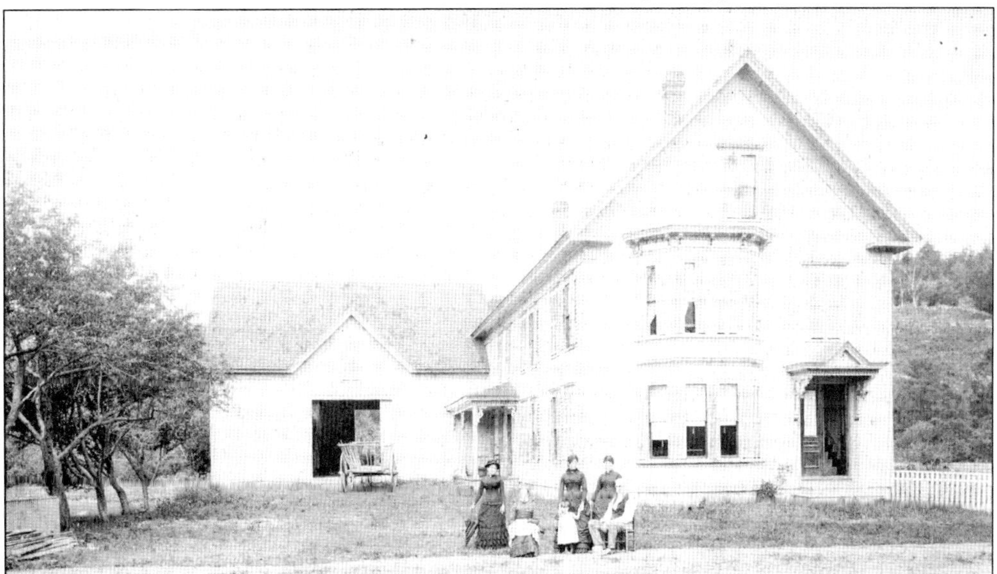

The Henry Morrill Homestead, in the Lower Village, is a Victorian farmhouse built in the late 1880s. In this 1887 family picture are, from left to right, Hazel, Mertie, Maria, Nan, Clarissa, and Henry Morrill.

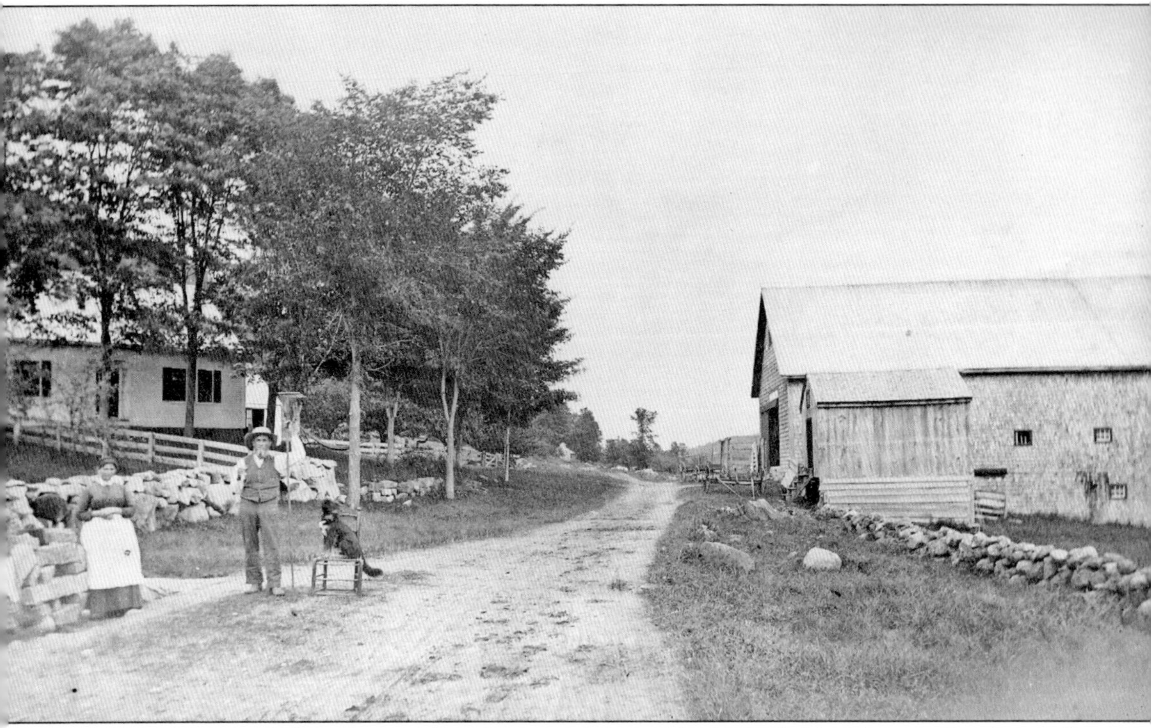

The Charles Pulsifer Homestead, in Campton Bog, was built in 1796 by Ebenezer Bartlett and is one of the oldest farms in town. Pulsifer bought the farm of 100 acres in 1856. When his family grew, he jacked the house up and added a new ground floor beneath. A new barn was built in 1867, with additions in 1889 and 1905. Over the years, more parcels of land were added to the farm. As the times have changed, so has the farm, but the one thing that has stood the test of time is the stone walls. Their legacy stands as true today as the day they were built. The people in this 1890s picture are, from left to right, Lizzie Pulsifer, Melvina Cook, and Charles W. Pulsifer. Members of the Pulsifer family still live on the farm today.

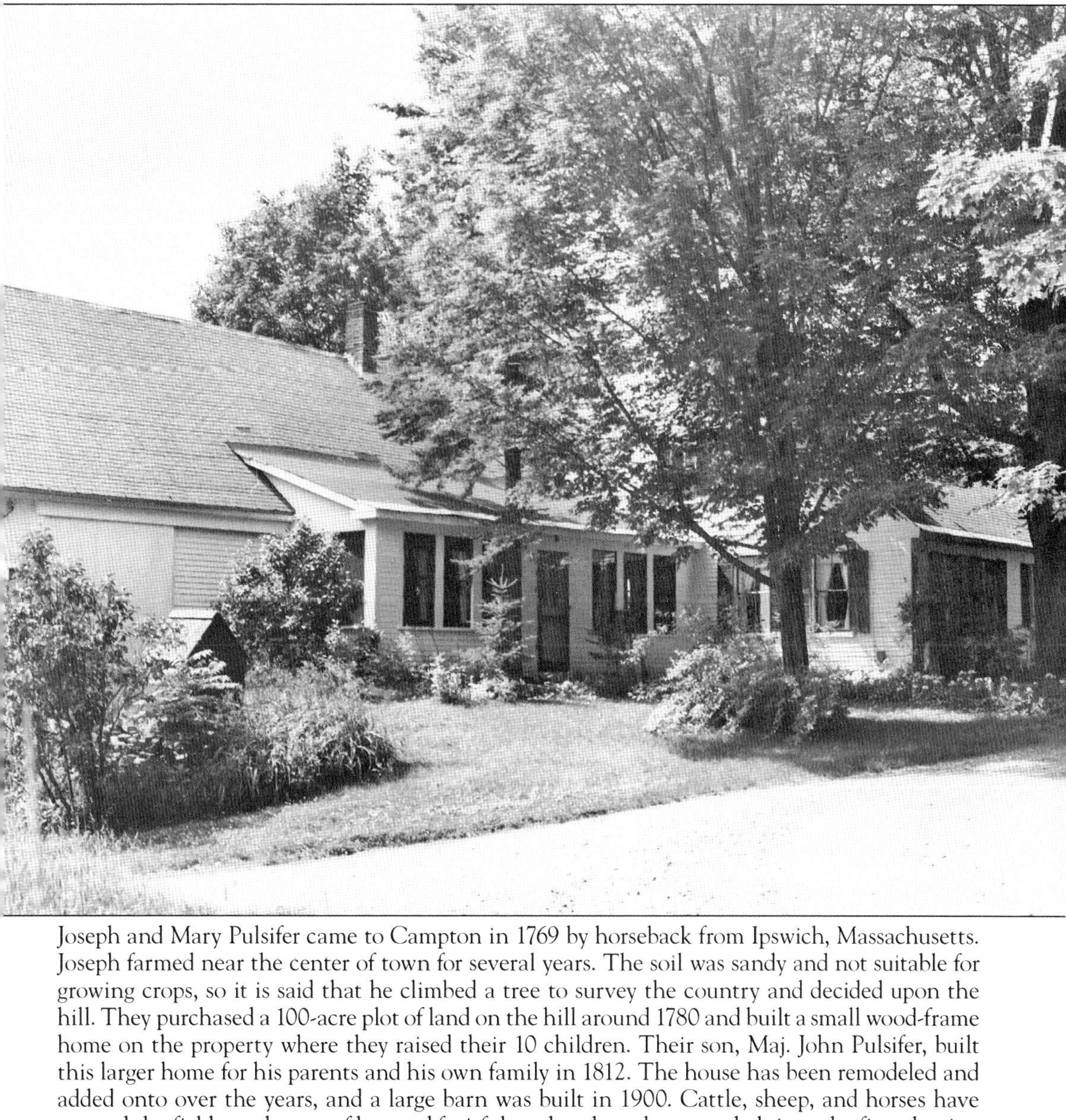

Joseph and Mary Pulsifer came to Campton in 1769 by horseback from Ipswich, Massachusetts. Joseph farmed near the center of town for several years. The soil was sandy and not suitable for growing crops, so it is said that he climbed a tree to survey the country and decided upon the hill. They purchased a 100-acre plot of land on the hill around 1780 and built a small wood-frame home on the property where they raised their 10 children. Their son, Maj. John Pulsifer, built this larger home for his parents and his own family in 1812. The house has been remodeled and added onto over the years, and a large barn was built in 1900. Cattle, sheep, and horses have roamed the fields, and crops of hay and fruitful gardens have been tended since the first clearing of the land in 1780. Many more acres were purchased and cleared over the decades, leaving miles of stone walls as monuments to their labor. The sixth generation of the Joseph Pulsifer family owns the property today.

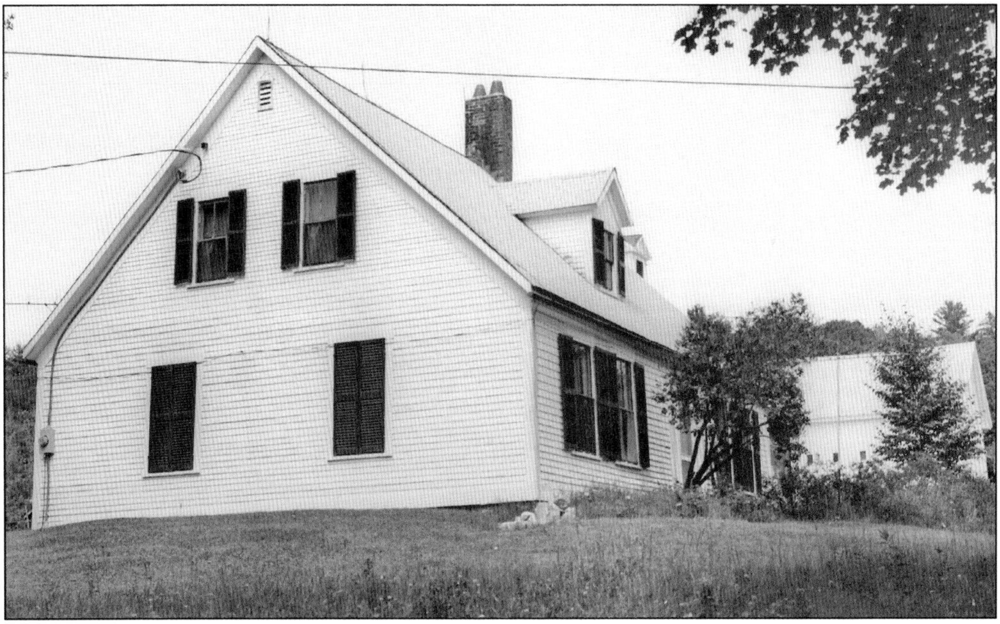

The Sanborn Farm was built in 1817 by Moses Pulsifer, son of Joseph Pulsifer. Moses started with 100 acres and later purchased an additional 100 acres that included Mount Prospect. A wagon road was laid to the top of the mountain, allowing local people and tourists trips to the summit. This home has come down through Pulsifer lineage; it was recently owned by Ralph and Blanche Pulsifer Sanborn and is now owned by their grandson.

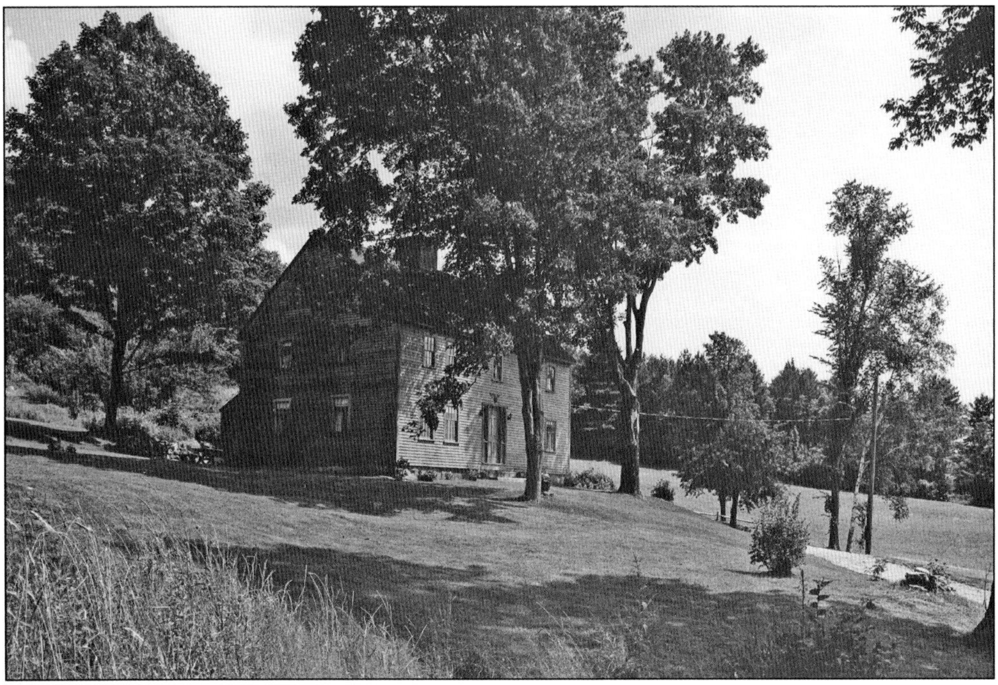

The Hodgdon Farm, on Route 175 near the entrance to Beebe River, was built in the early 1800s and is one of the oldest houses in town. In the 20th century, the farm was known for raising Angus cattle.

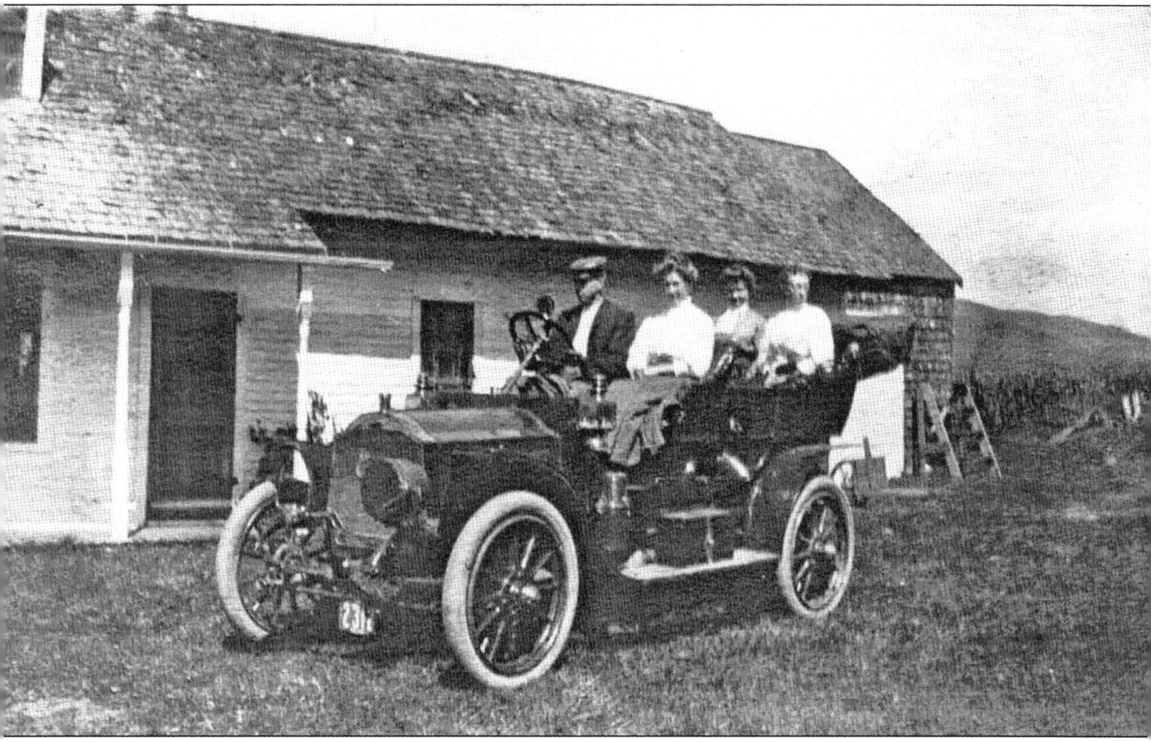

The Stickney Homestead was built around 1798 by Joseph Palmer. His daughter, Polly, married John Pulsifer (1806), and the home became the Stickney Homestead in 1831, when their daughter, Phebe, married Benjamin Franklin Stickney, from Massachusetts. At the time, the homestead, on what is now Stickney Hill, was about 300 acres; it was expanded in subsequent generations with purchases on the Bump Intervale. The farm was a dairy operation from its inception. Benjamin and Phebe's son, B. Frank, inherited the property in 1868. He and his wife, Laura, had three children—Annie, Mary, and Henry. Henry married Daisy Morgan and had two children—Alice Phebe and Morgan Andrew. In 1902, the barn was doubled in size. After inheriting the farm in 1950, Morgan built two pole barns, a milking parlor, a hay dryer, and a silo. Although members of the Stickney family still live on the property, the farm ceased operation in the 1990s when family farming could no longer provide a living. Pictured are Henry and Daisy in the front seat and Annie and Mary in the back.

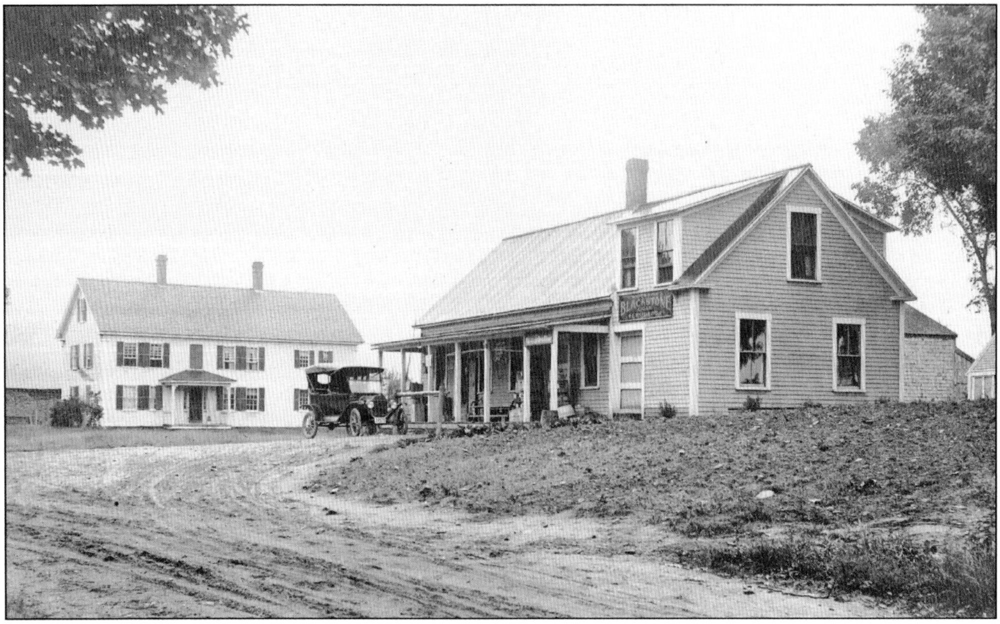

The Blaisdell House (c. 1820–1950) is in the background, at the top of Wishman's Hill. The general store is in the foreground. Over the years, several stores have been at this location, with new buildings constructed soon after the previous ones burned.

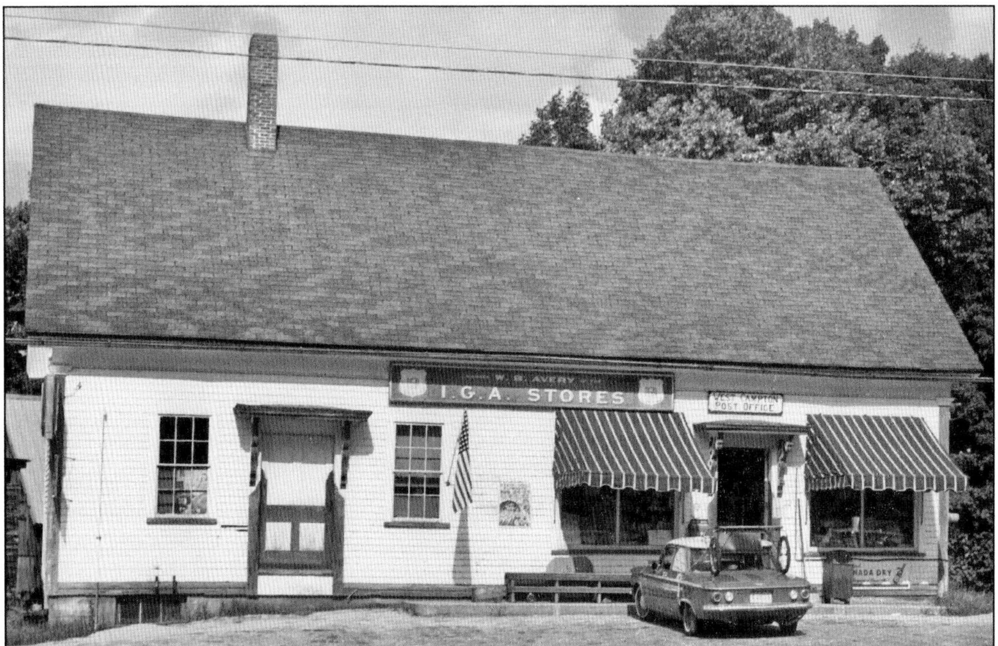

Avery's General Store and Post Office, in West Campton, was run by Will Avery and his son, Ralph, for many years. The store was a gathering spot, with people from all over the west side of town stopping in to meet friends, chat with Will, and learn the latest news. Will served as a selectman from 1932 to 1962, so he certainly knew what was happening in town. Will's parents owned and operated the Maples Inn, across the street from the store, from 1885 to 1925.

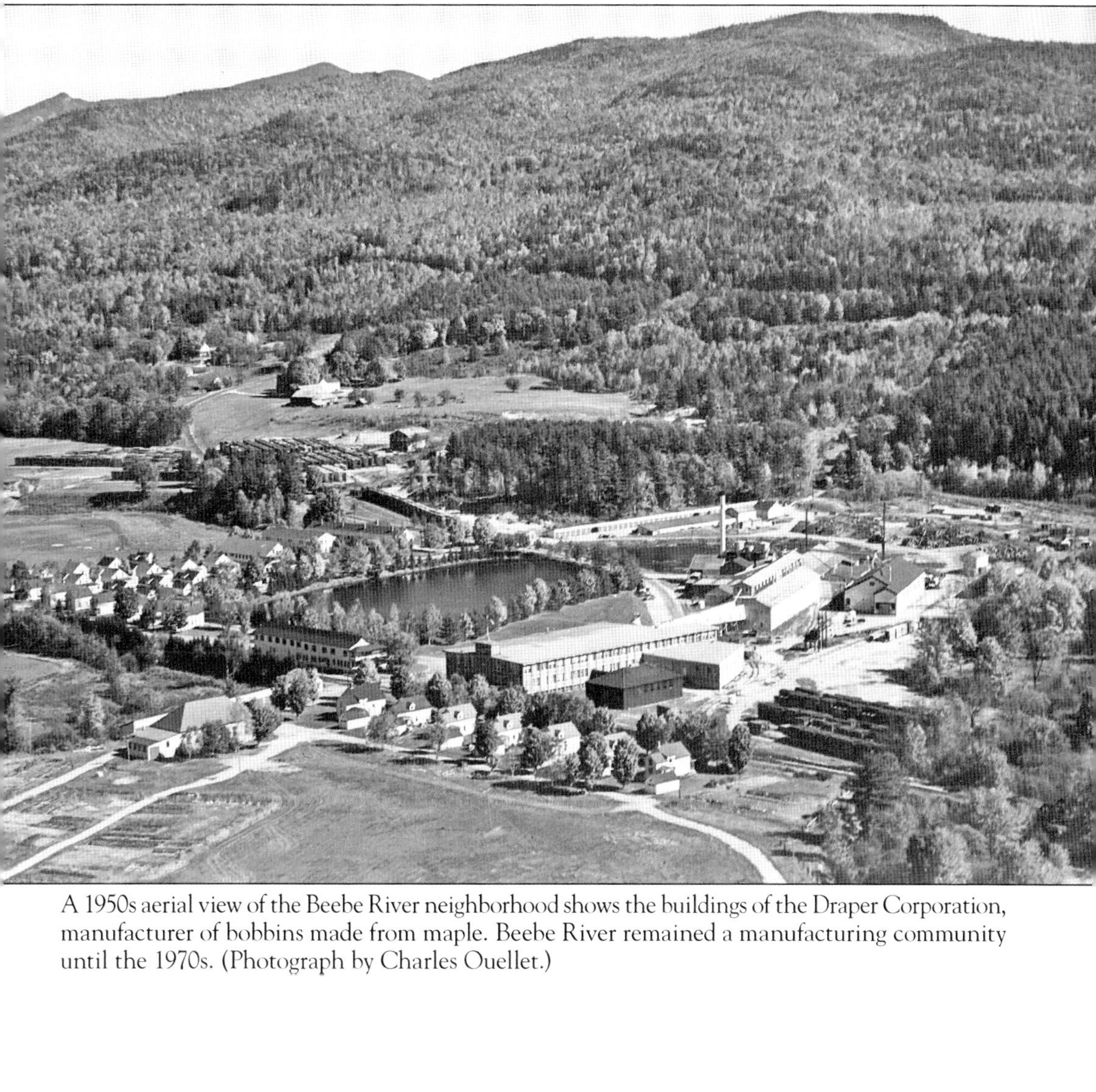

A 1950s aerial view of the Beebe River neighborhood shows the buildings of the Draper Corporation, manufacturer of bobbins made from maple. Beebe River remained a manufacturing community until the 1970s. (Photograph by Charles Ouellet.)

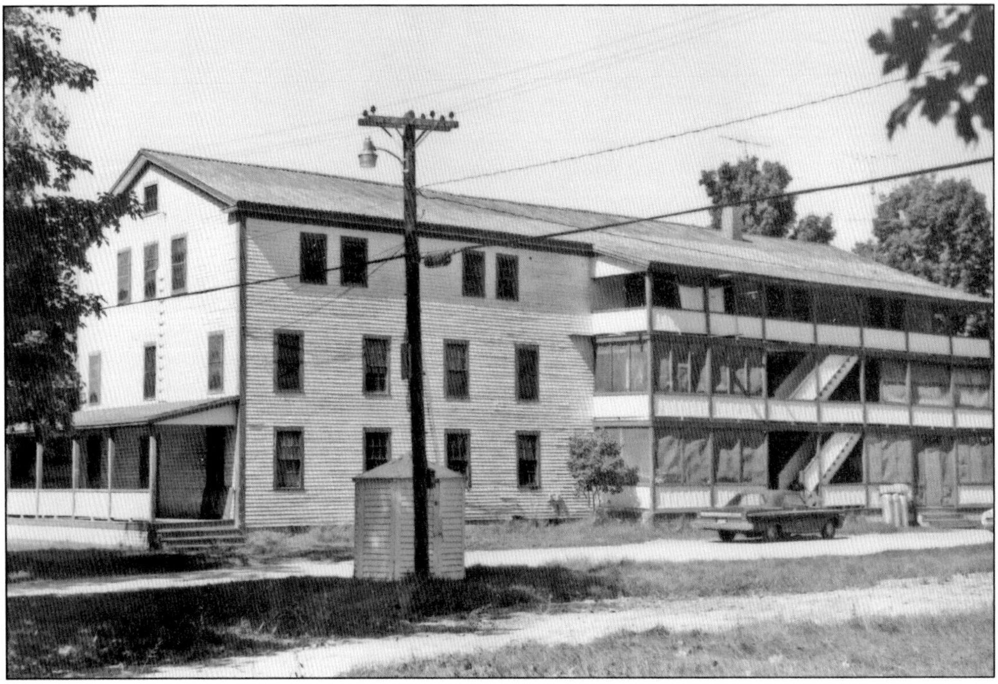

This Beebe River boardinghouse had a dining room and kitchen on the first floor and rooms on the upper floors that were originally designed for single men.

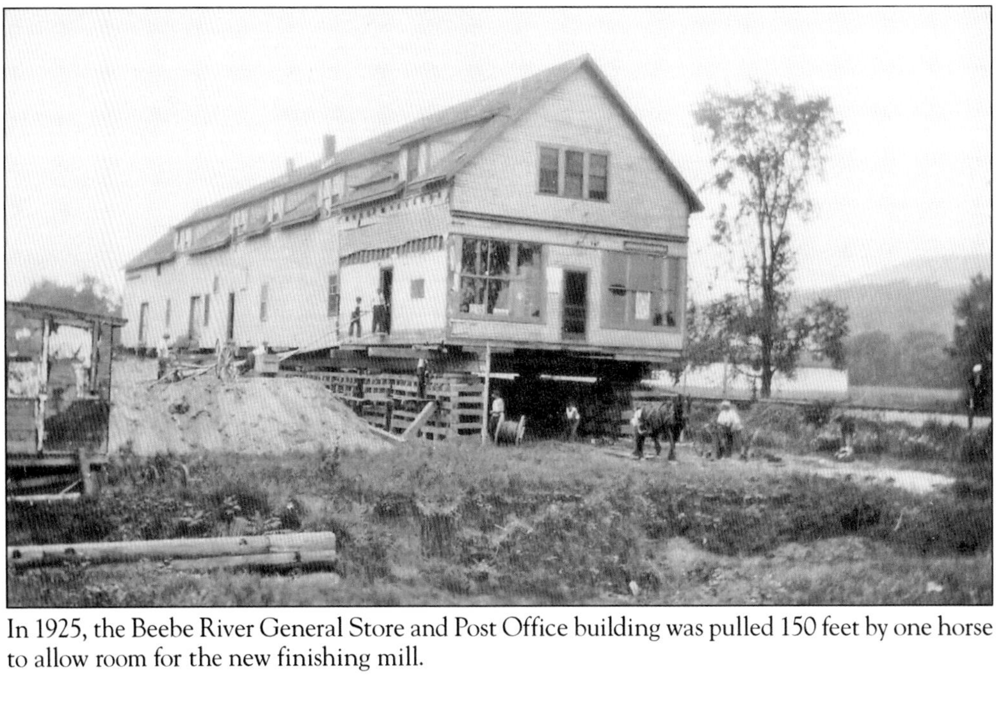

In 1925, the Beebe River General Store and Post Office building was pulled 150 feet by one horse to allow room for the new finishing mill.

Two

EVERYDAY LIFE

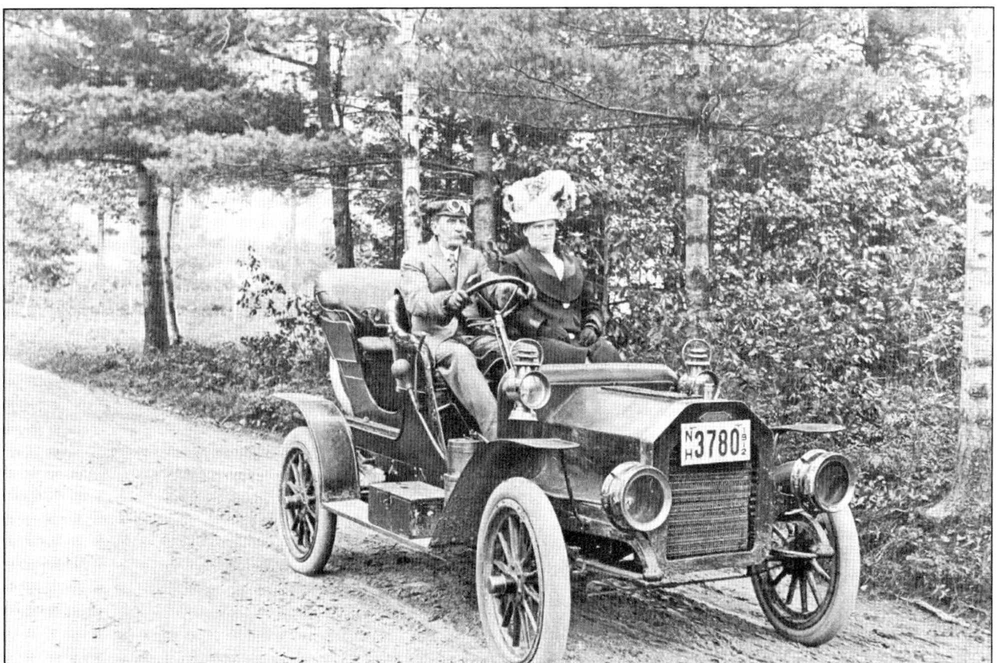

The cost of this 1912 REO would have been about $2,000, and gas was 7¢ a gallon. Here, Bob Cummings and Ella Fox are enjoying a Sunday outing. Apparently, the speed of the open car did not interfere with a lady wearing a fancy hat.

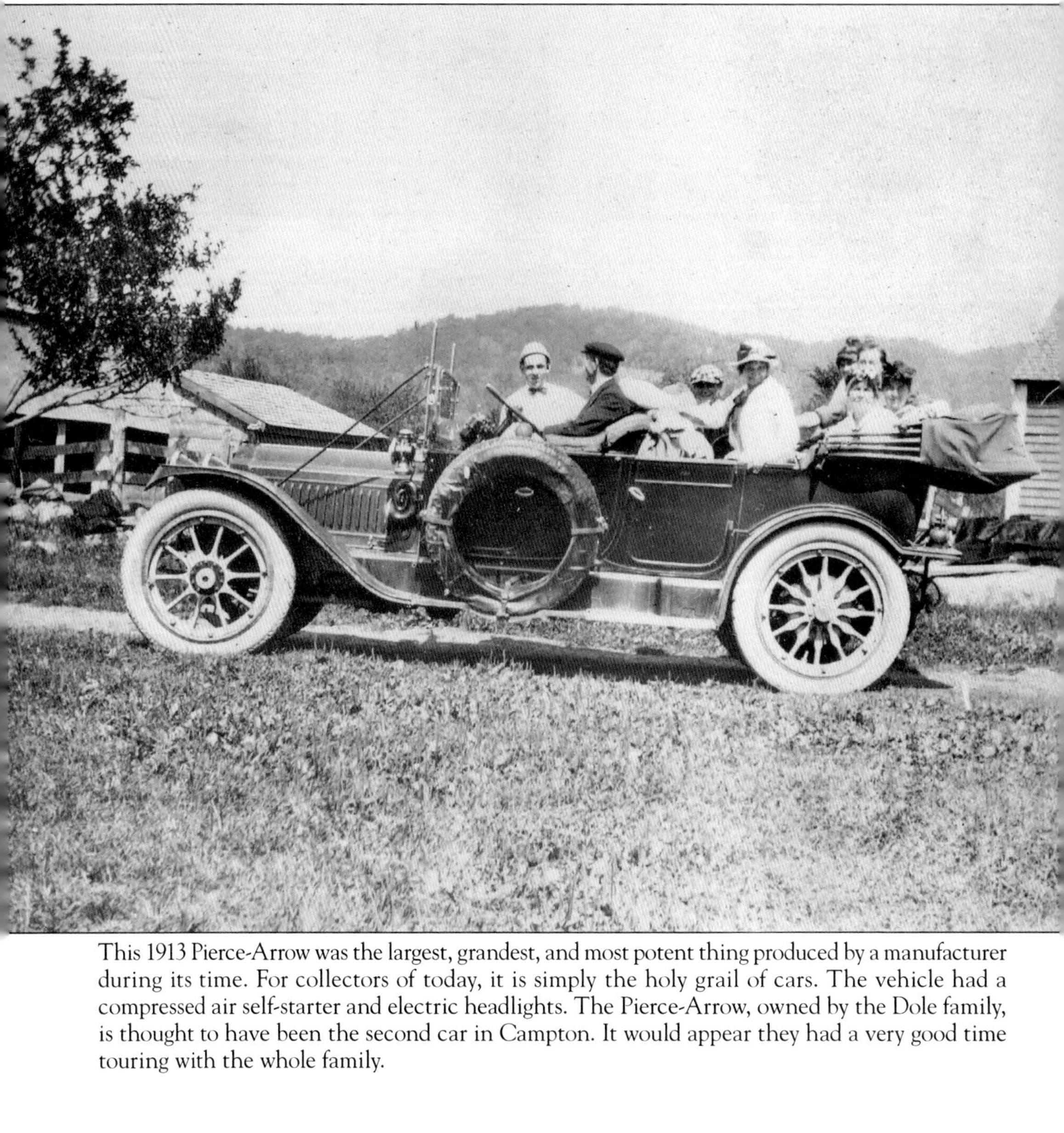

This 1913 Pierce-Arrow was the largest, grandest, and most potent thing produced by a manufacturer during its time. For collectors of today, it is simply the holy grail of cars. The vehicle had a compressed air self-starter and electric headlights. The Pierce-Arrow, owned by the Dole family, is thought to have been the second car in Campton. It would appear they had a very good time touring with the whole family.

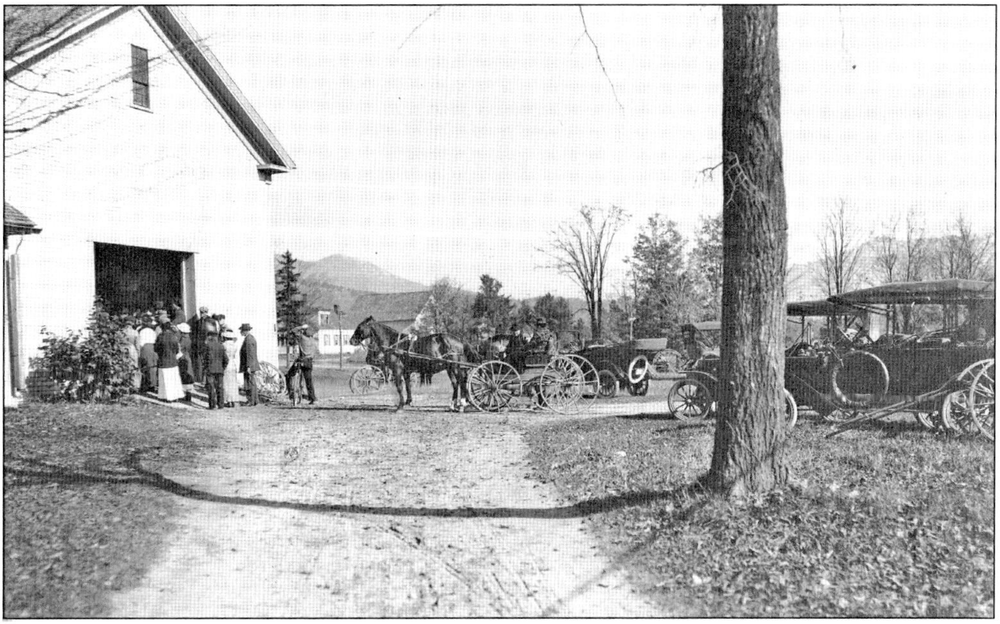

Neighbors arrive by buggy and automobile to attend an auction at Pettingill's barn in 1915. By the early 1900s, the number of automobiles had surpassed the number of horse-drawn buggies in some parts of the country, but in Campton and other rural areas, the use of buggies continued well into the 1920s.

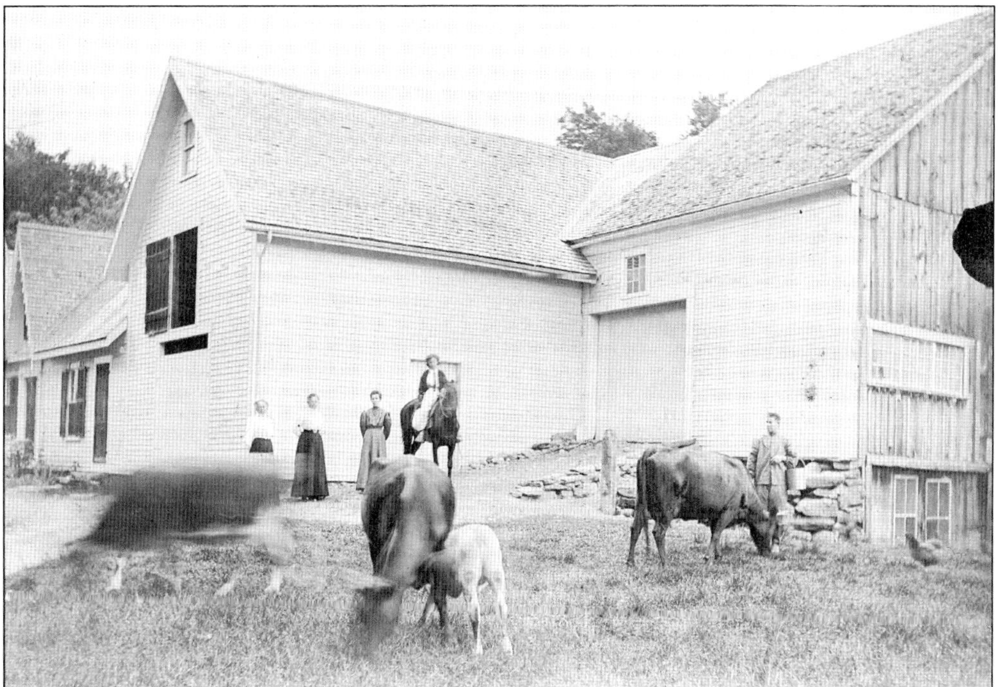

D.S. Moulton, a professional Campton photographer, took this picture of the Robie sisters' farm on Route 175. The road along the east side of the Pemi was an important route for stagecoaches in the mid-1800s, and this house served as a tavern along the way.

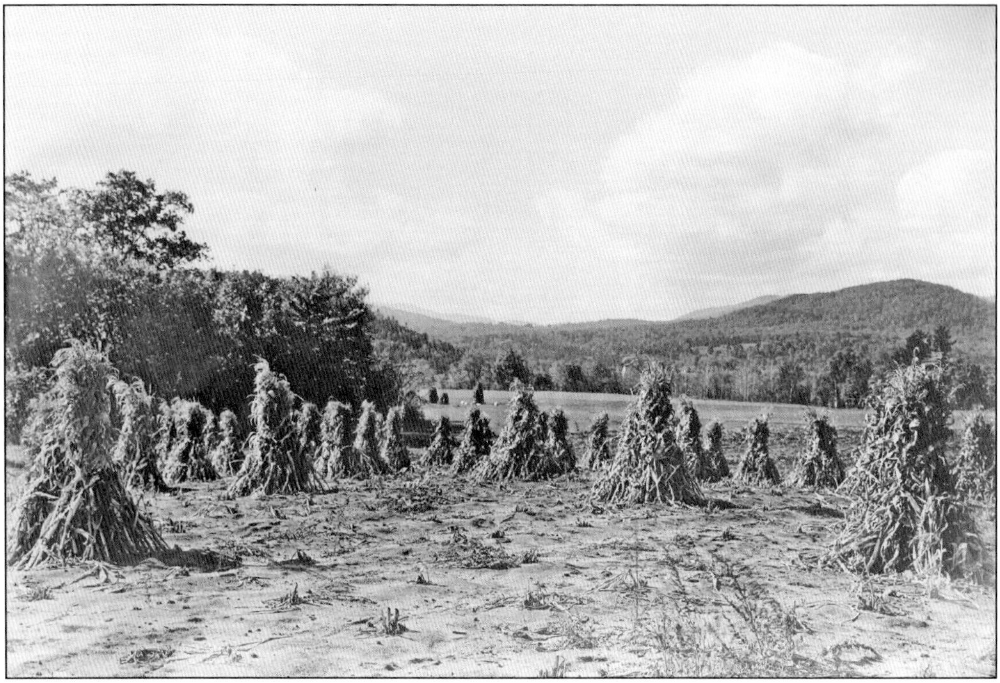

Imagine the physical labor that went into this pastoral scene of Sawyer's cornfield around 1910. Harvesting was a very important time for the American farmer. It was when the rewards of the growing season could be clearly seen. Harvest had its own beautiful colors and smells.

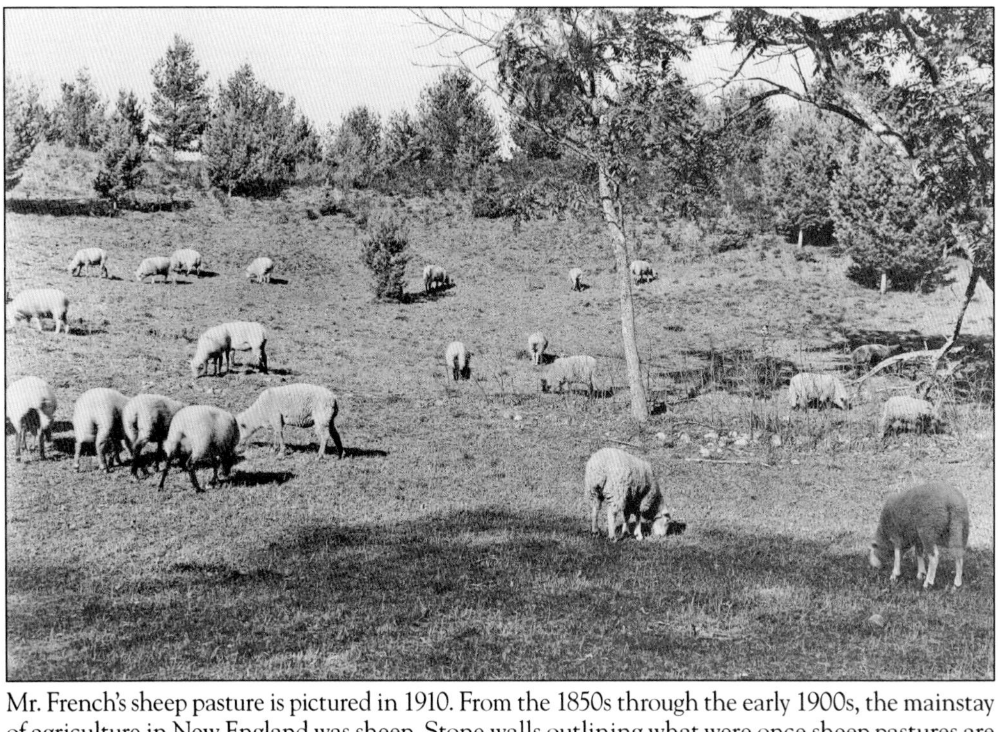

Mr. French's sheep pasture is pictured in 1910. From the 1850s through the early 1900s, the mainstay of agriculture in New England was sheep. Stone walls outlining what were once sheep pastures are seen all across New Hampshire as lasting tributes to the sheep industry's heyday in the state.

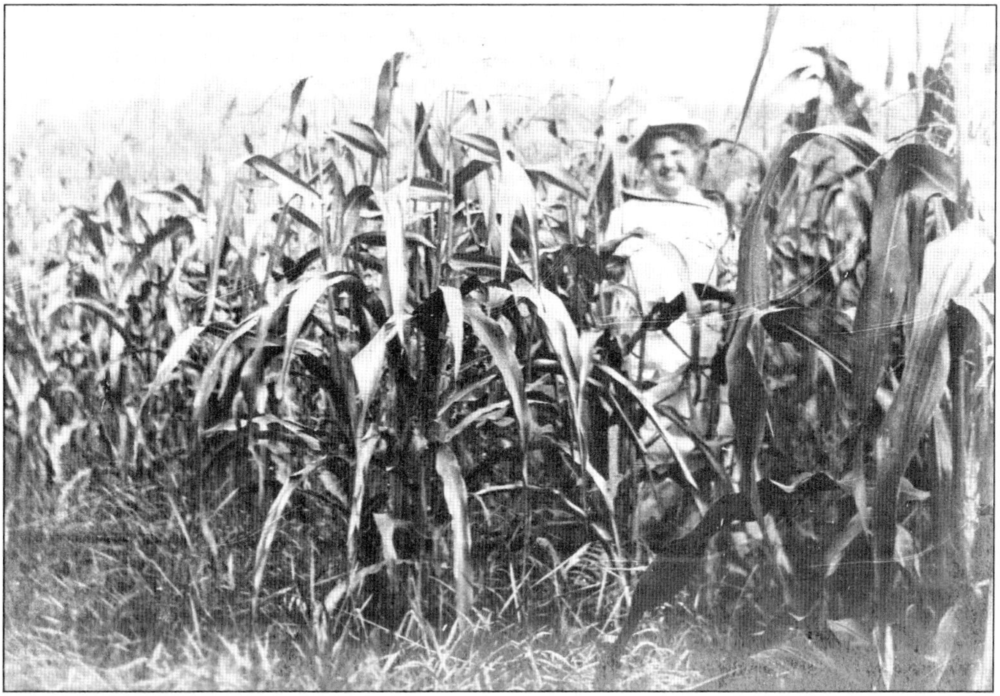

In 1902, Bertha Nichols Brown enjoys a moment in the cornfield. This photograph, part of a very old Kodak Photographs scrapbook, was entitled *Laugh for the Lady.*

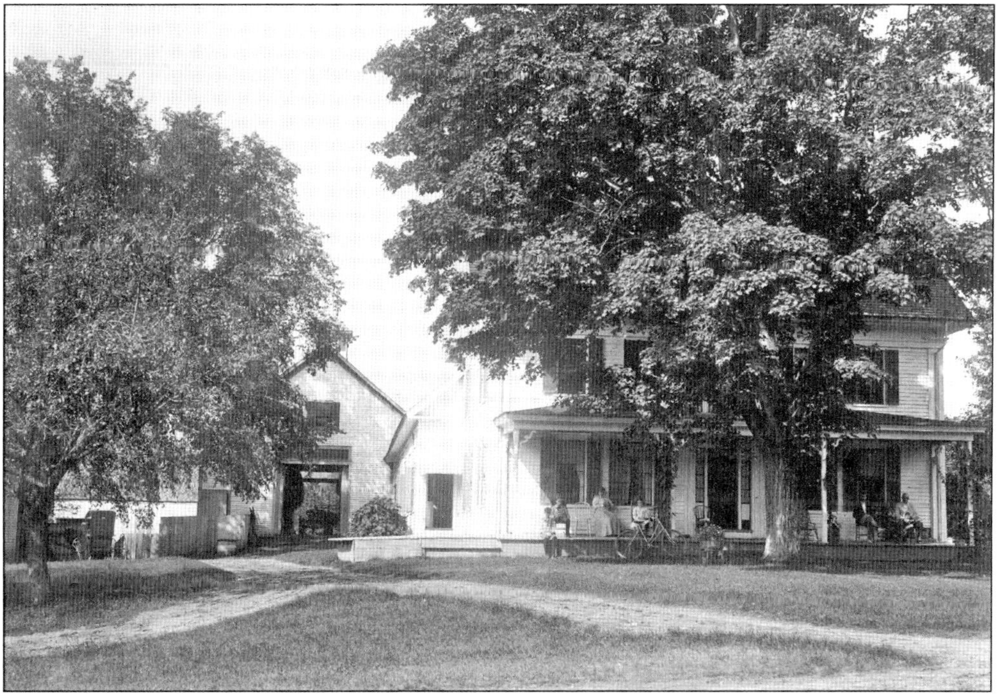

The tractor is in the barn; the buggy is parked; the lawn is mowed. It is Sunday afternoon and time to relax, and how nice to have a big front porch to accommodate the Haartz family and friends. And, of course, there is a big old shade tree to keep everyone cool.

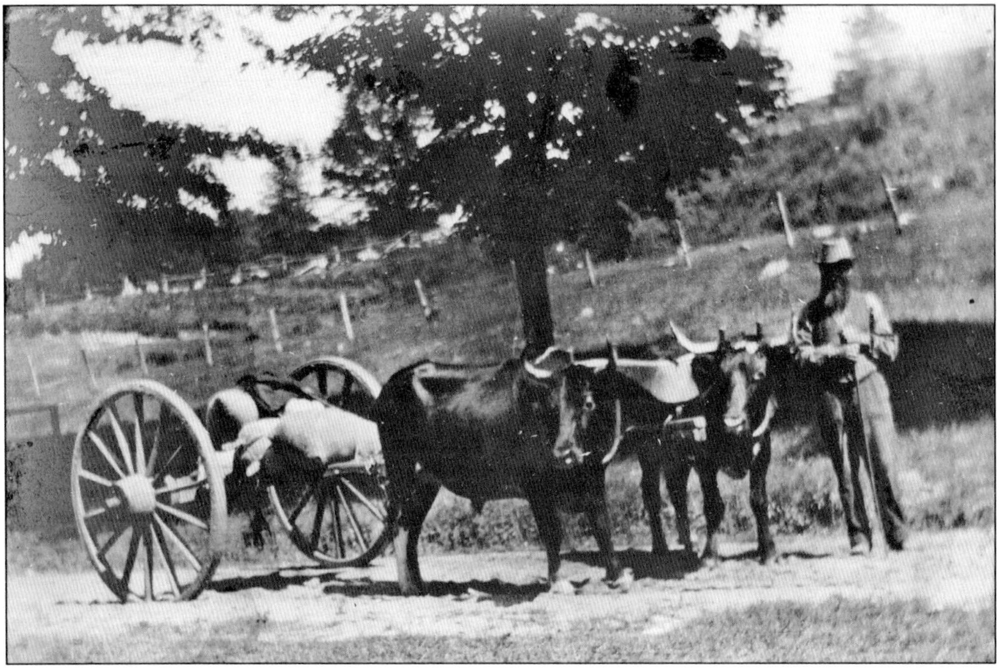

This photograph comes from a very old Kodak Photographs album. Every picture was meticulously labeled with titles, names, and dates. Pictured here is Charles Shute, and the photograph is entitled *Just Coming from the Grist Mill, 1901.*

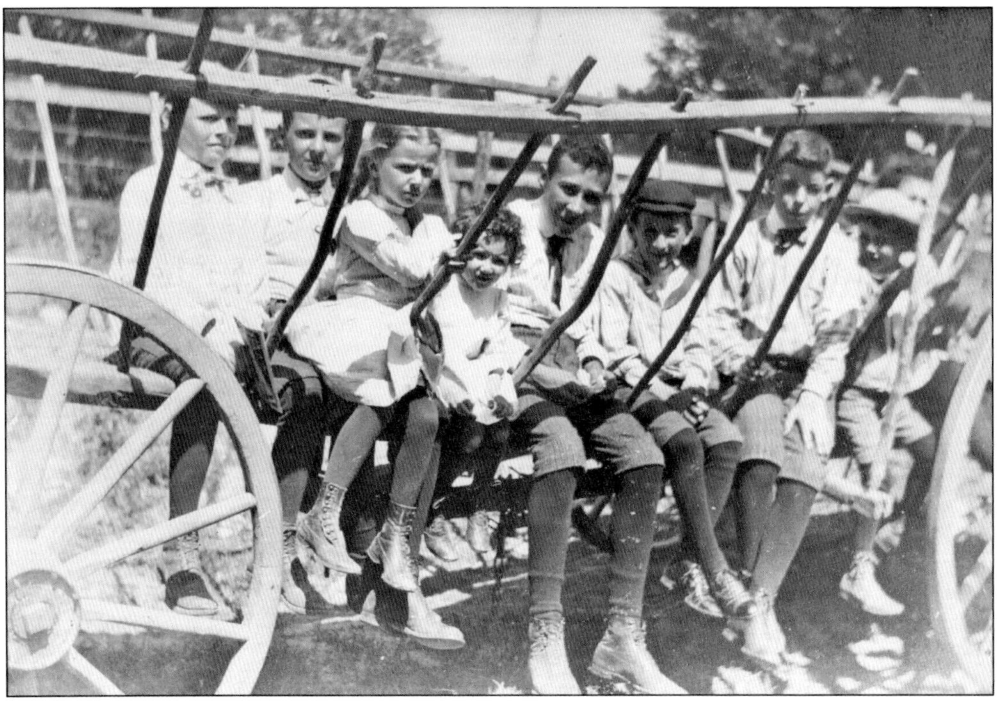

A *Study in Legs, Campton, 1901* is from the same Kodak Photographs album. One may surmise that the day was a special occasion as the children are all dressed in their Sunday best. The hay wagon is a perfect setting.

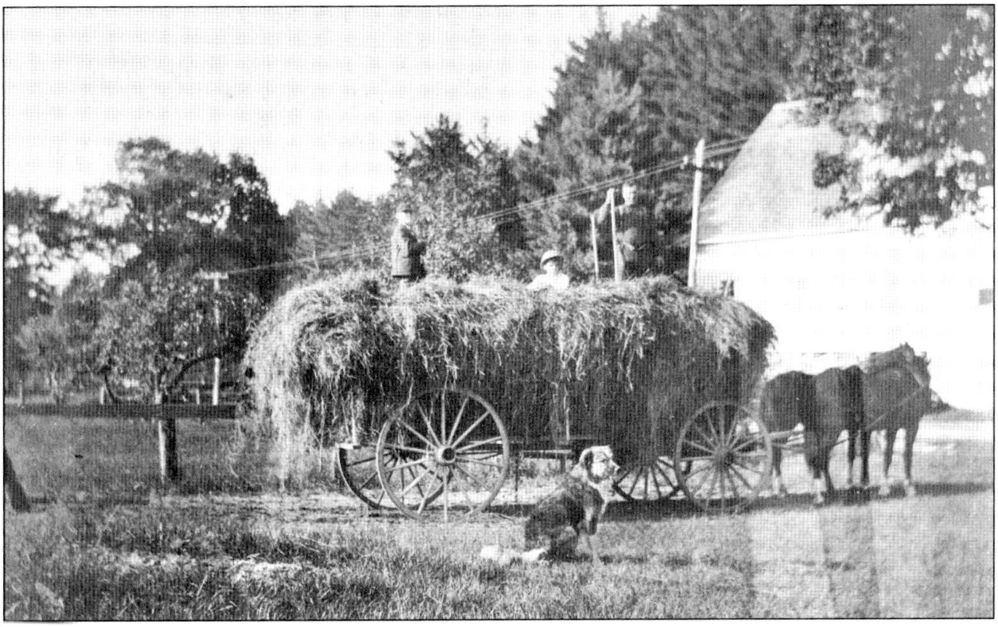

This c. 1900 photograph, taken at the Sunset House on Owl Street, is titled *On the Way to the Barn*. No doubt local inns and guesthouses provided numerous employment opportunities for local folks. The Sunset House employed outside as well as inside workers.

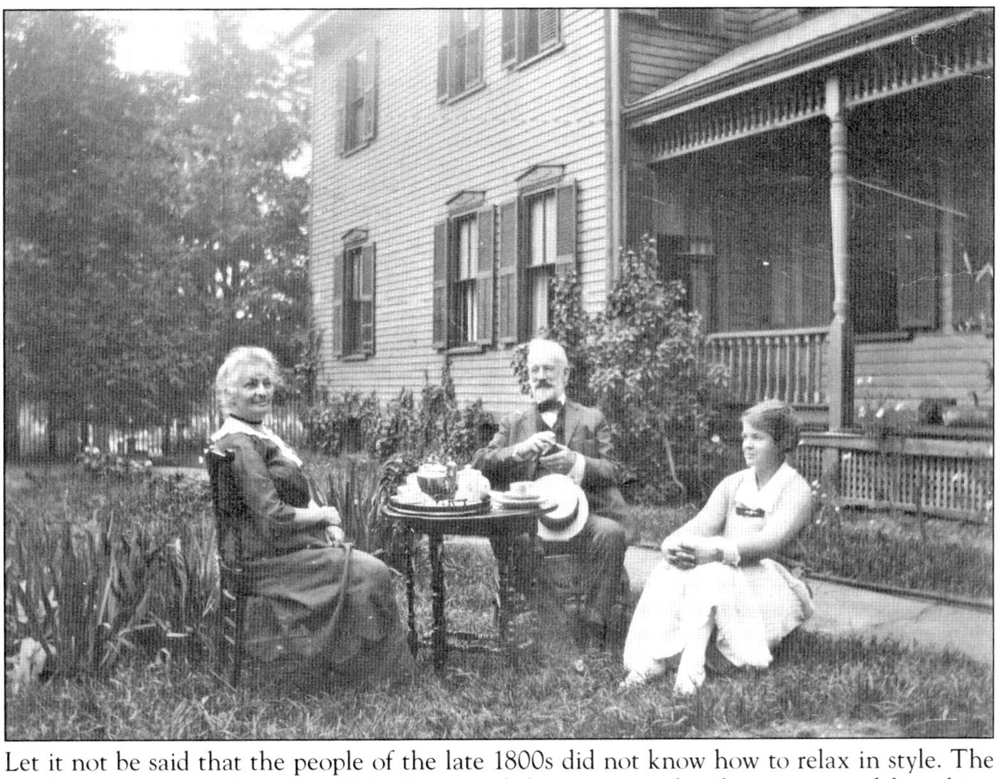

Let it not be said that the people of the late 1800s did not know how to relax in style. The gentleman wearing a bow tie and frockcoat and the presence of a silver teapot and fine china cups tell otherwise.

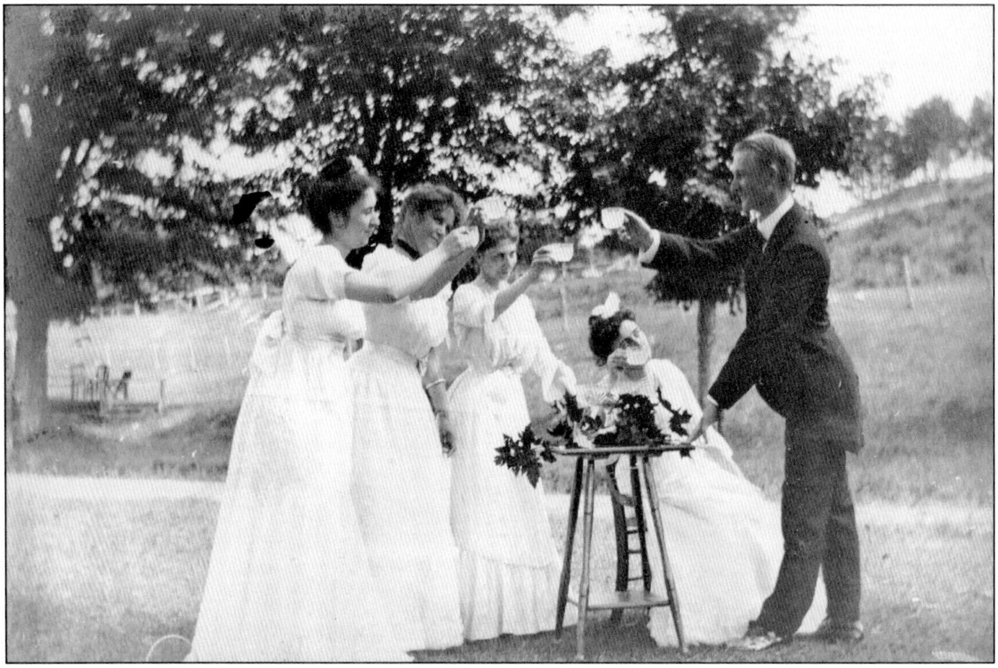

From left to right, Bernice Mayhew Brown, Miss Patterson, Maude Weyman, Leone Crosby, and John Haartz, of Campton, pose for a bachelors' supper tableau in 1901.

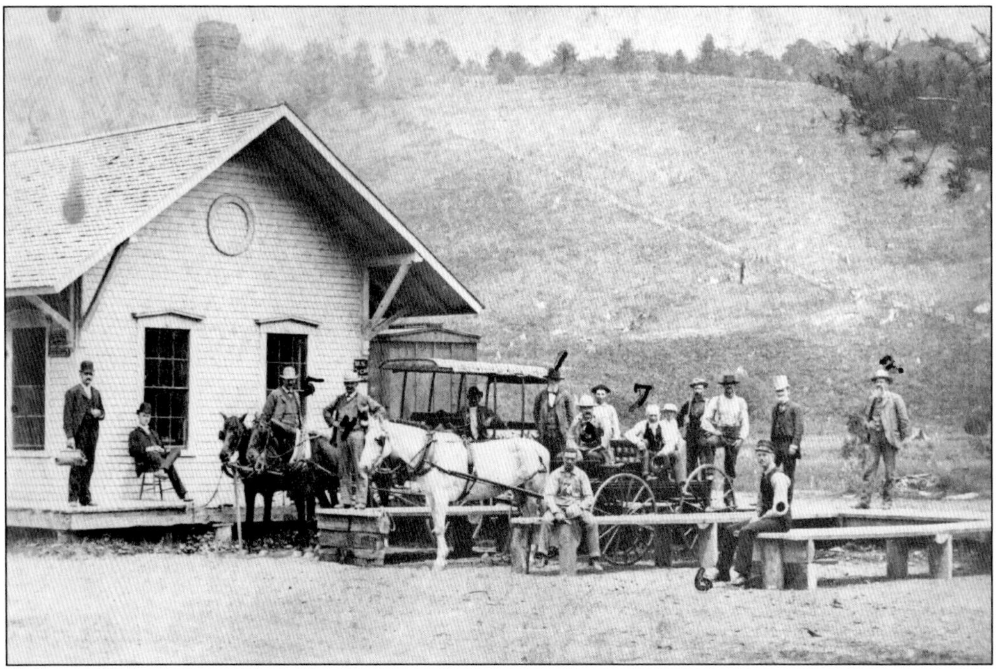

The Pemigewasset Valley Railroad Station was located across the road from what is now Mount Prospect Academy. Pictured around the wagon are, from left to right, Ephrim Elliott, Erastus Emerson, Charles Clark, David Foss, James McCoy, Fred James, and Erastus Dole.

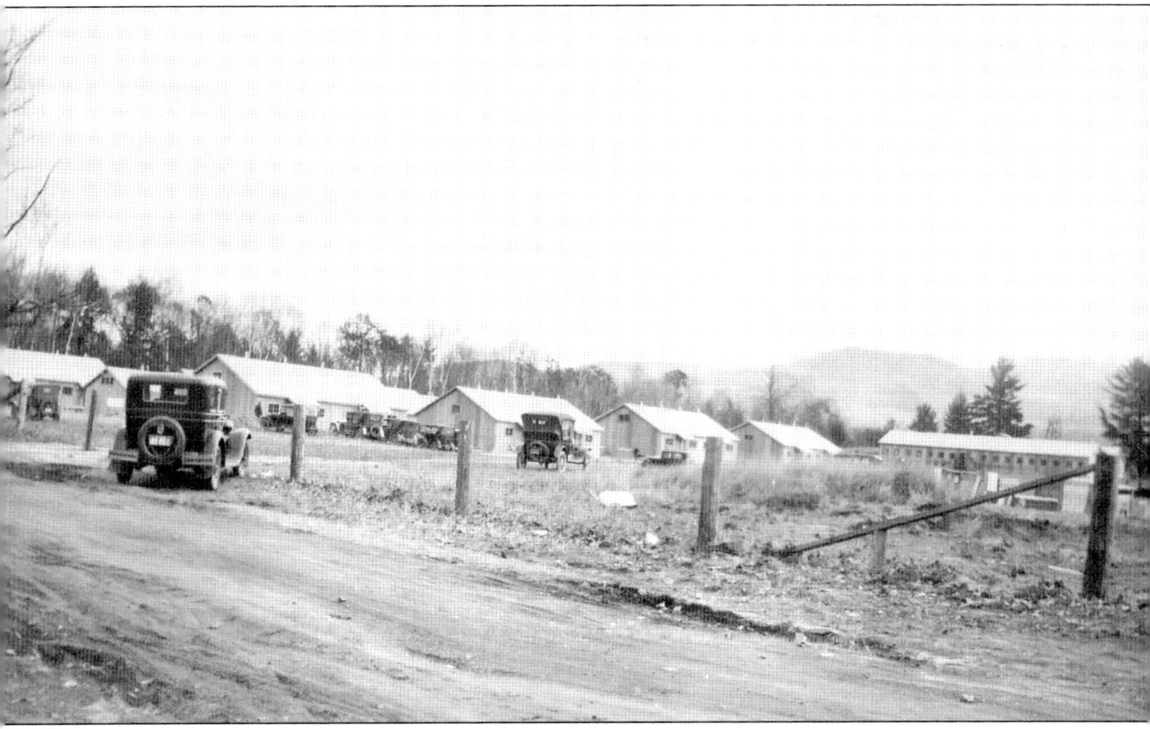

The Civilian Conservation Corps (CCC) public work relief program operated in the United States from 1933 to 1942, during the Great Depression, for unemployed and unmarried men 17 to 28 years old. Modern tenets of environmental preservation are an outgrowth of the conservation work begun by the young men of the CCC camps. Pictured here is the camp on Route 3 in Campton, just below the Thornton town line. The Campton Dam was built by the CCC in 1935. The men of the corps also worked on extending Tripoli Road into Waterville Valley.

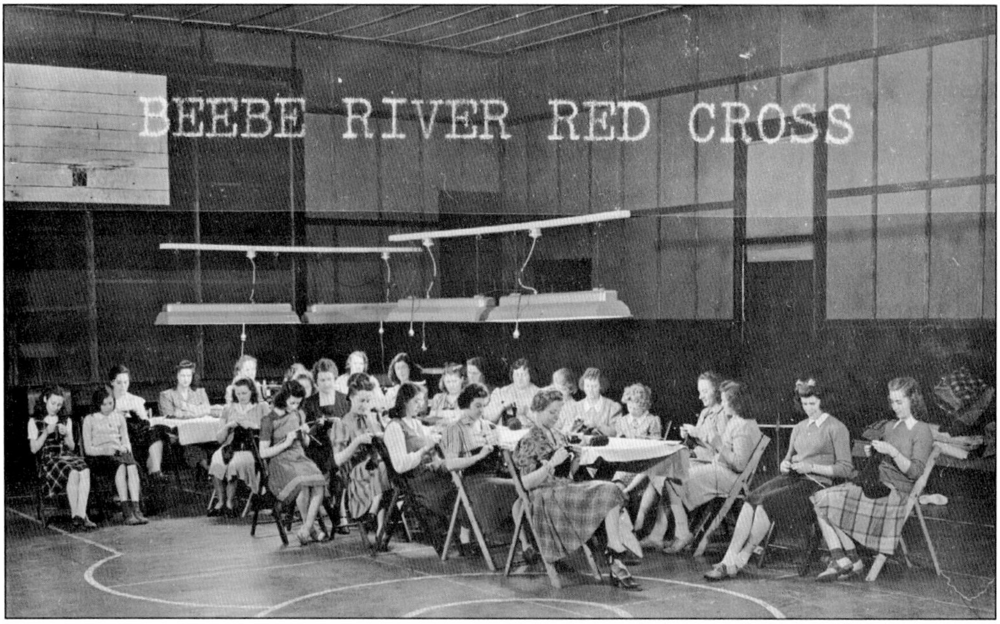

On the home front during World War II (1941–1945), knitting to keep American soldiers warm and to support the war effort was an important preoccupation of Americans, particularly women. Pictured are the women and girls of the Beebe River Red Cross.

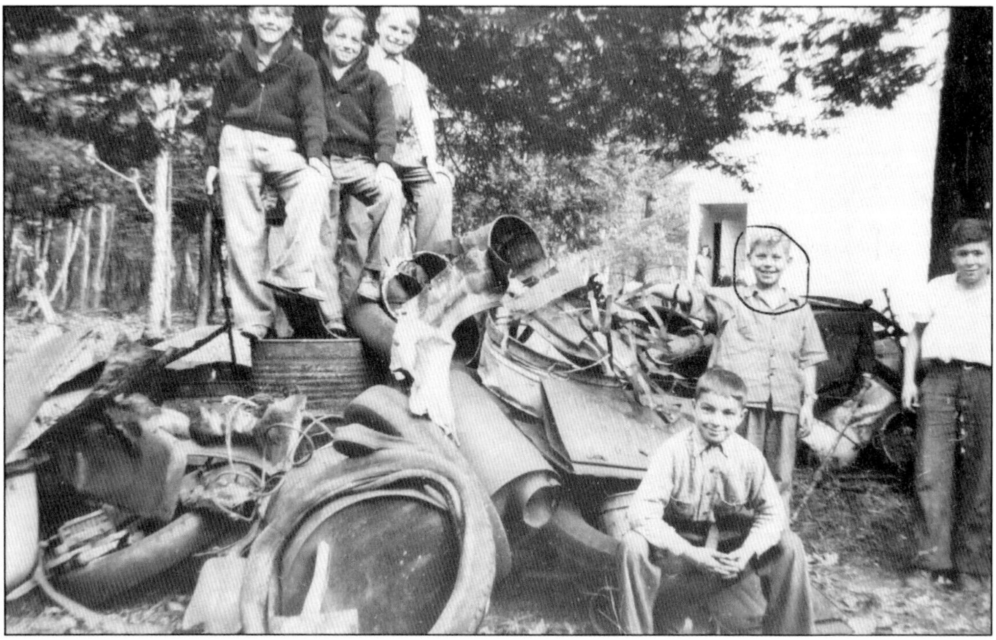

Livermore School students stand proudly with metal collected for the war effort. Americans were urged to turn in scrap metal for recycling, and schools and other groups across the country held scrap metal drives. The drives generated a strong sense of community and a patriotic feeling that everyone was helping in the war effort.

Three

Hotels, Inns, and Guesthouses

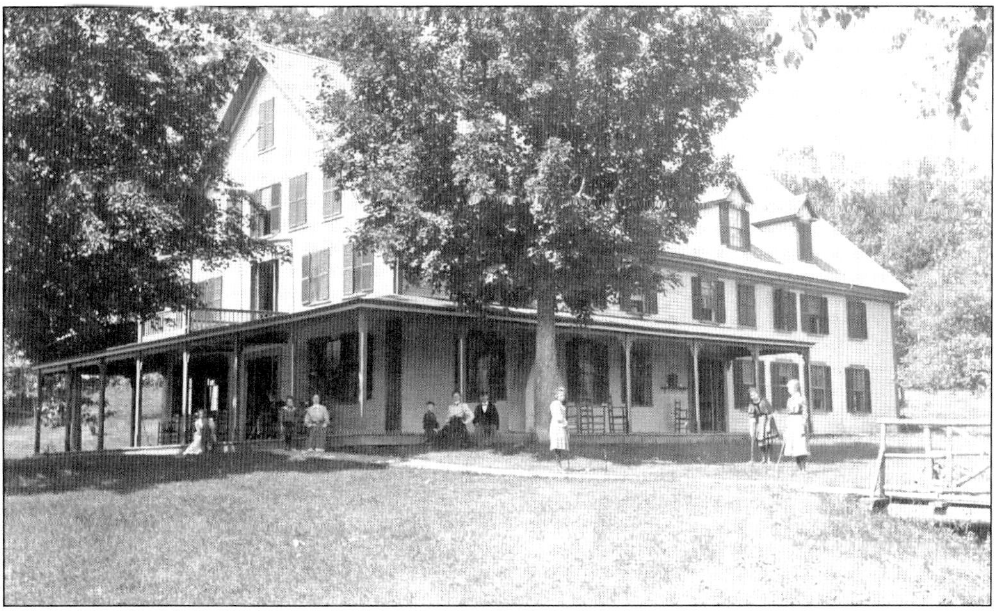

The Blair House, pictured around 1890, was located in the section of town called Blair after the Blair family, who were among the first settlers. The Blair neighborhood had its own post office, located in the hotel. The hotel was owned and operated by members of the Blair family. Until it burned in 1908, the hotel was located on Route 3, north of the current Days Inn location.

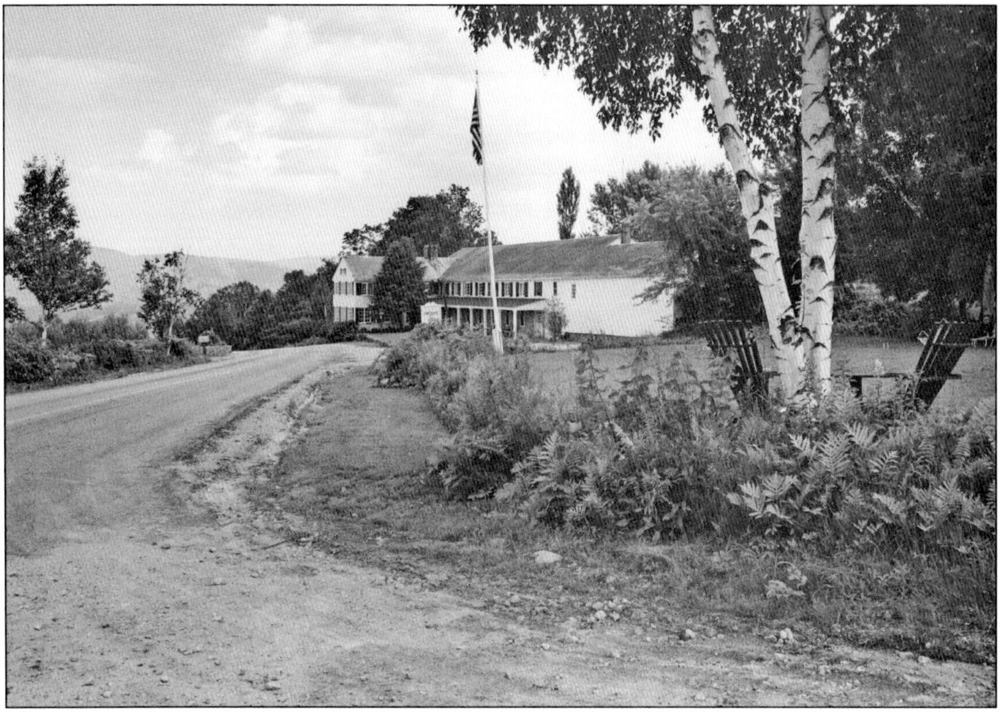

The Armont Inn, in West Campton, started as a dairy farm in the 1930s; one of the first milking machines in New Hampshire was used here. It later became an inn and operated as such until it was destroyed by fire in the fall of 2015. The last proprietor was Richard Murphy.

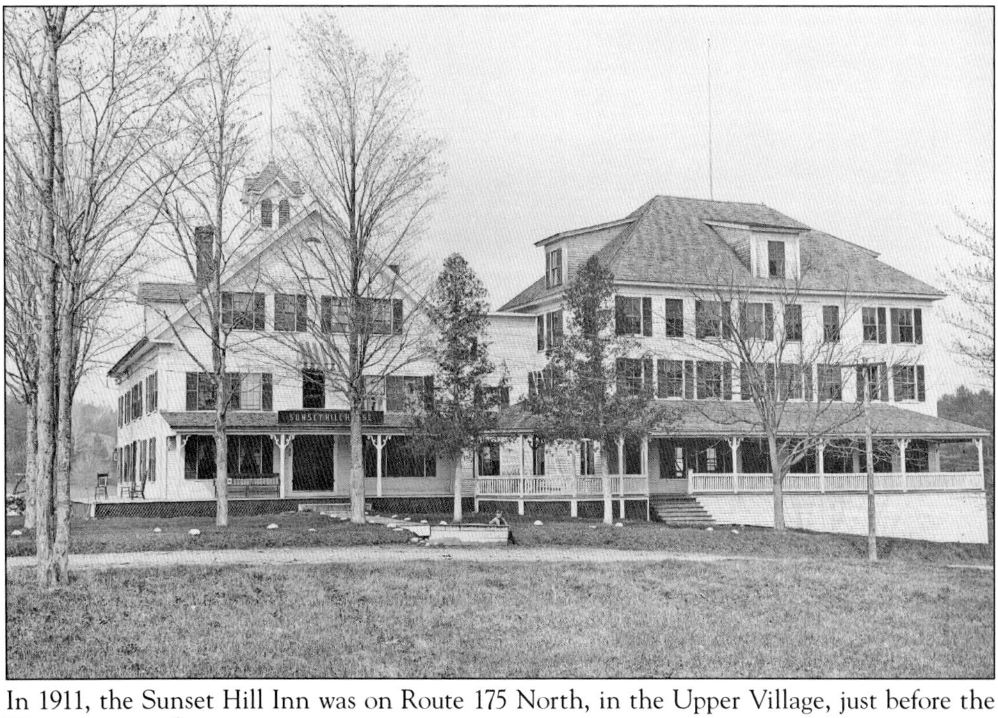

In 1911, the Sunset Hill Inn was on Route 175 North, in the Upper Village, just before the Thornton town line.

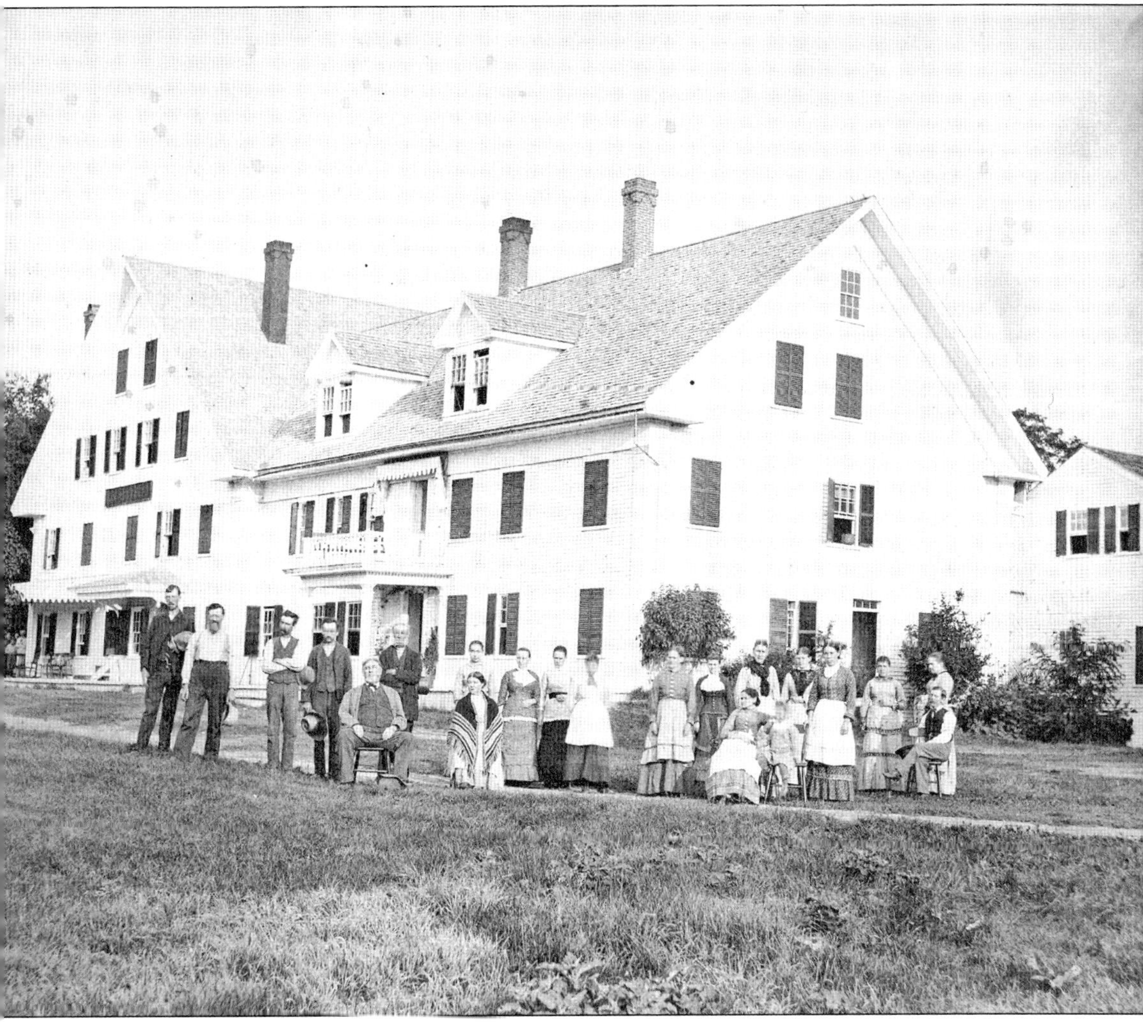

The main building of the Stag and Hounds Hotel stood close to where Chesley's Store is today. It replaced the original inn, a large, square, center-chimney Colonial that was destroyed by fire, in 1895. The Sanborn family had opened their home to the public in 1850, calling it the Maple Villa and Sanborn Hall. This second building, shown here, burned in 1902.

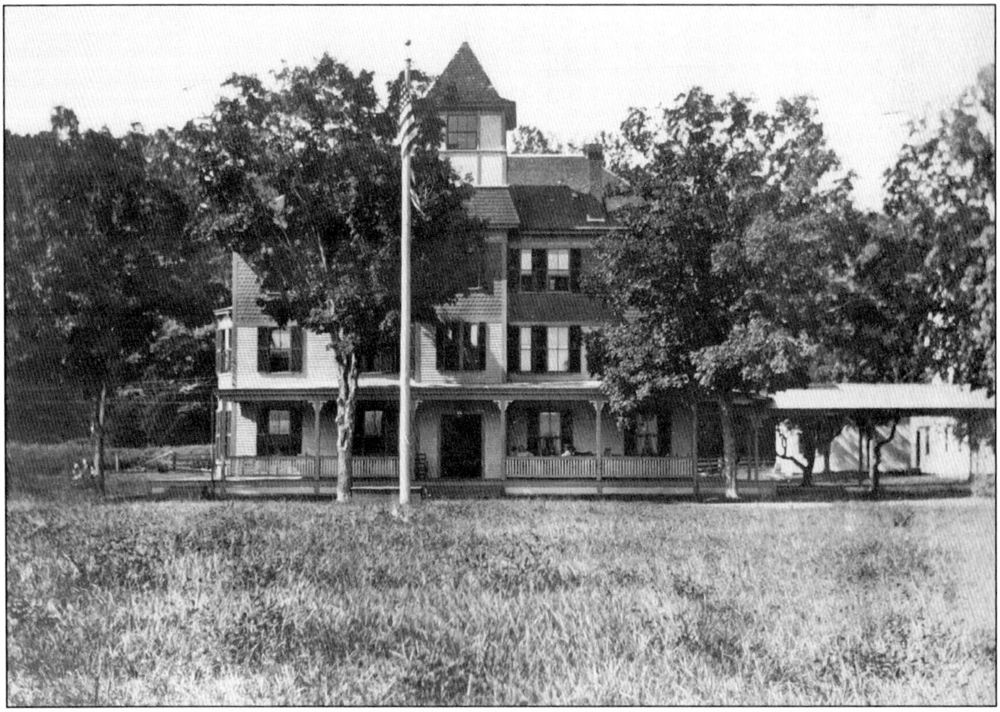

This Stag and Hounds Hotel (pictured in 1901) was almost directly across the road from the main hotel on the spot where Thornton Collision is today. These two buildings, along with the guest cottage (below), made up this large inn that flourished until the 1920s.

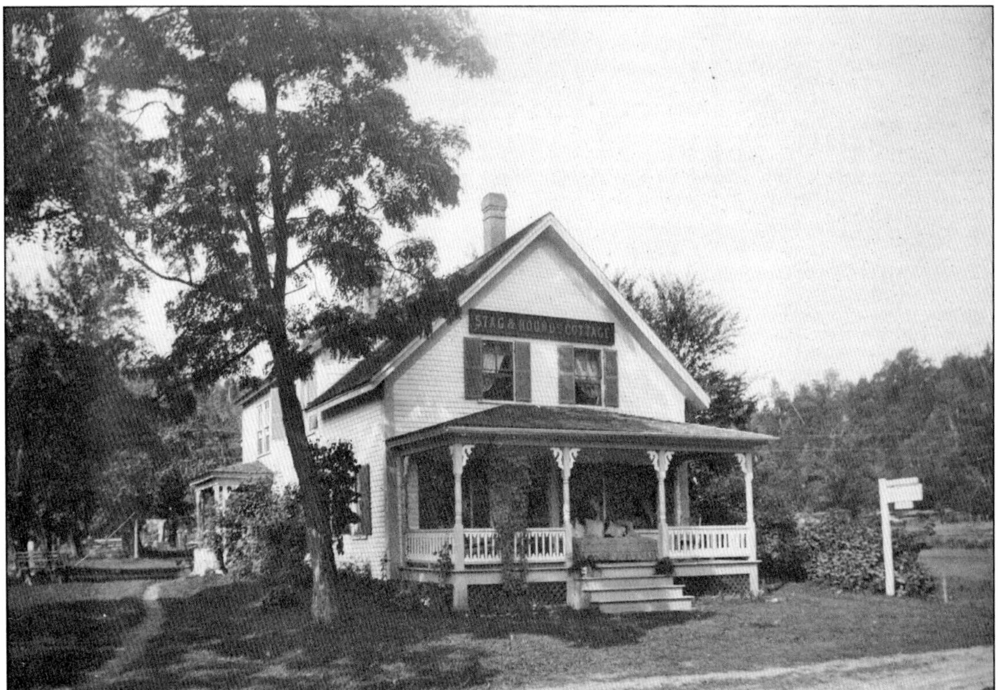

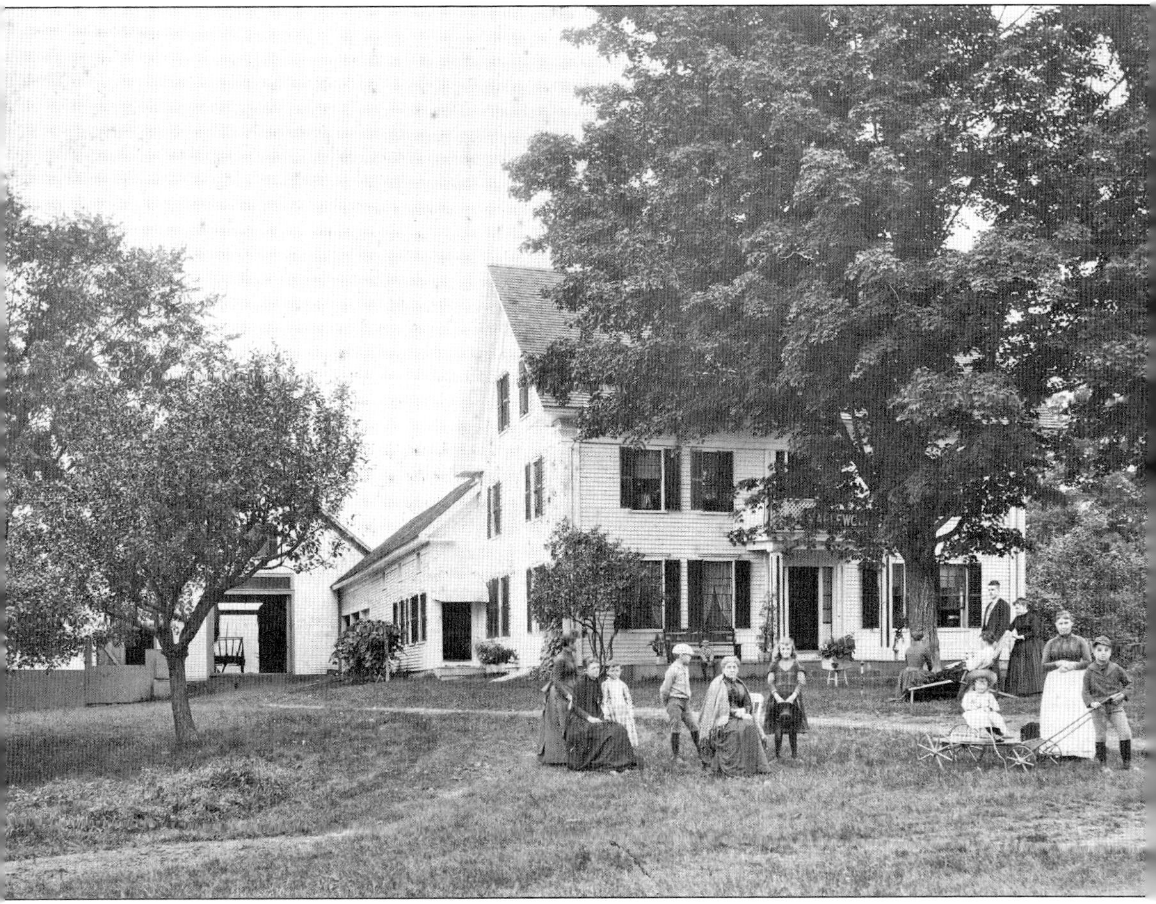

In 1876, Joseph Morrison purchased the home that would become Maplewood and began taking summer boarders. It is located near the present site of Owl's Nest Golf Course. In 1880, he was listed as having room for 25 guests at $7 to $10 a week. The Morrisons sold Maplewood in 1885, and the property continued to change hands many times. The Cook family, who sold the property in 1905, is believed to have been the last to have taken in guests. It has remained a private home ever since.

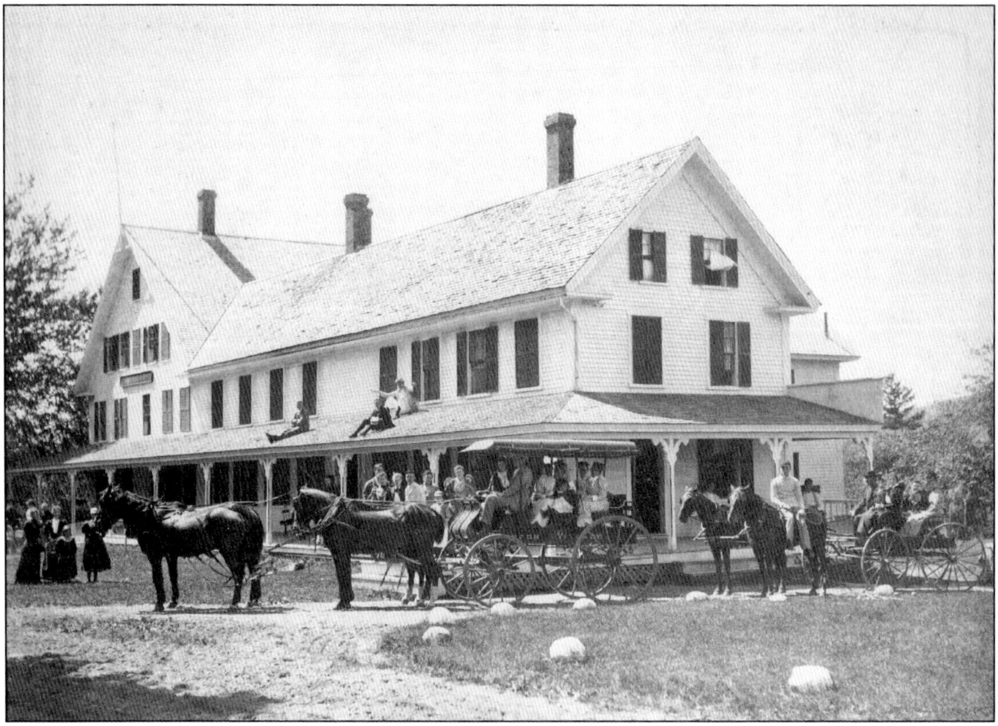

The Hillside House (pictured in 1901) was on Owl Street near the former McAveeney Greenhouses. It began operating as a summer resort in 1880, when it was purchased by Frank Chase, and it continued to operate as a guesthouse until the last owner lost the property for financial reasons. It was auctioned off and then torn down in the early 1940s.

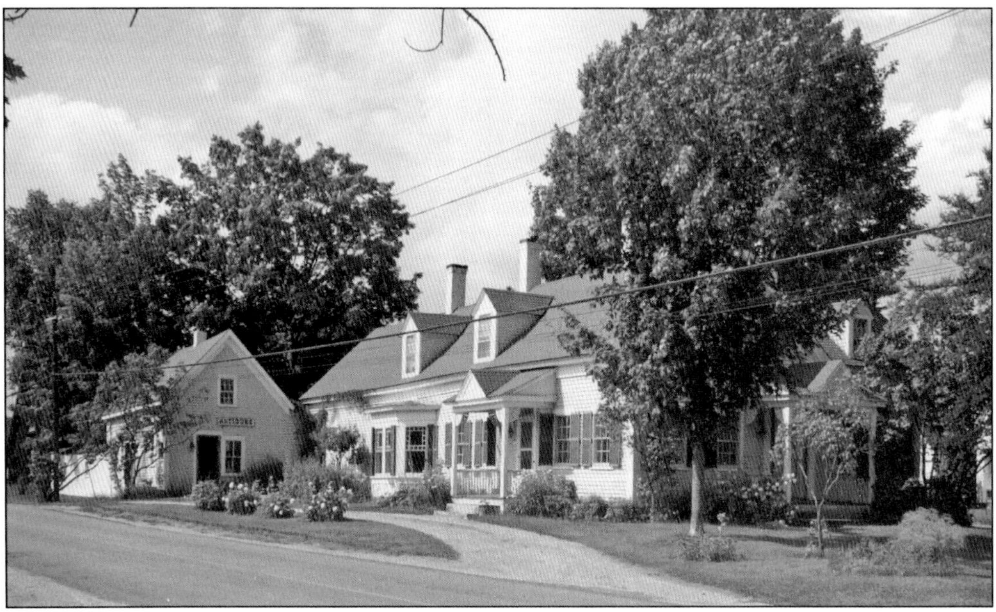

The Damon Tavern, located at the intersection of Route 175 and Mad River Road, was a tavern and inn in the 1880s. The tavern could accommodate 12 guests at $3 to $6 a week. Today, the building is the Sunny Grange Bed and Breakfast.

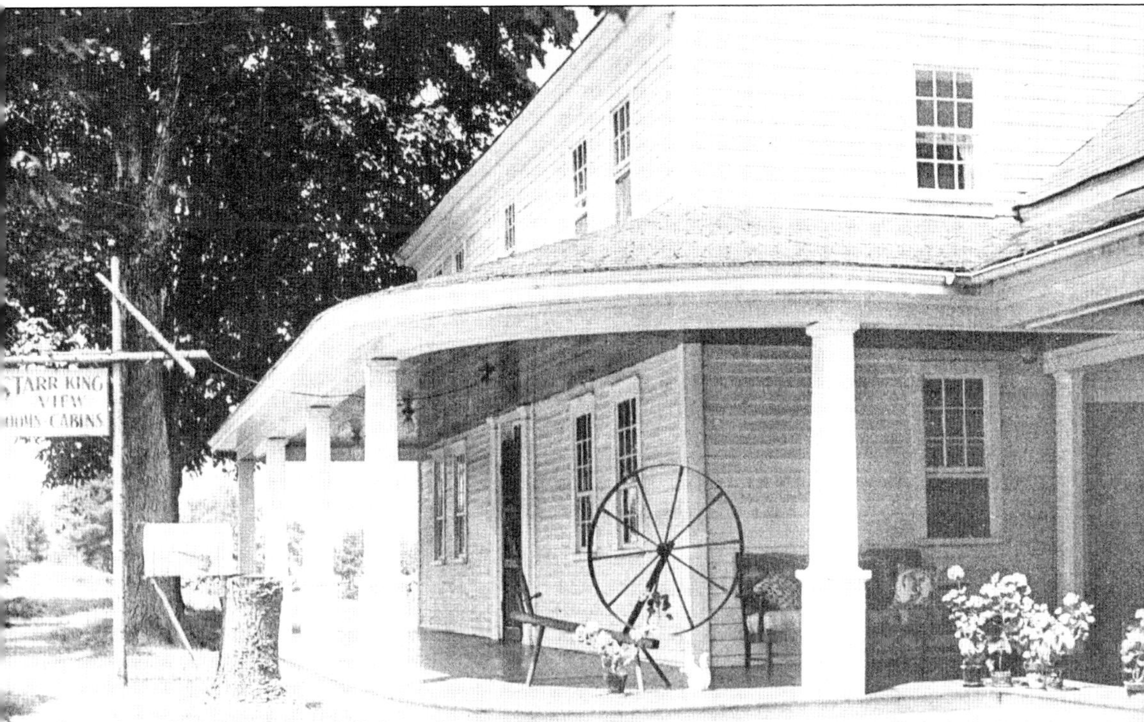

Starr King View Rooms and Cabins, D. W. Highway, Route 3
West Campton, N. H. Mail Address RFD No. 4, Plymouth, N. H.

Starr King View is in West Campton. Rev. Thomas Starr King was a well-known Unitarian Universalist minister who vacationed in the White Mountains in the mid-1800s and wrote a book titled *The White Hills: Their Legends, Landscapes, and Poetry*. King enjoyed sitting by the West Branch Schoolhouse and studying the mountains. When Felix and Mamie McCarthy opened their nearby farm to guests, it was appropriate for them to name it the Starr King View. The house, one of the oldest in town, is still standing but is no longer operating as an inn.

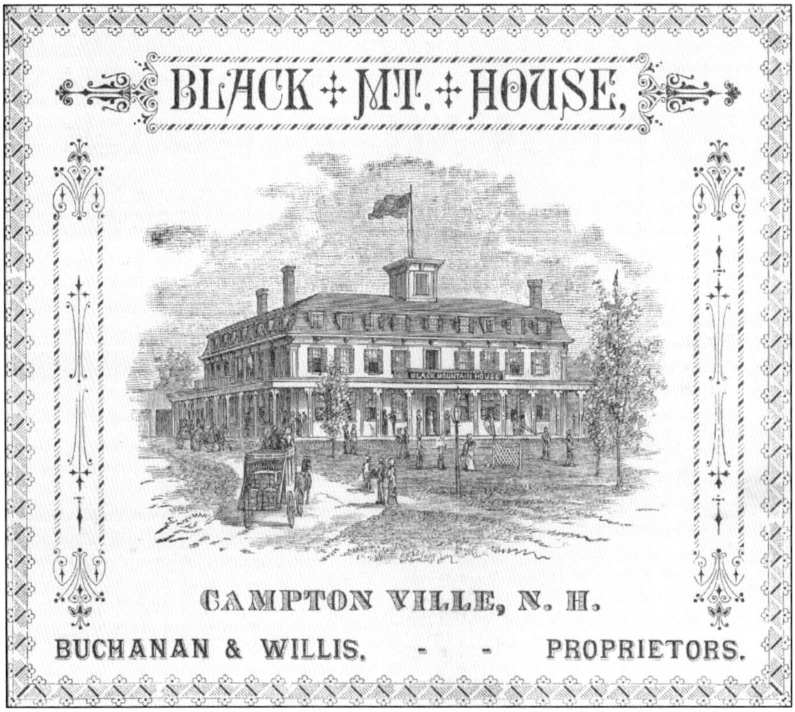

The Black Mountain House was located on the Campton-Thornton line on Mad River Road. It was built in 1870 but burned to the ground in 1885. It was celebrated for its beautiful grounds and panoramic views of Franconia Notch and the Waterville Mountains.

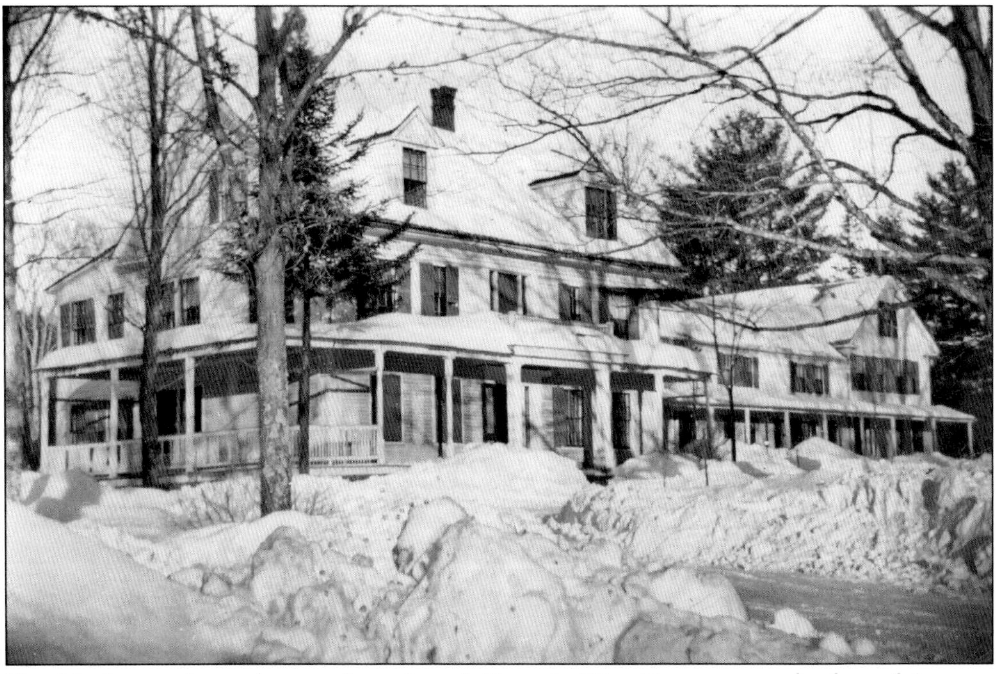

The Maples was located across from Avery's Store in West Campton, at the foot of Armont Hill. In 1885, the house was purchased by Charles Avery and opened to guests. The inn ceased operation sometime between 1938 and 1940. The main part of the house remains as a private home today. It is seen here in 1901.

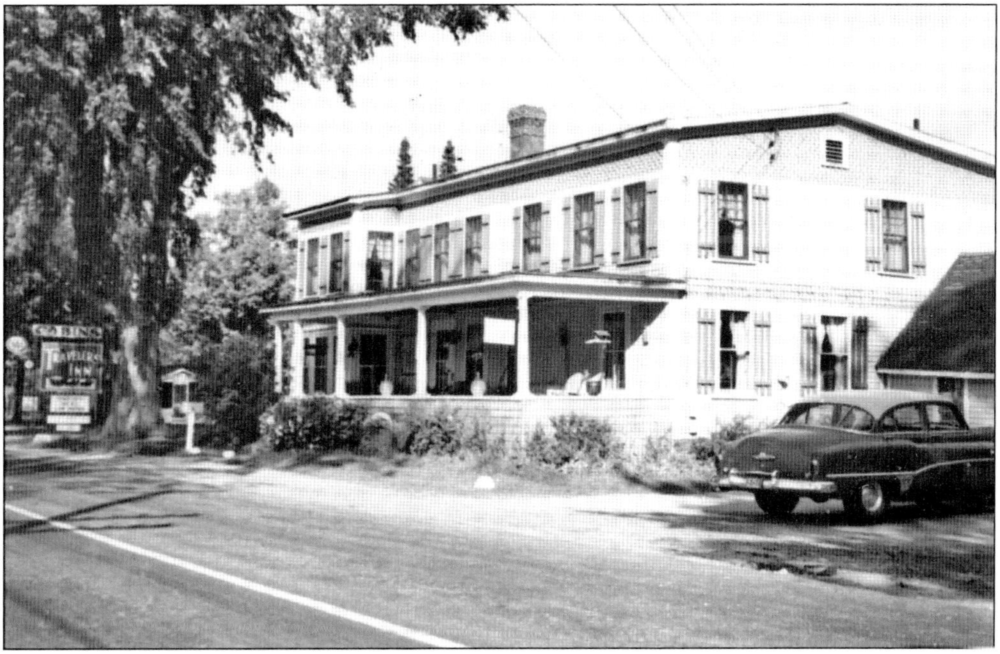

The Traveler's Inn, in Blair, was on the east side of Route 3 at the intersection of Blair Road. This property was originally owned by Samuel Cook, one of the town's early settlers. In 1922, Charles Muzzey bought the property and took in summer guests. In 1955, the last owner sold it to the state, and it was torn down to make way for road improvements.

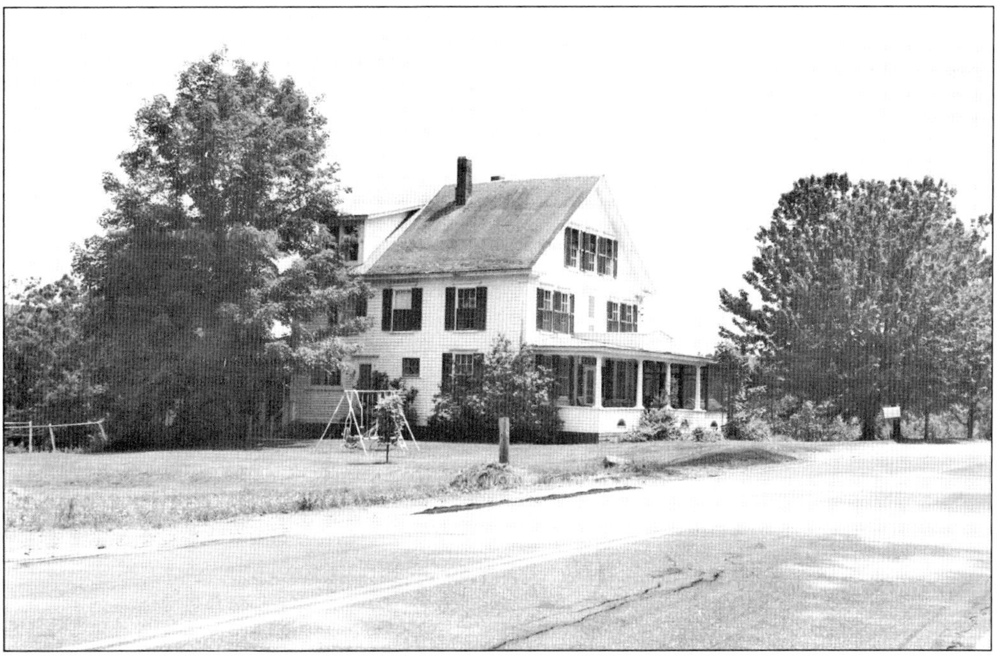

The Riverview Farm guesthouse, in Blair, was about a mile south of the Blair Covered Bridge and the Blair Railroad Station, on Route 3, the main route to the mountains at the time. It was operated by the Garland family until the 1950s. Notice the second-floor entrance for unloading luggage from the roofs of the coaches.

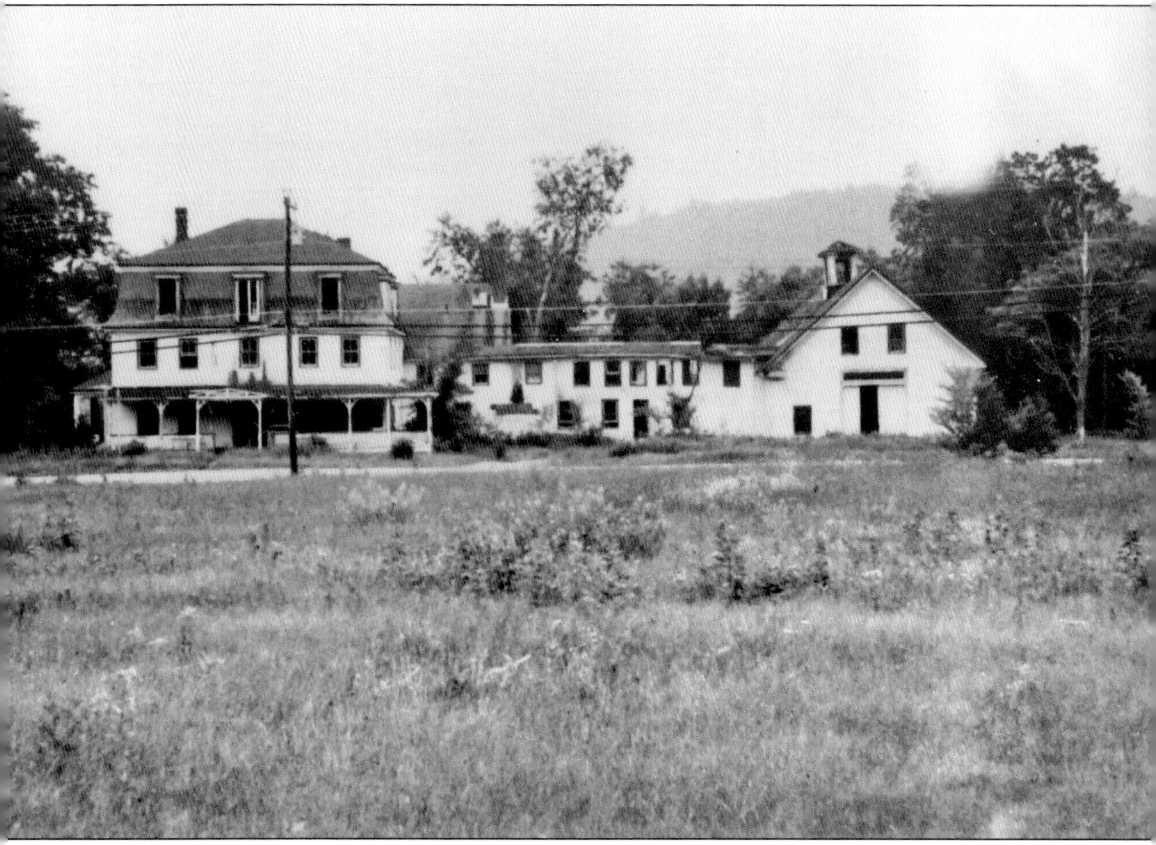

The Judge Livermore home, in Blair, was purchased by Joseph Holmes in 1853 and opened to summer guests as the Riverview Hotel. It continued as a summer guesthouse until 1920, when it became the Emily Balch Soldiers and Sailors Memorial Hospital. It remained the area hospital until a new hospital was built in Plymouth in 1951. The building burned down in 1974.

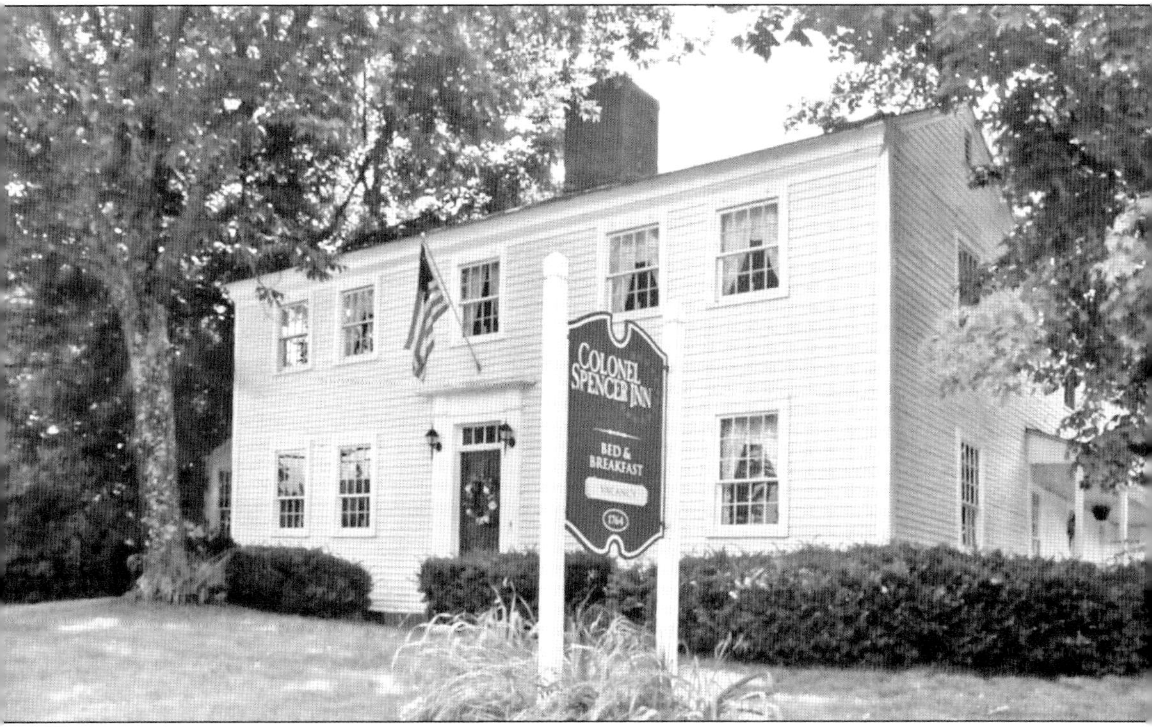

Today, the guesthouse tradition is still evident in Campton, and this is shown through two of the town's vibrant bed-and-breakfast establishments. Colonel Spencer Inn was built as a private residence in 1764 on land owned by Col. Joseph Spencer of Connecticut, who served in the French and Indian War and was the first town clerk and one of the charter grantees of the town of Campton. He was later promoted to brigadier general and served under Gen. George Washington in the Siege of Boston in 1776. Joseph Spencer went on to be the first delegate from Connecticut to the Continental Congress. The Campton property was sold to Benjamin Baker, who also served with distinction in the Revolutionary War and played prominent roles in the early days of the republic. Since the late 1980s, the home has served as a cozy 18th-century bed-and-breakfast, steeped in rich American history, and it continues to welcome travelers from around the world.

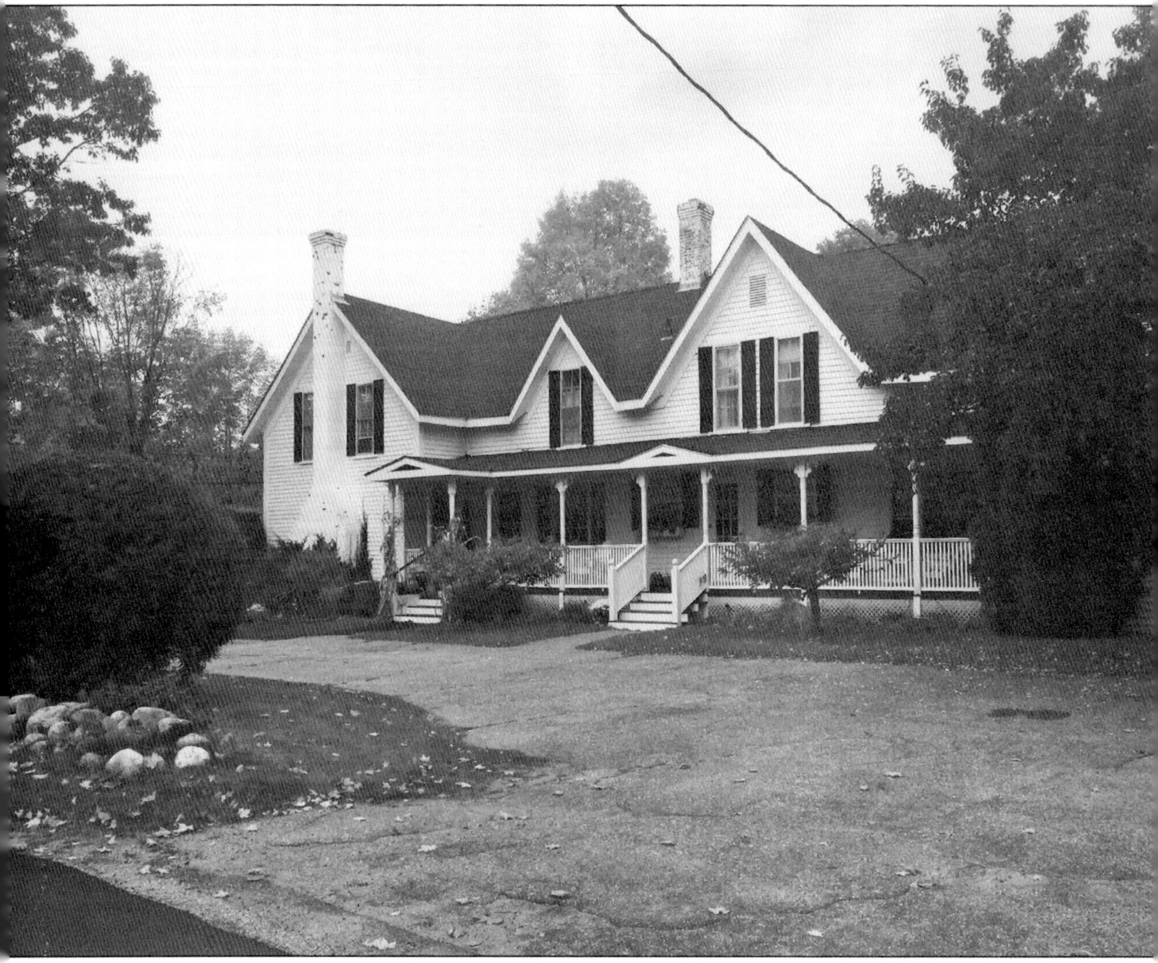

Mountain Fare Inn, originally built as a family home by Elijah Mitchell, has provided welcome respite for city dwellers since the 1880s. It was formerly known as Thompsons' Valley Inn; the old Waterville Road passed right by its doors. As the most popular spot to stop for dinner and lodging en route to Waterville's ski trails, the inn welcomed Robert Kennedy and his family, who often skied in the valley. In 1980, the present owners, Nick and Susan Preston, took jobs as freestyle ski coaches with the Waterville Valley Ski Club and rented a room at what was then Andersons' Inn. In 1982, the Prestons bought the property and began renovations, renaming it Mountain Fare Inn. True to its history, the charming property continues to host travelers, skiers, hikers, and ski teams to this day.

Four

Life, Death, and Everything in Between

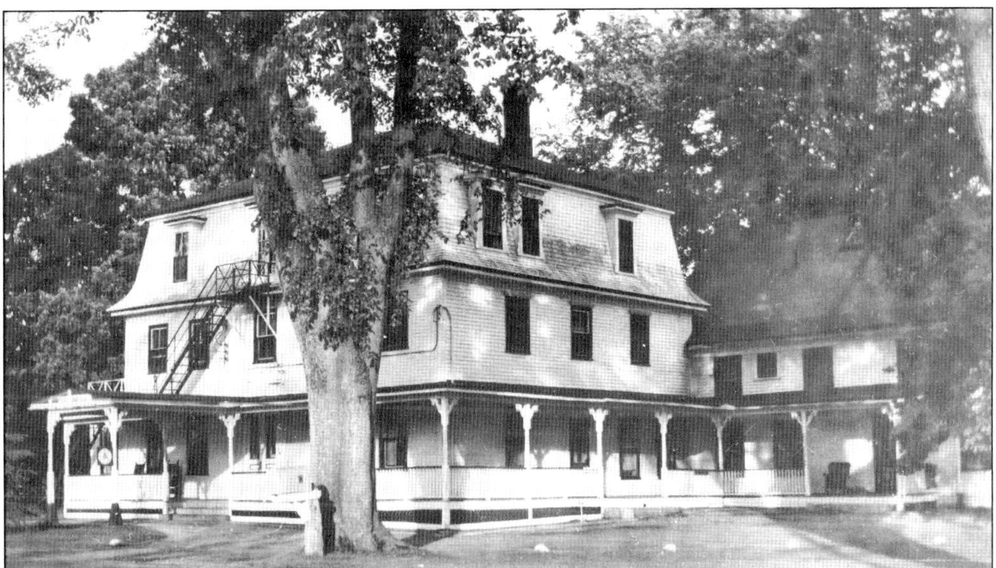

In 1911, the Emily Balch Cottage Hospital was severely damaged by fire. In 1919, the Schofield property in Campton was purchased for the establishment of a new hospital. The hospital would be named the Emily Balch Soldiers and Sailors Memorial Hospital to honor the veterans of World War I. It was in operation until the present Speare Memorial Hospital was built in 1951.

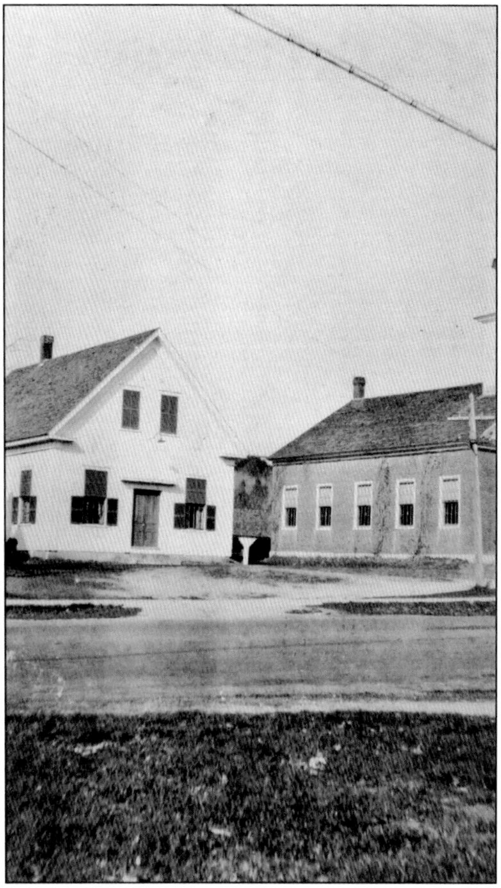

The Campton Baptist Church, in the Upper Village, was built in 1826. The church was formed in 1811 with the Reverend Shubael Tripp as the first pastor. The horse barns can be seen behind the church.

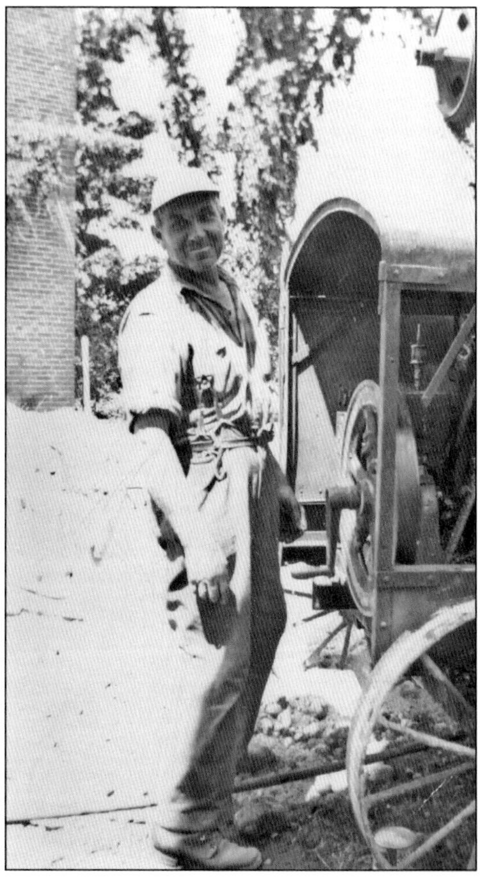

Dave Rogers, of Campton, is seen here working on the Campton Baptist Church vestry. In 1948, Dave, a local carpenter, stands before a cement mixer, preparing to commence work connecting the vestry to the church.

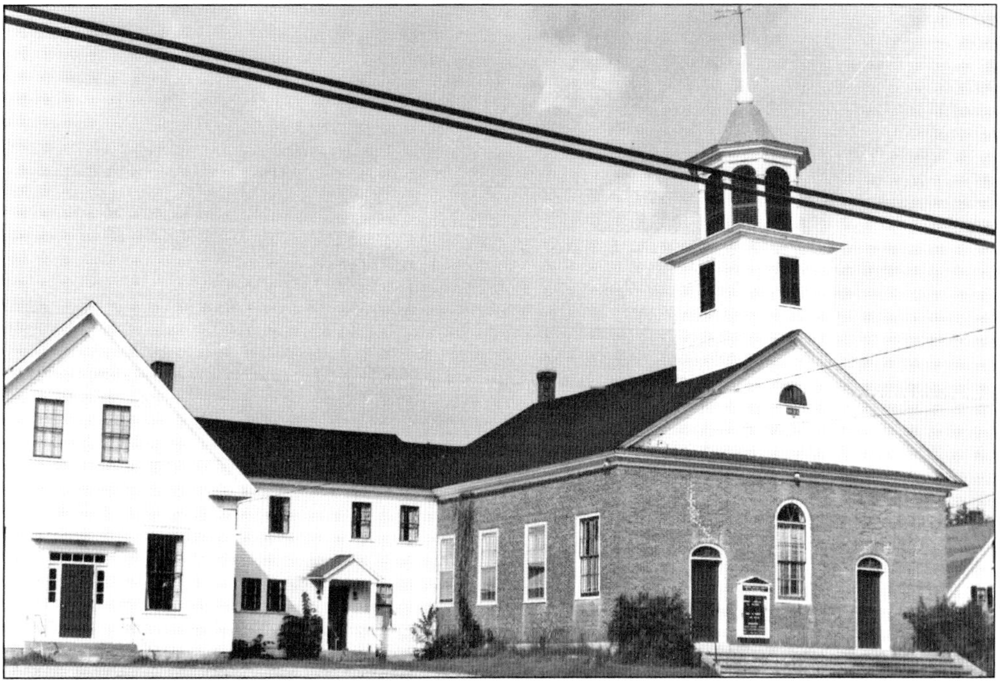

Pictured here is the Campton Baptist Church in 1948 after the vestry was remodeled and joined to the church. The new addition featured a small auditorium named the Frank Fogg Room, a modern kitchen, and much-needed Sunday school rooms.

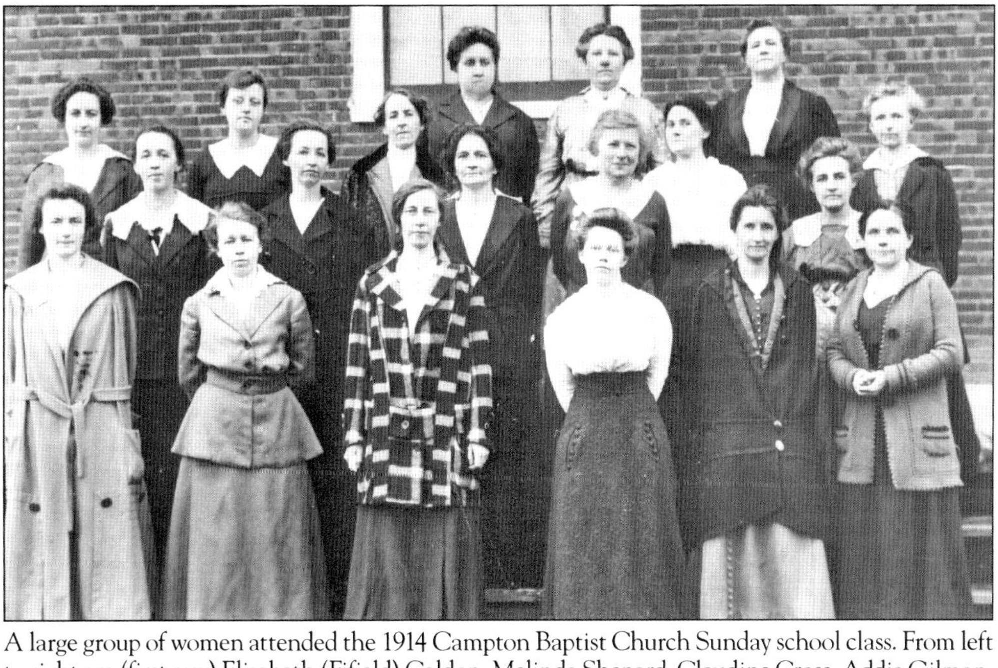

A large group of women attended the 1914 Campton Baptist Church Sunday school class. From left to right are (first row) Elizabeth (Fifield) Caldon, Melinda Shepard, Claudine Cross, Addie Gilman, Mildred (Adams) Townes, and Anna Little; (second row) Nora McCoy, Nattie Bump, Florence Russell, Mrs. Albert Elliott, Minnie Washburn, Sarah Cheney, and Nettie Bigelow; (third row) Del MacGowan, Lottie Webster, Leona Bump, Edna Page, L. Ridelle Morrison, and Kate Simpson.

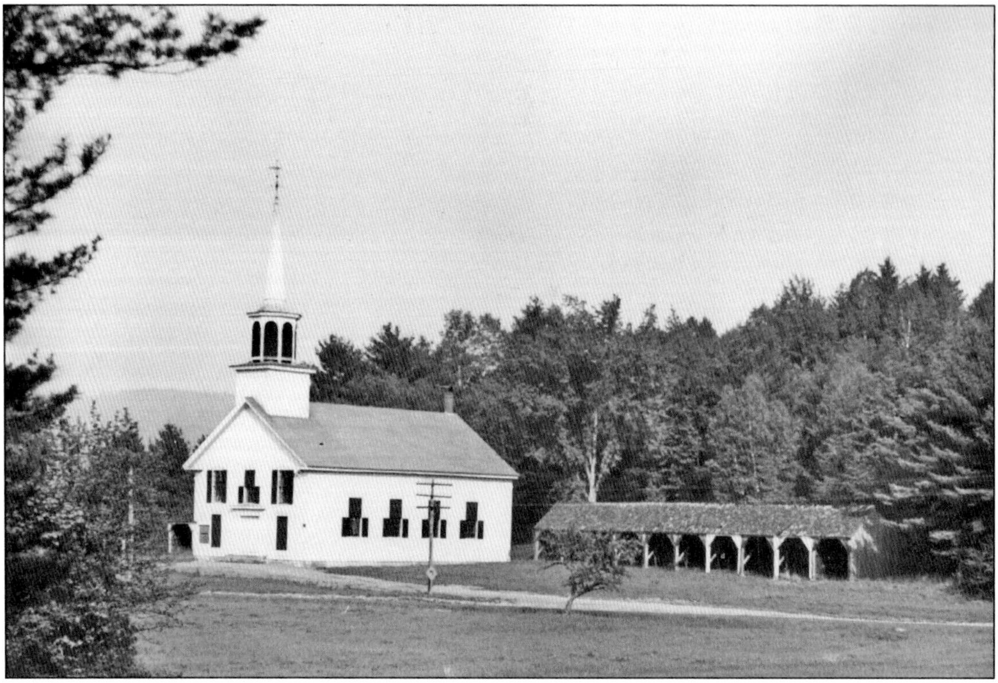

The Campton Congregational Church, in Campton Hollow, was built on the west side of the river and was moved by very industrious parishioners in 1858 to its present location on New Hampshire Route 175. The horse sheds were torn down during World War II. The hearty parishioners kept warm in the cold winter months by means of two woodstoves, one near the altar and one at the back of the church. Rumor has it that one Saturday night the fellow responsible for getting the stoves going had a bit too much to drink, and early Sunday morning, after stoking the stoves, he lay down for a nap in a pew. When parishioners arrived for church, both stoves were cherry red and the building very hot.

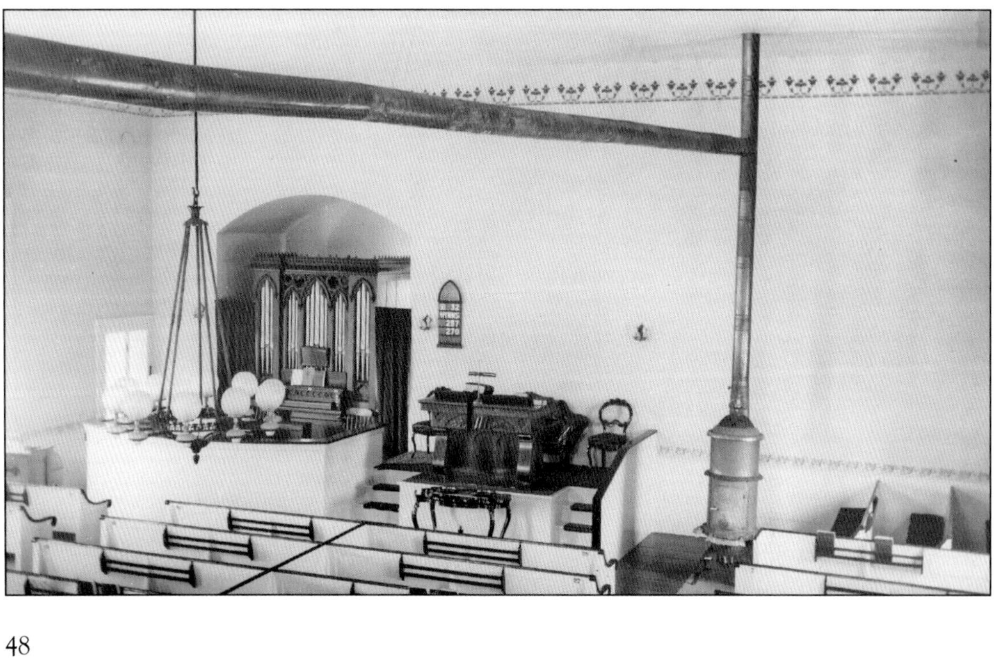

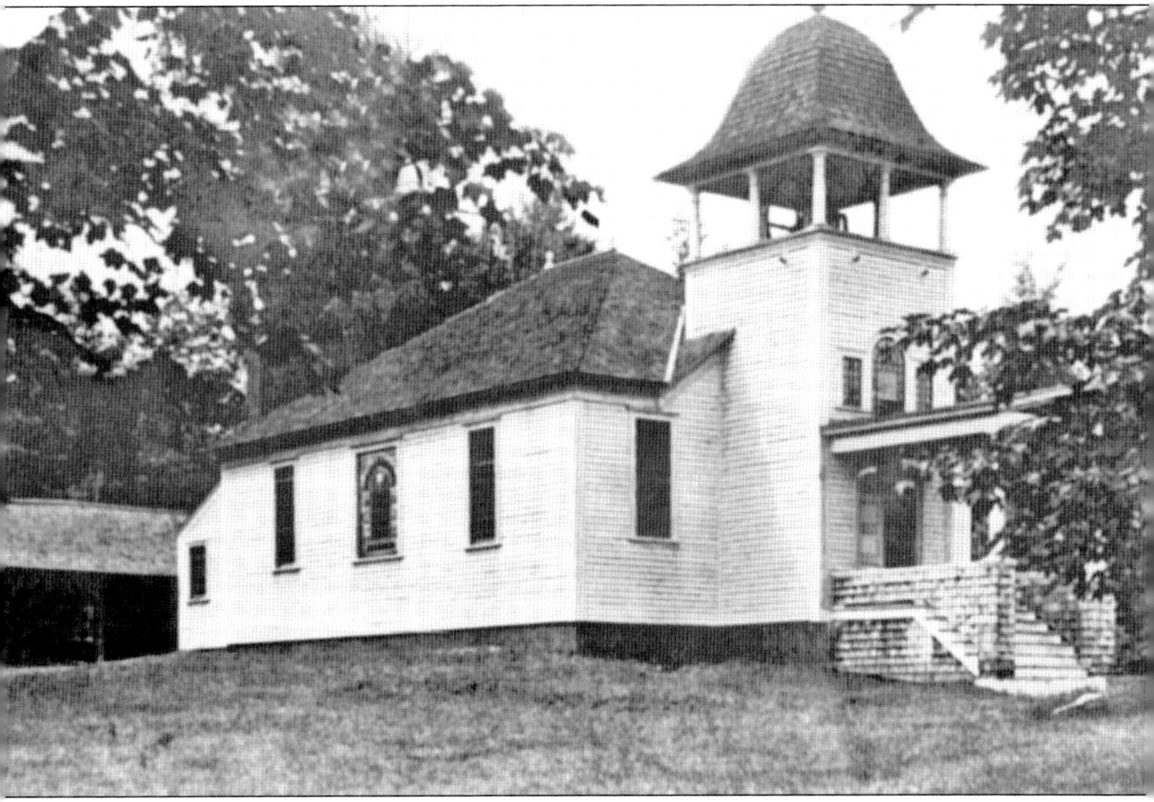

Blair Chapel, on Route 3 in Campton, was constructed in 1883. It was a nondenominational church built for the convenience of the guests staying at Blair House. Services were held in the church until 1911; after that time, the building was used solely for community gatherings. The chapel was purchased by Dr. Fred and Maude Gray in 1929, and Maude Gray immediately set about remodeling the church into their home and summer guesthouse. The Grays made an effort to return the pews and artifacts to their rightful owners, and a beautiful Madonna stained-glass window was returned to the artist, F. Schuyler Mathews. Woodland Rooms and Cabins opened in 1932. Dr. Gray, a veterinarian, passed away in 1935. Maude Gray and her daughter, Leah, continued to run the guesthouse until 1982, renting rooms at $10 per night. Leah Gray stills owns the property and resides there summers.

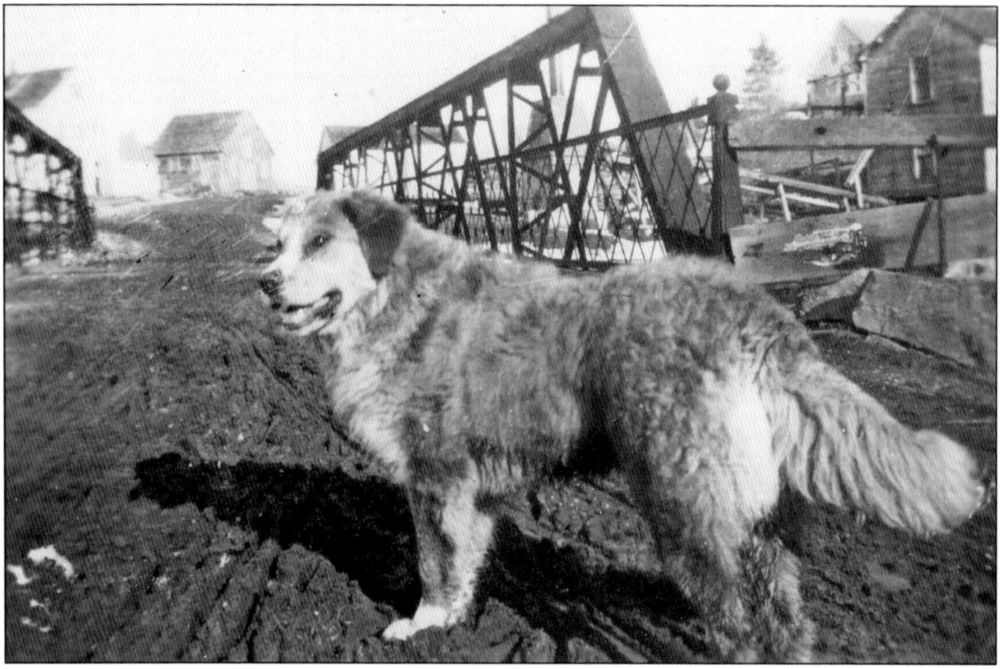

The building at the top of the hill, as seen from across the Mad River, is purported to be the first school in Campton. Imagine how difficult it was to travel on the muddy roads.

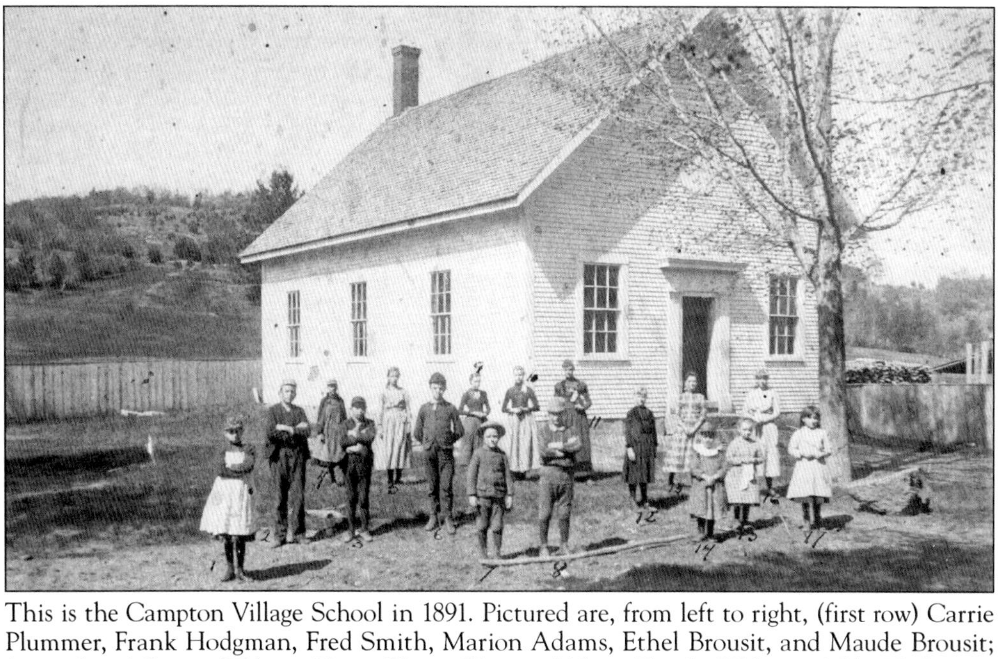

This is the Campton Village School in 1891. Pictured are, from left to right, (first row) Carrie Plummer, Frank Hodgman, Fred Smith, Marion Adams, Ethel Brousit, and Maude Brousit; (second row) George Webster, Harry Chase, Clinton Abbott, Phoebe Webster, Addie Hodgman, and Flossie Whiten; (third row) Helen Adams, Flossie Brousit, Fannie Cook, Alice Whitney, and Molly Pillsbury (teacher).

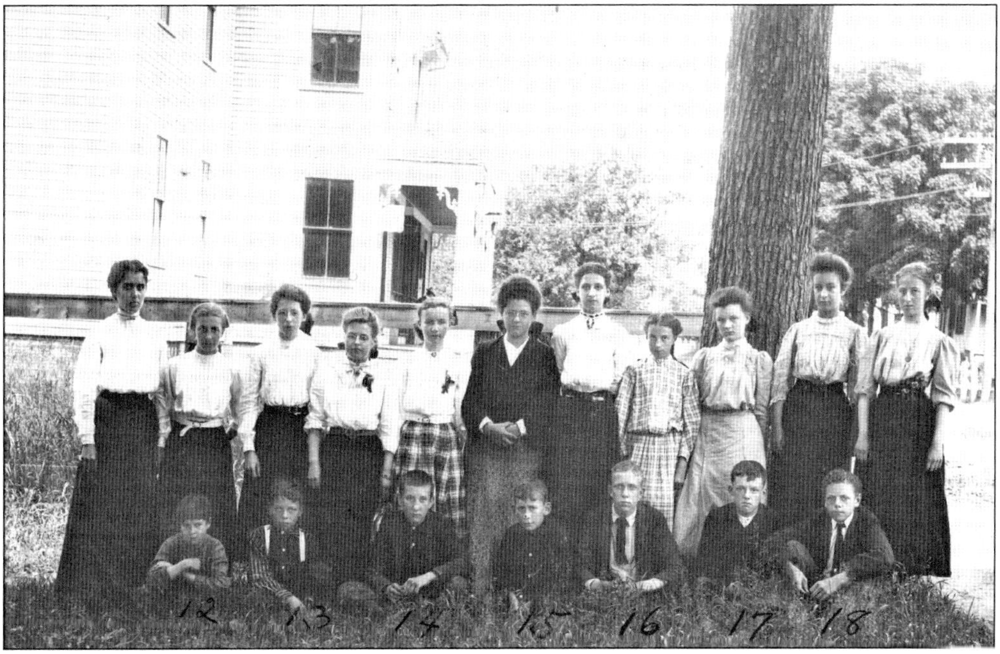

Students attending the Campton Upper Village School in 1900 pose for a photograph. Pictured are, from left to right, (back row) Grace Dole Lawlor (teacher), Alena Fifield, Nina Saunders, Florence Dole, Elizabeth Fifield, Hazel Smith, Clara Saunders, Mildred Simpson, Bertha Chase, Dell Russell, and Margaret Simpson; (front row) Tommy Smith, Lee McCoy, Henry Benton, Ramsey Pettengill, Scott Holmes, Lewis Chase, and Ernest Gilman.

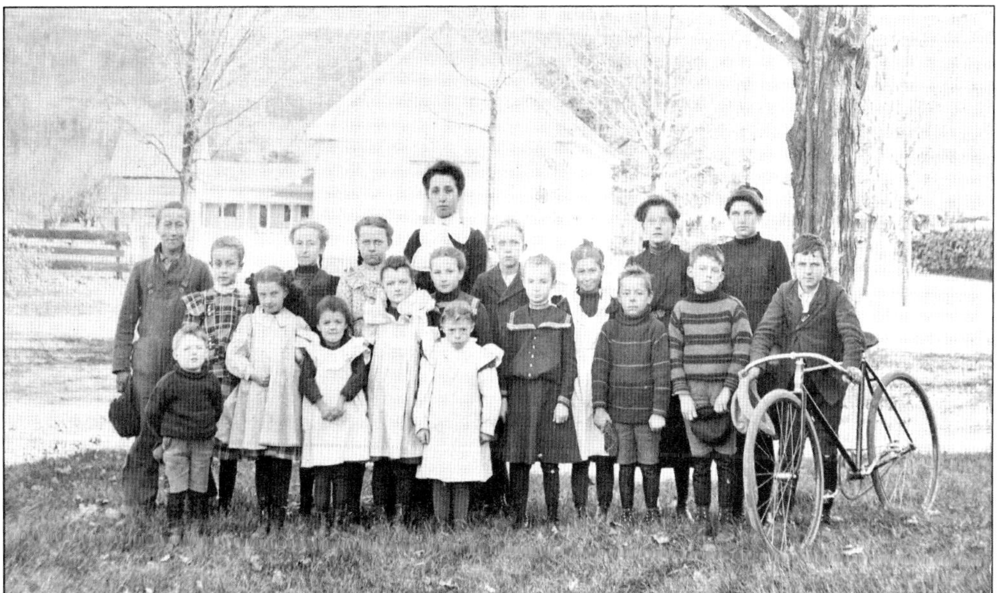

Amy Brown Hill poses with her students at the Lower Village School around 1890. It was a big responsibility for a young teacher to instruct 18 children of varying ages, development, and intellectual abilities. Although the young boy on the right is happy to show off his fancy bicycle, perhaps the little girl in the front is sad because she wants her own bicycle.

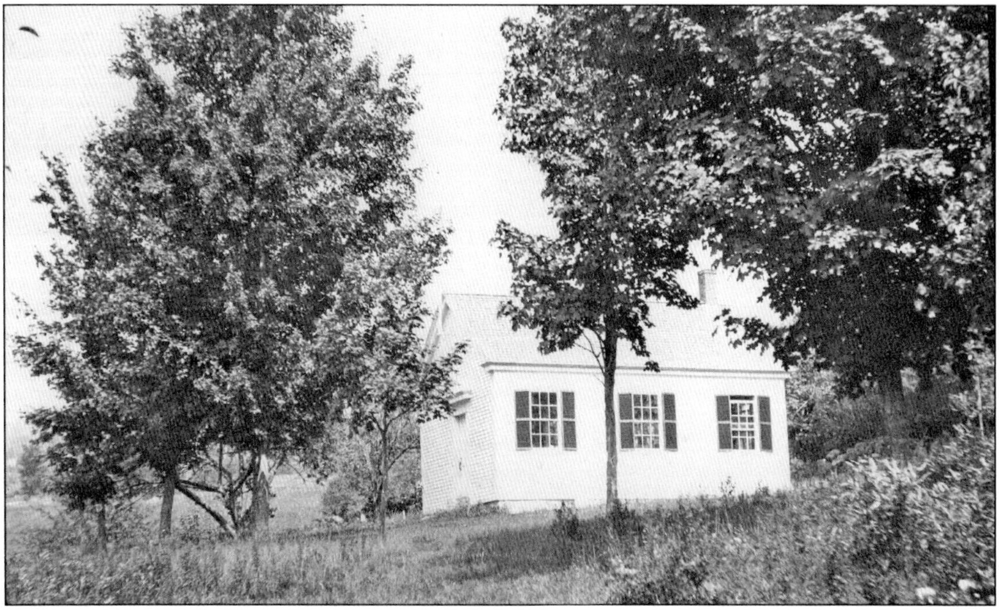

The Campton Bog School, which is a private home today, is located on Bog Road between the Pulsifer and Mitchell farms. There are records of a school on this site in 1828 although the present building dates from approximately 1856. In the 1930s, John Jennings, an American historical author, wrote *Next to Valour* while staying at the old schoolhouse that he rented from the Pulsifers.

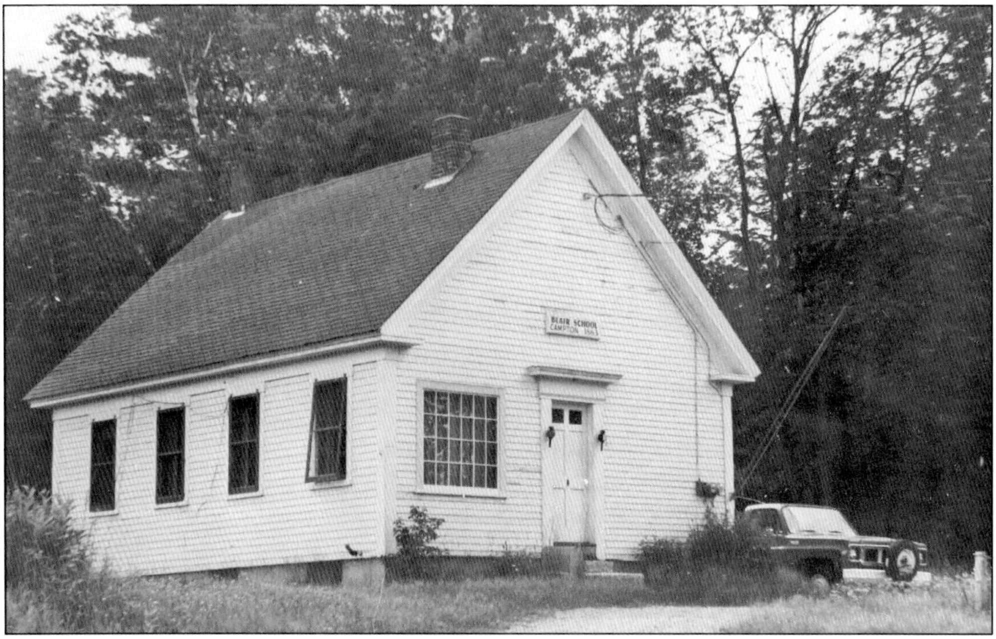

The Blair School was located on Route 3, half a mile south of the Blair Covered Bridge. This was the site of one of the earliest schools in town. The Baker family, early owners of what is now the Colonel Spencer Inn, conveyed the northwest corner of their property for a school as early as 1802 and again in 1814. The original school burned, but the second school building, now a private home, was built in 1863. The first teacher in Campton was brought to town by Col. Moses Baker and lived with the Baker family.

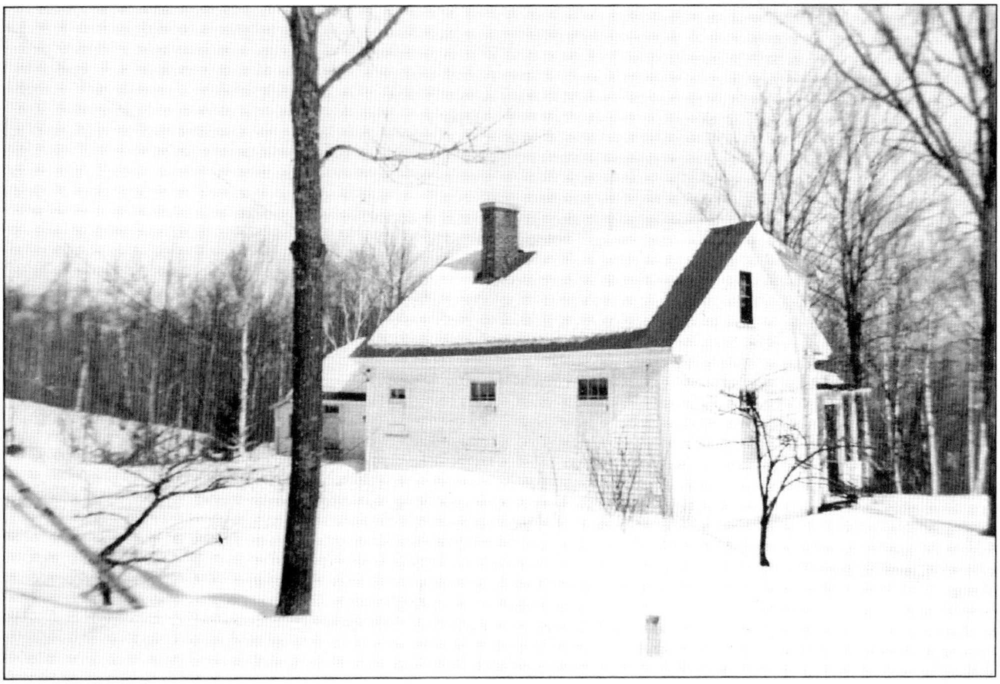

The Hildreth School was on Mason Road, just beyond the White Mountain Orchard. The school's founder, Mary Hildreth, was a compassionate Campton woman who believed that all children should have good homes. Mary left her career in art to devote herself to the 11 orphans she adopted and to whom she provided a safe and loving home on Butternut Farm (see page 119). The Hildreth School was so named because most of the attending students were Hildreth children. Today, the school is a private home.

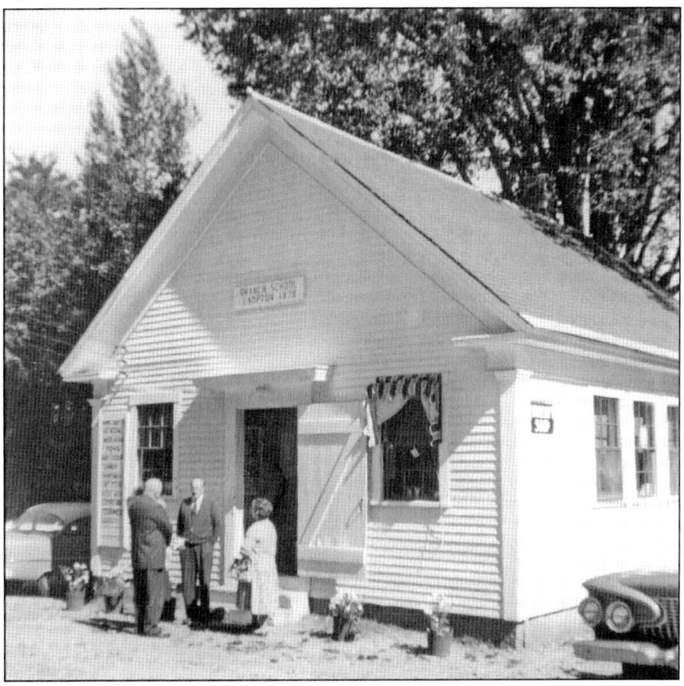

The Branch School in West Campton was built in 1878. It later became well known as the Little Red School House Arts and Crafts Center. It has recently become the Little Red School House Restaurant.

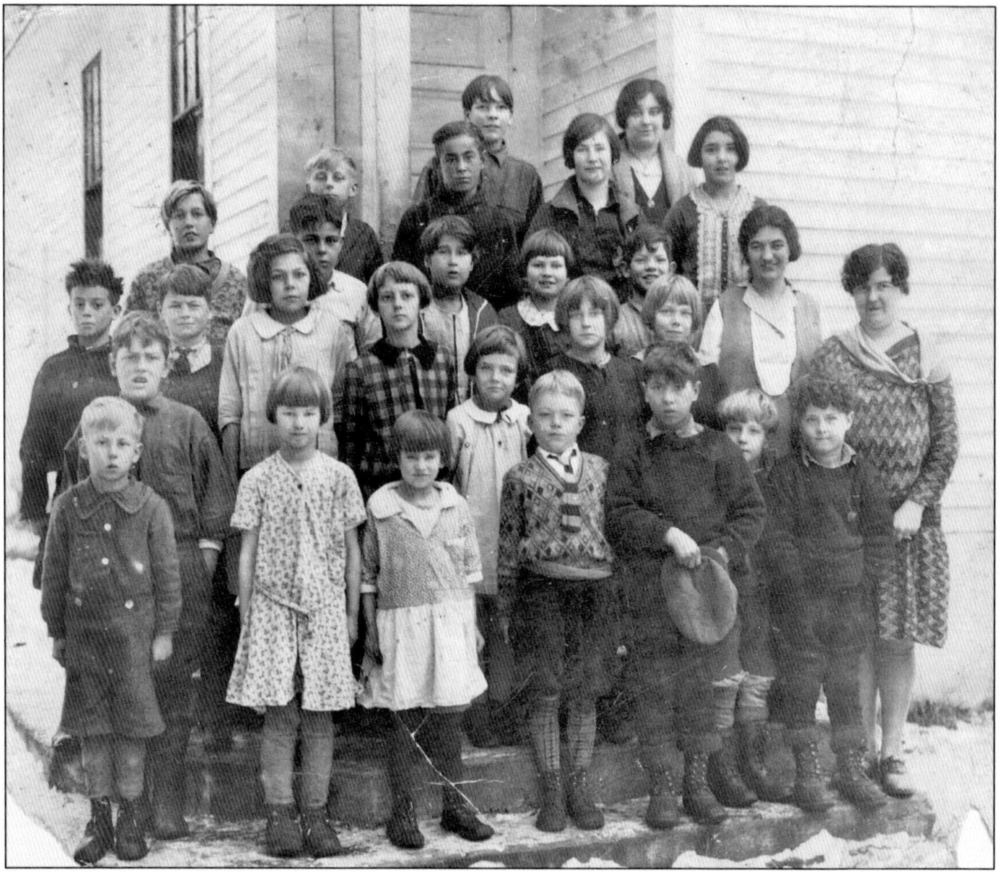

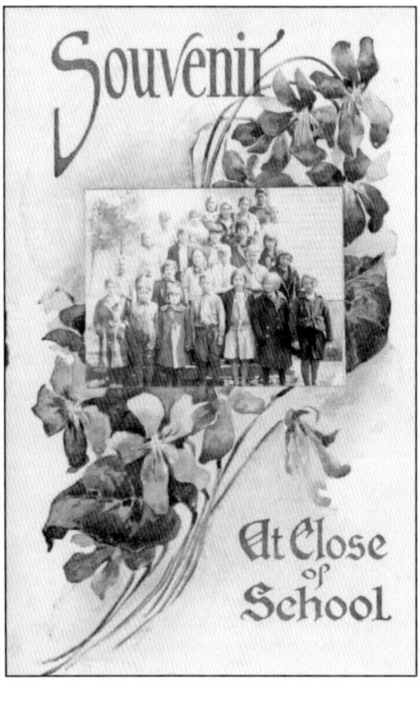

The first Livermore Falls School was built near the Holderness town line on New Hampshire Route 175. A later school was built south of Pulsifer Road. This building is now a private residence. The children of Livermore Falls School are pictured above in 1929 and include, from left to right, (first row) Roger Pierce, William Cilley (behind Pierce), Dorothy Moulton, Margaret Moulton, Edward Pattee, Dora Clark (behind Pattee), Ellsworth Wiggett, Ephram Salls, Jackie Wiggett, and Miss Ramsdell (teacher); (second row) Forrest Jenkins, Clifton Moulton, Hazel Cilley, Thelma Pierce, Gerite Salls, Velma Salls, and Miss Tolman (teacher); (third row) Erwin Salls, John Driscoll, Ina Driscoll, Louis Moulton, and Carl Mitchell; (fourth row) John Chartier, Mildred Moulton, Vivian Dustin, and Richard Pierce; (fifth row) Horace Mitchell and Miss Fellows (teacher). Pictured at the left is a souvenir booklet that each student would receive at the exercises held at the end of the school year. It would include names of the teachers, students, district administrators, and winners of academic awards.

The Beebe River School (pictured) was built in the mid-1930s. The Campton Village School was an identical two-room school built in 1934.

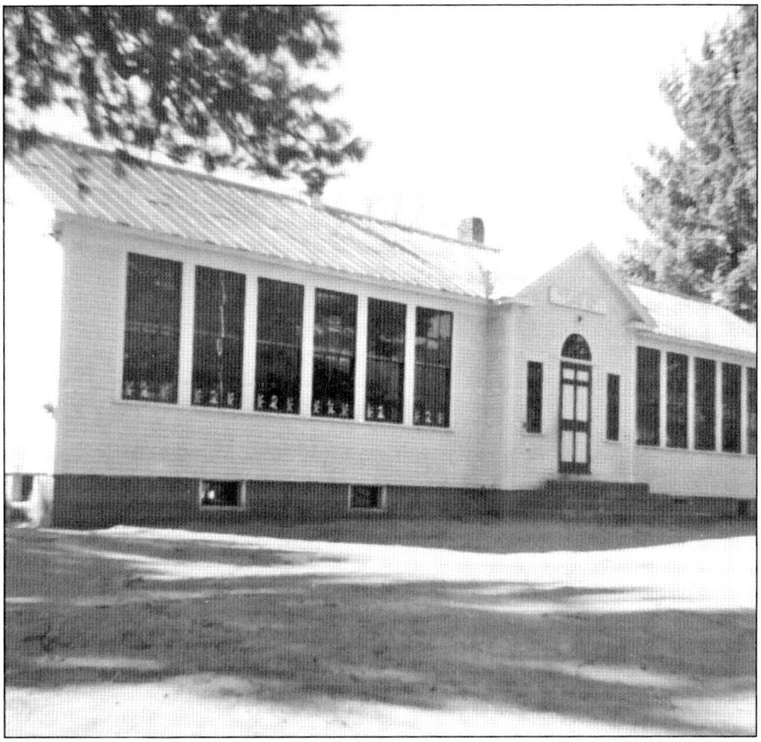

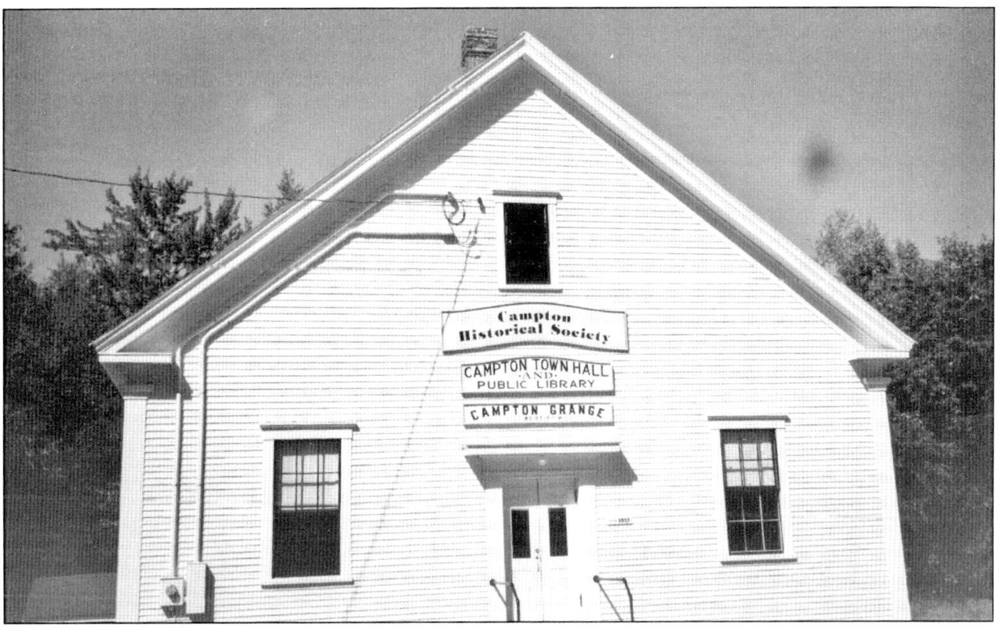

The town library was located in the town house in Campton Hollow. Today, the building is the home of the Campton Historical Society. When the Grange gave up its charter in 1974, the library was moved to the Grange Hall, which is attached to the town house. It was then called the Grange Public Library. Abigail Ewins served as the librarian from 1907 until 1937, when her daughter took over the post. Laura Ewins Pulsifer continued as librarian until the library was moved to the elementary school in 1986.

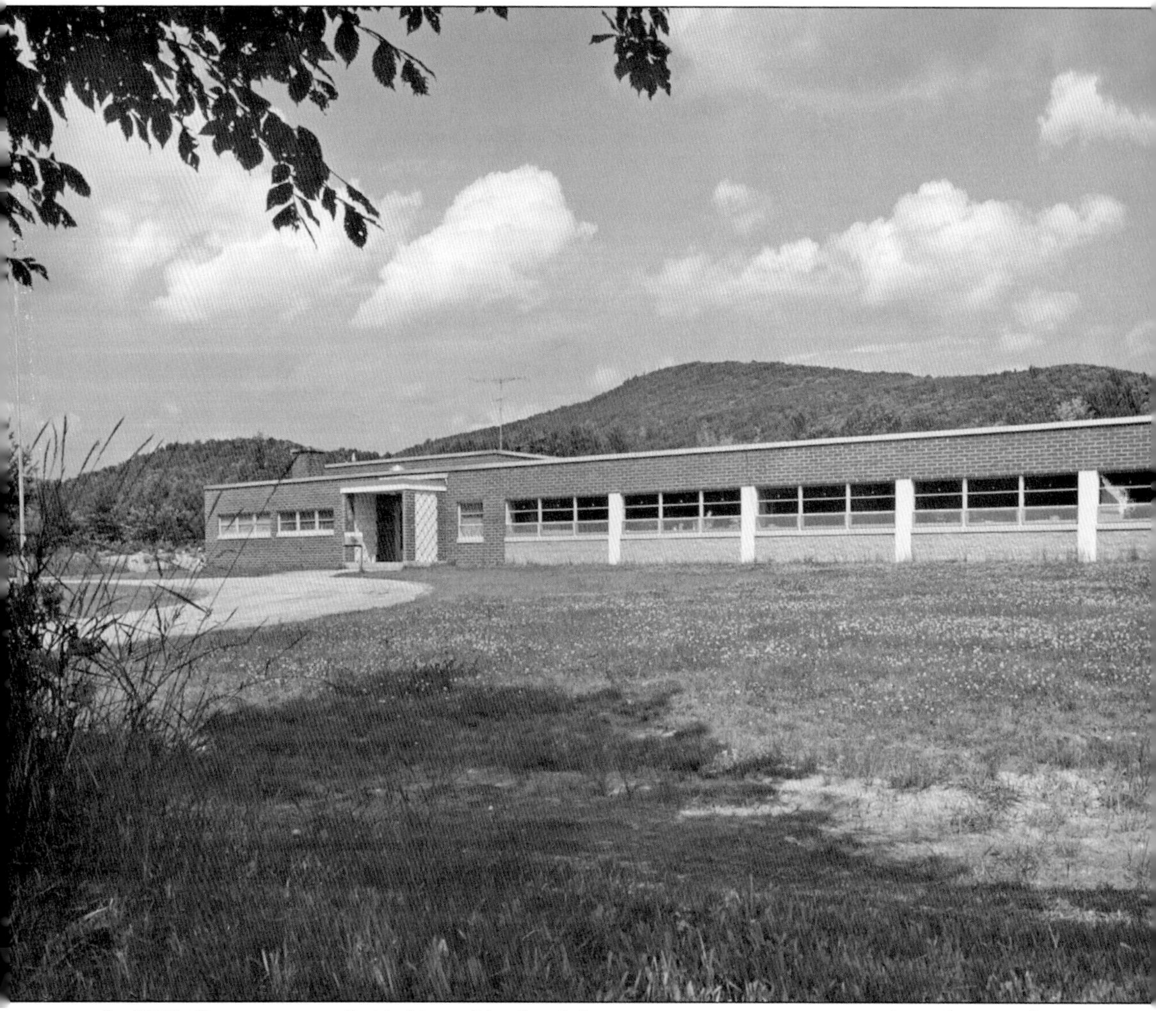

In 1875, Campton was divided into 14 school districts, necessary at a time when the population was scattered hither and yon over difficult-to-navigate roads. As life became less complicated, employment more lucrative, and transportation easier, schools closed one by one, until early in 1930, only four schools remained: two on the west side of town—one at Blair, one in West Campton—and two on the east side of town, at Livermore and Campton Hollow. In 1962, this modern six-room school was built on Route 175 in the lower part of Campton Village, and all pupils were then transported by bus. The school has been added onto and remodeled over the years and presently has over 300 students ranging from preschool through eighth grade.

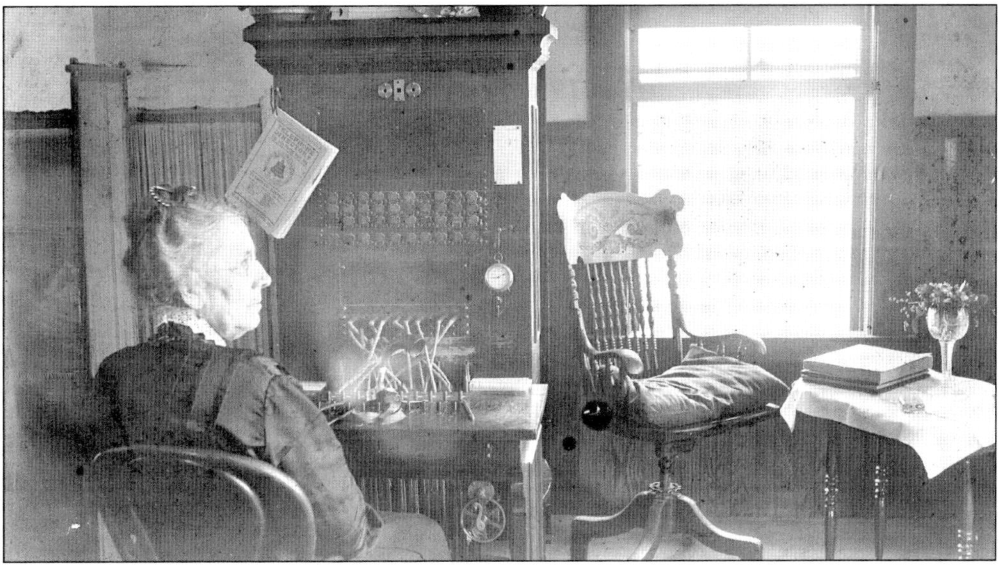

"October 9, 1897, We the undersigned citizens of the town of Campton in the State of New Hampshire, do respectfully petition to the selectmen of the town of Campton that we be granted the right to set poles and hang wires thereon side of the public highways anywhere within the boundary lines of said town of Campton for telephone purposes." Shortly thereafter, the first telephones came to Campton. Shown here is Mrs. Osgood, busy at the switchboard.

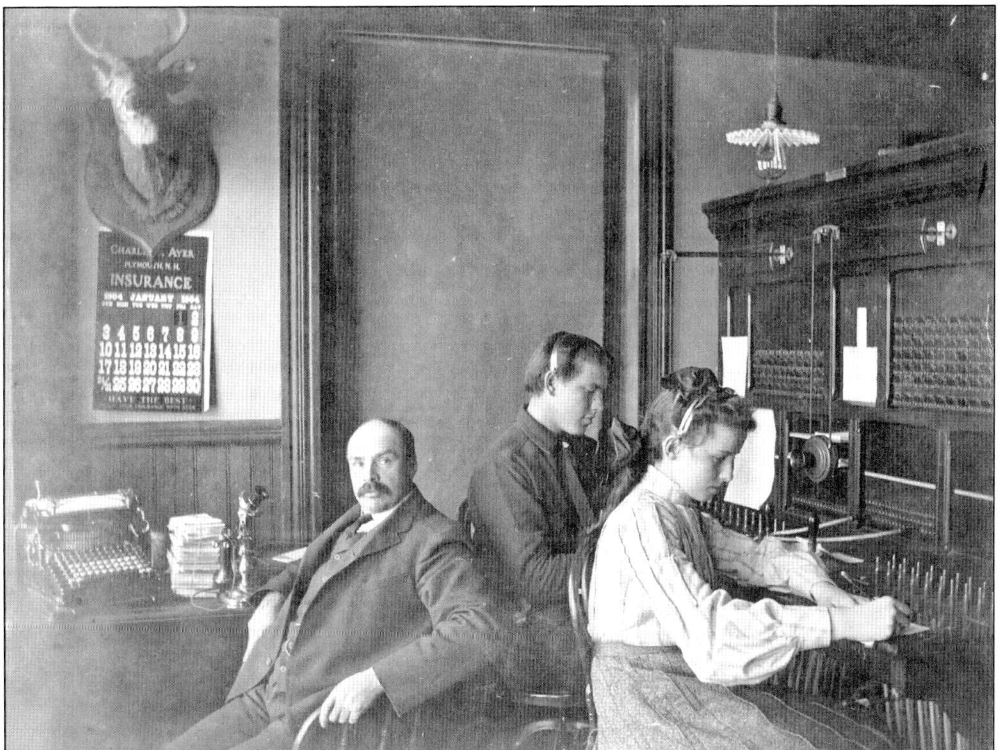

It is January 1904, and Walter Isaiah Lee sits at his desk in the Campton Telephone office. There appears to be one less buck roaming the Campton woods.

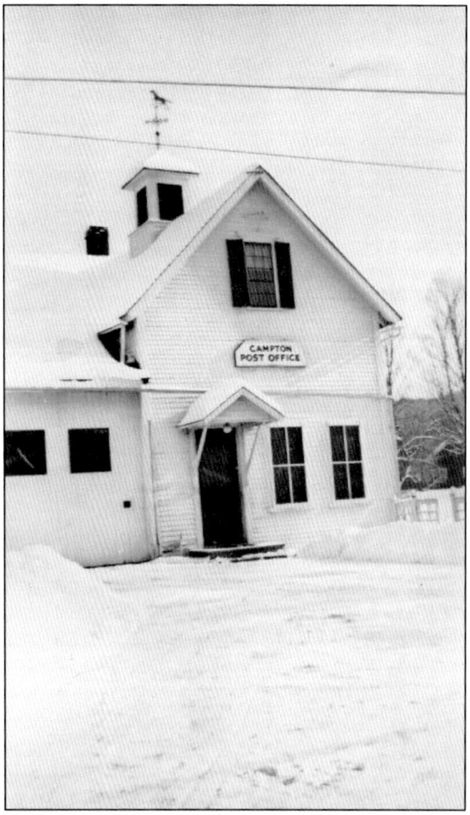

This building served as the post office when Irving Brown (1884–1987) became postmaster of Campton. The post office was physically attached to Brown's house on Main Street in Upper Campton Village. Upon Irving's retirement, Sadie Kilbourn Brown, his wife (1891–1995), became postmistress. This building still stands on Main Street and is owned today by the Bracketts.

The town jail, seen here around the 1960s, was also known as the Lumberjack Hotel. The jail is referred to as "the Lobby" in the old Campton town reports. The reports make reference to wood and other supplies needed for the Lobby and meals being served to the tramps. These tramps, otherwise known as lumberjacks, spent the night in the Lobby on their way on foot in or out of Waterville Valley, looking for or having finished up work. Of course, it also served as the town jail in the late 19th and early 20th centuries and was then in better structural condition.

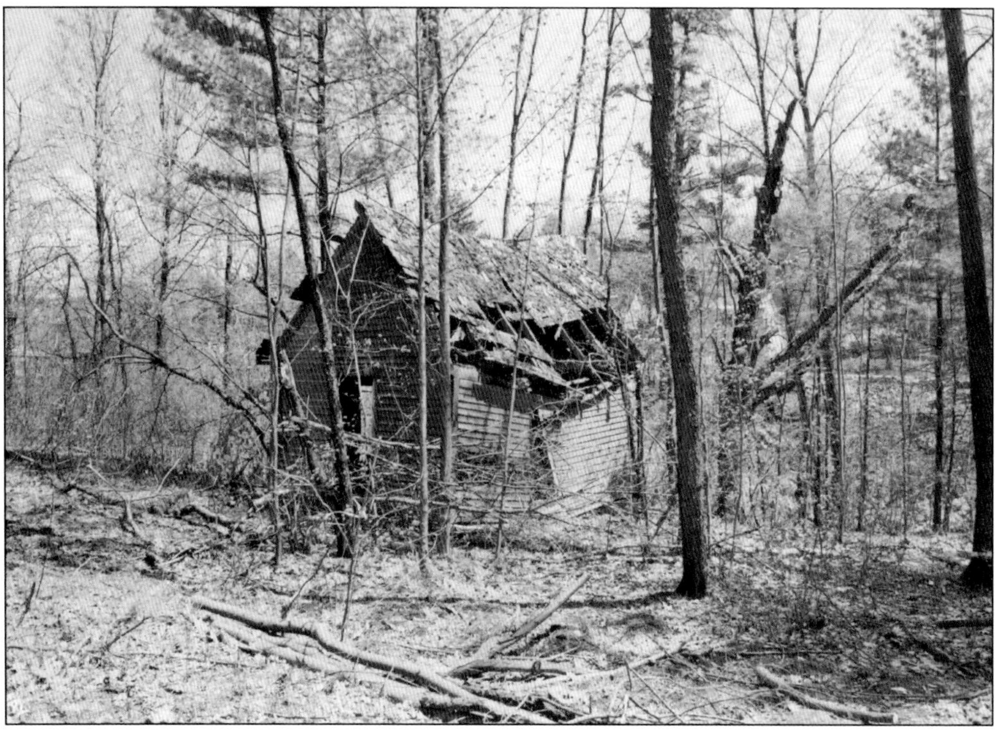

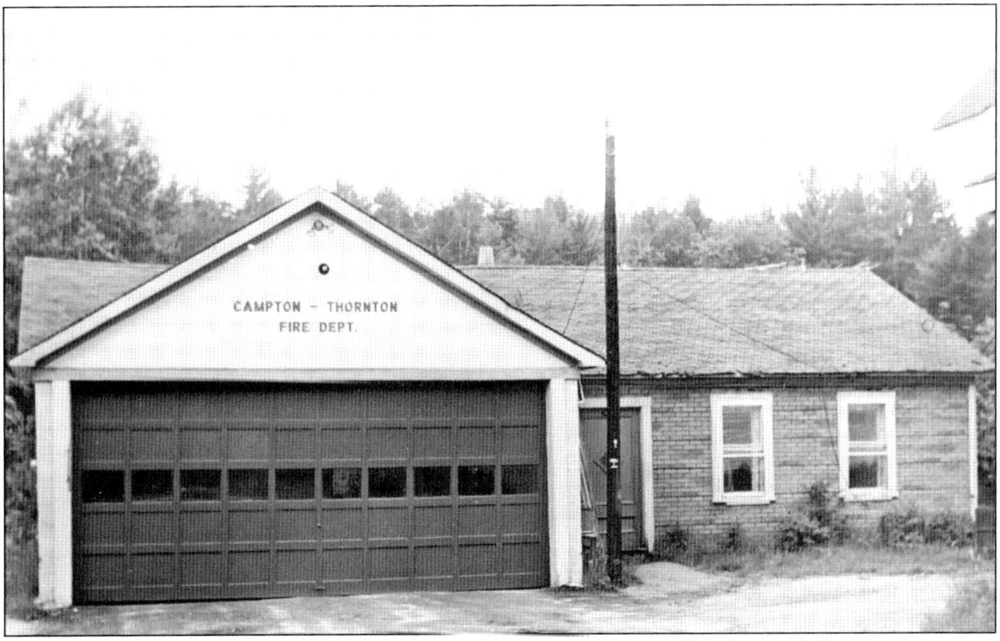

The Campton-Thornton Volunteer Fire Department was organized and recorded as a corporation on April 10, 1947. Shirley Tracy, Sterle Cheney, Richard Bean, George Estabrook, and Pascoe Roberts signed as officers. Land was deeded to the town by the Estabrook family for the building of the firehouse, and the first portable pump and attachments were donated by the Haartz family. In 1948, the fire department wives organized the Campton Firemen Women's Auxiliary.

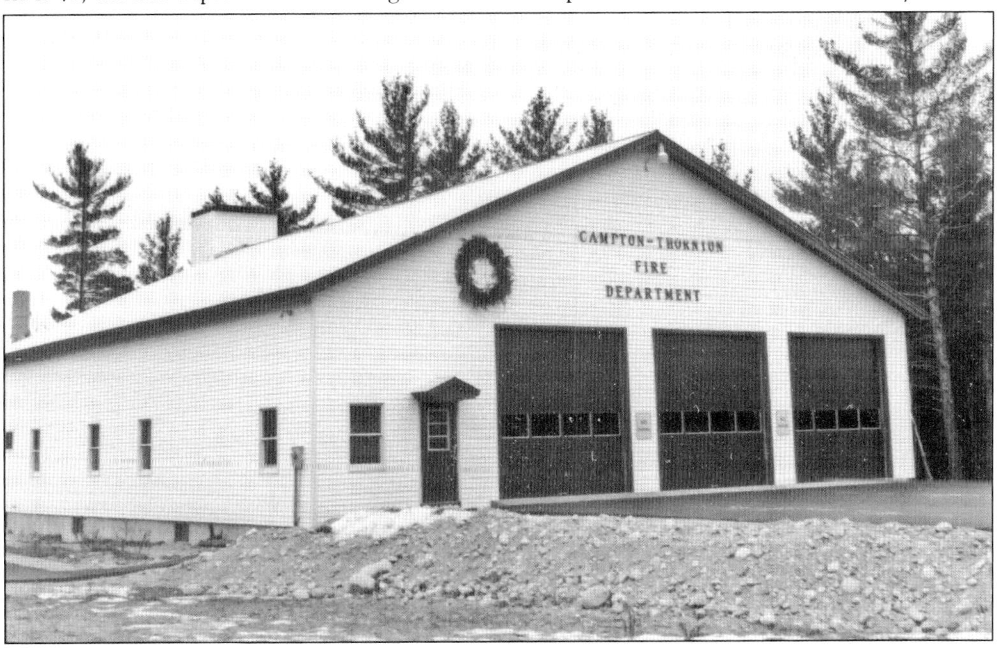

In March 1978, the people of Campton voted to "raise and appropriate $65,000 to build a new fire station." The fire station was built on land owned by the Town of Campton on Route 49. This department is an active member of Lakes Region Mutual Fire Aid Association, part of 35 communities in the Lakes Region.

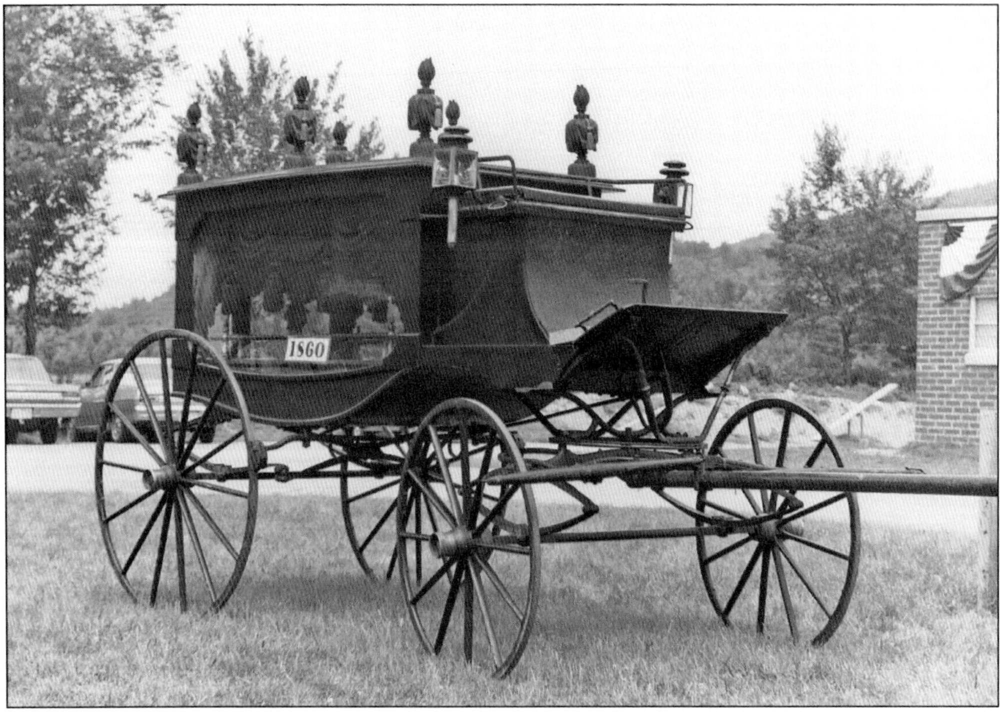

Campton's funeral coach was used to carry town residents to their final resting place. The coach remains today as part of Campton Historical Society's museum collection.

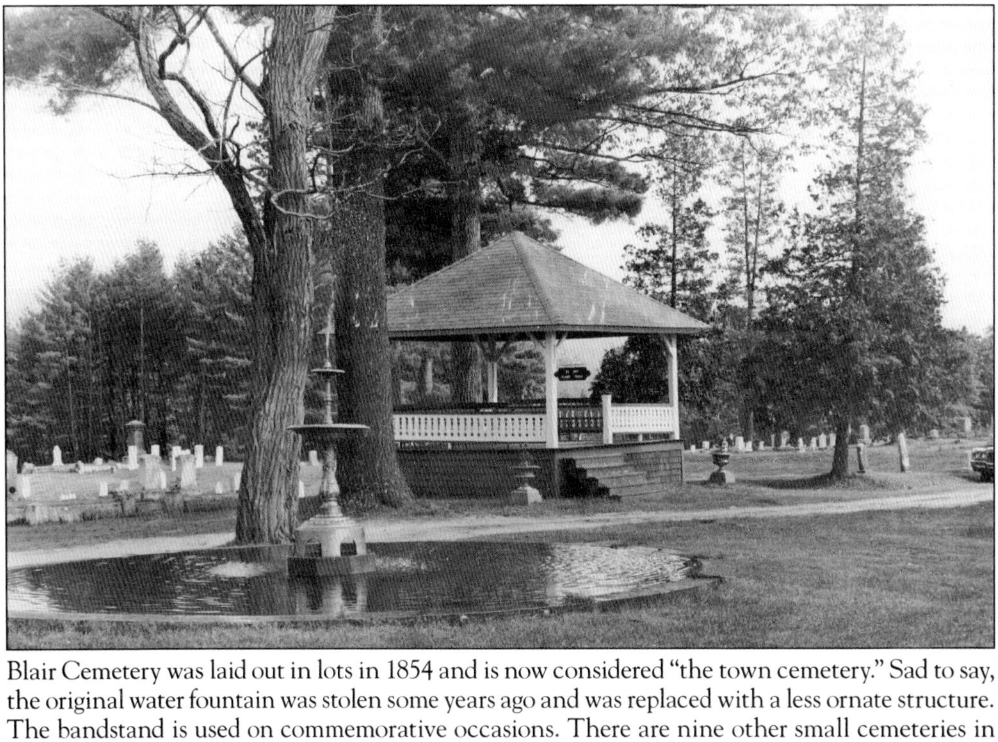

Blair Cemetery was laid out in lots in 1854 and is now considered "the town cemetery." Sad to say, the original water fountain was stolen some years ago and was replaced with a less ornate structure. The bandstand is used on commemorative occasions. There are nine other small cemeteries in town, once used mainly by families living in the immediate area.

Five

Mother Nature and Father's Follies

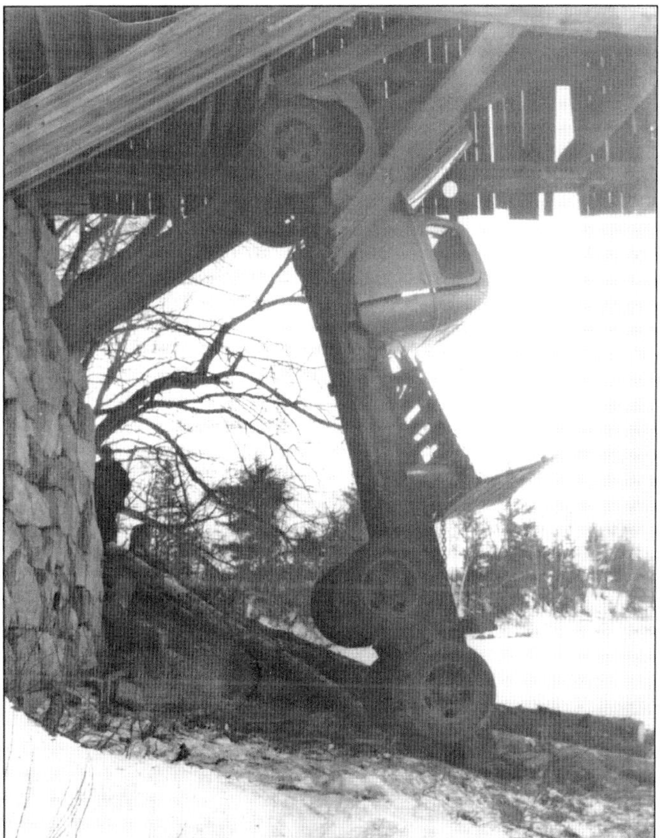

In 1944, a logging truck went through Blair Covered Bridge. Although large trucks were not allowed on the covered bridge, it was late in the day and the driver was running late. What choice did he have but to take a shortcut?

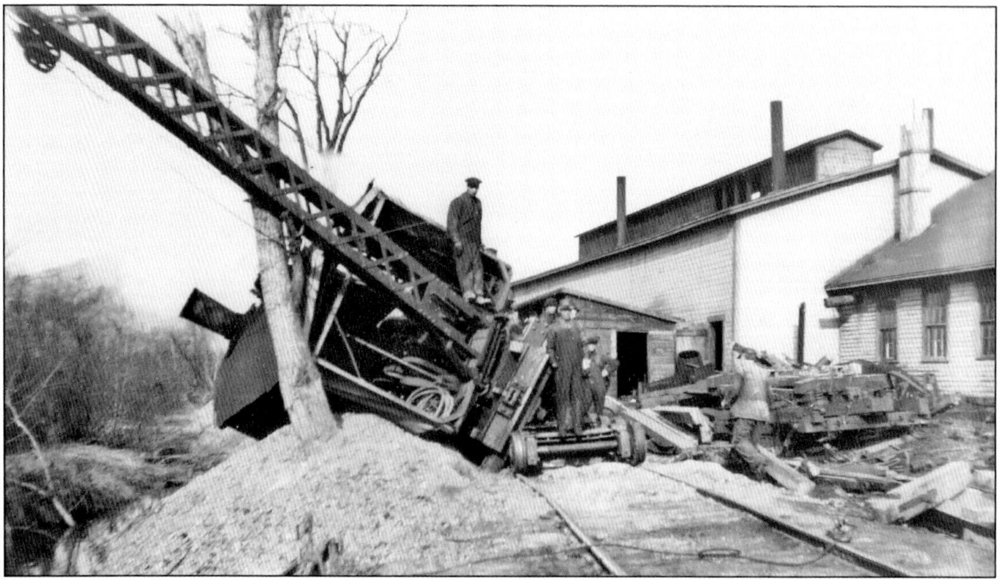

In April 1923, this steam operated, non-self-propelled steam crane tipped over on the spur track beside the Beebe River Railroad Engine House.

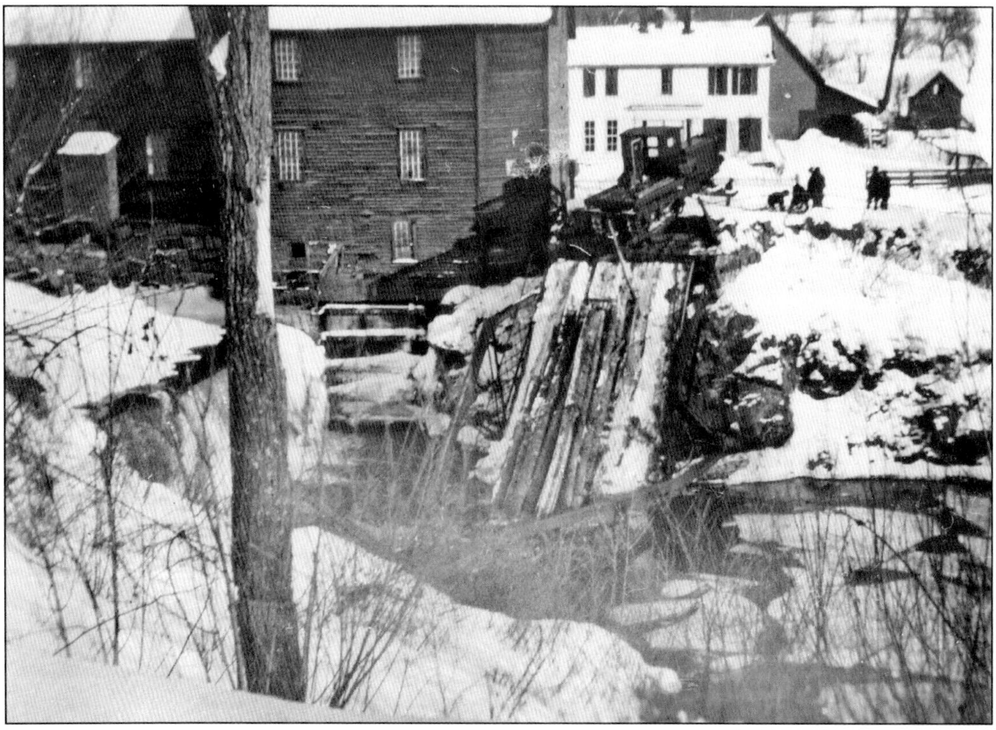

This 1926 view of the Campton Dam shows a log hauler carrying two loads of logs after it went through the bridge near the dam.

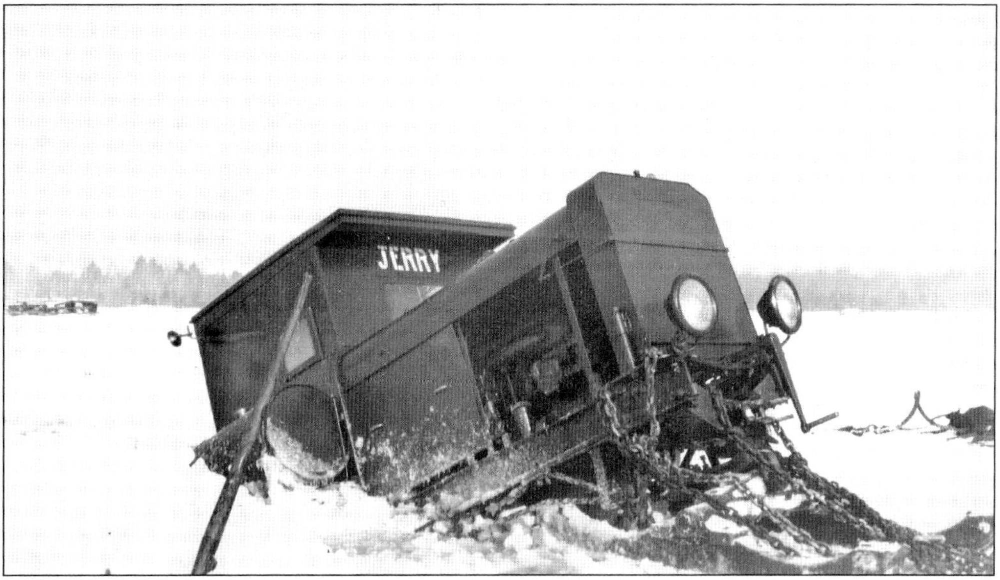

Jerry, the log hauler, went through the ice on Campton Pond in 1926 while attempting to rescue the first log hauler.

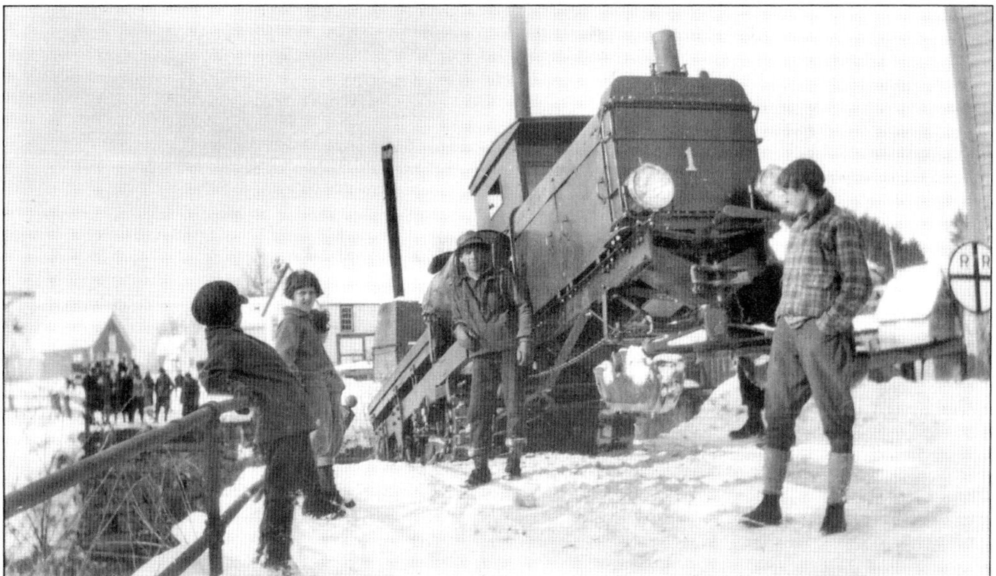

Just six years later, in 1932, another Lombard engine went through the bridge at the Campton Dam. This seems to have been a common occurrence. Once again, the bridge was destroyed, making it difficult to get from the Upper Village to the Lower Village until a new bridge was built.

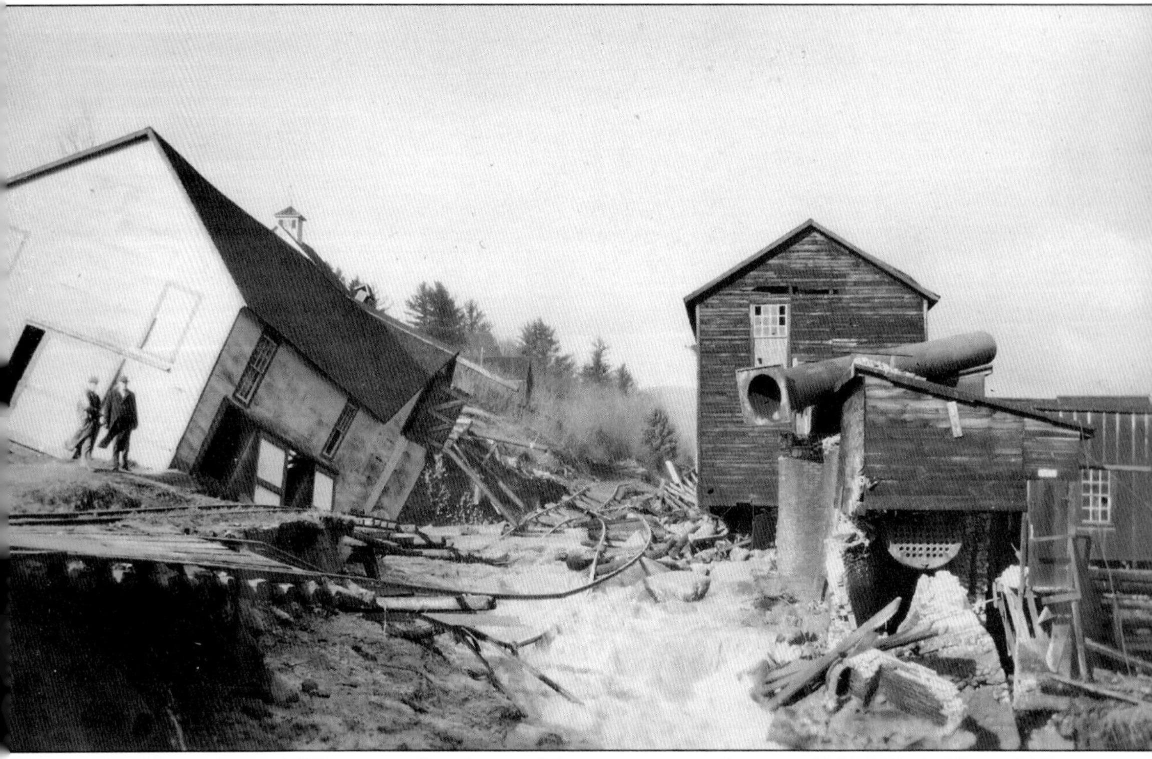

On November 4, 1927, a severe flood caused damage estimated at over $100,000. At Upper Village, a break in Campton Pond carried away the loading dock at Parker Young Company, causing the storehouse to tip into the cavity. The waters cleared a channel down to the cement bridge, washing out the approaches to the bridge. Four Campton covered bridges were lost in this flood.

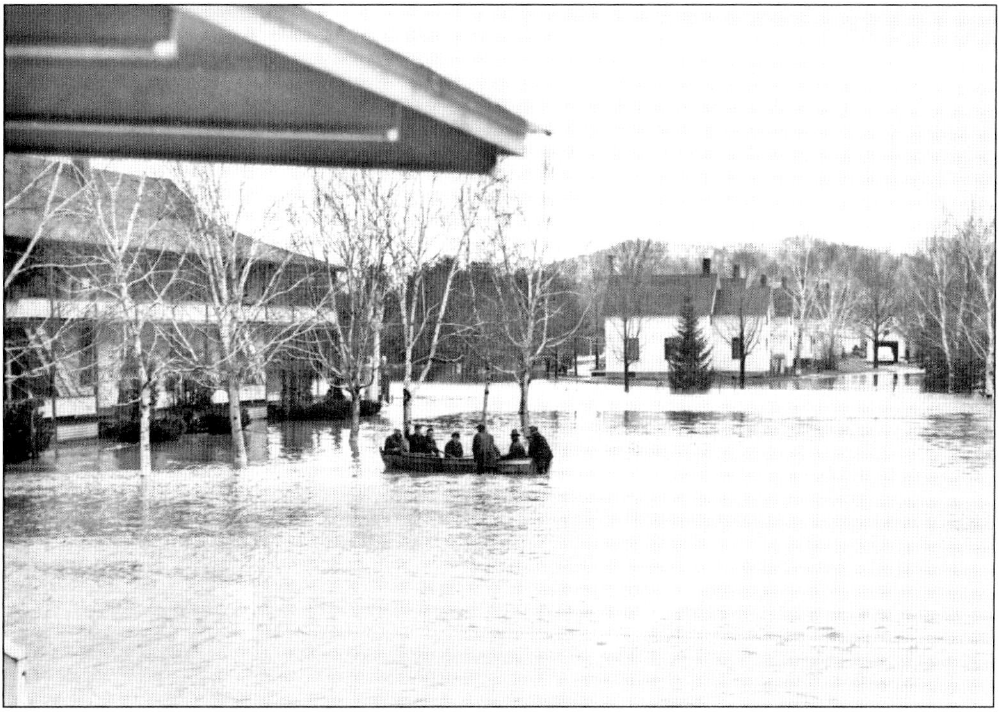

The Beebe River community experienced many floods during the 20th century. It is believed that this picture shows the flood of 1927. The building housing the company's offices, the store, and the post office is on the left, with people being evacuated by boat in the foreground. Company houses are to the right.

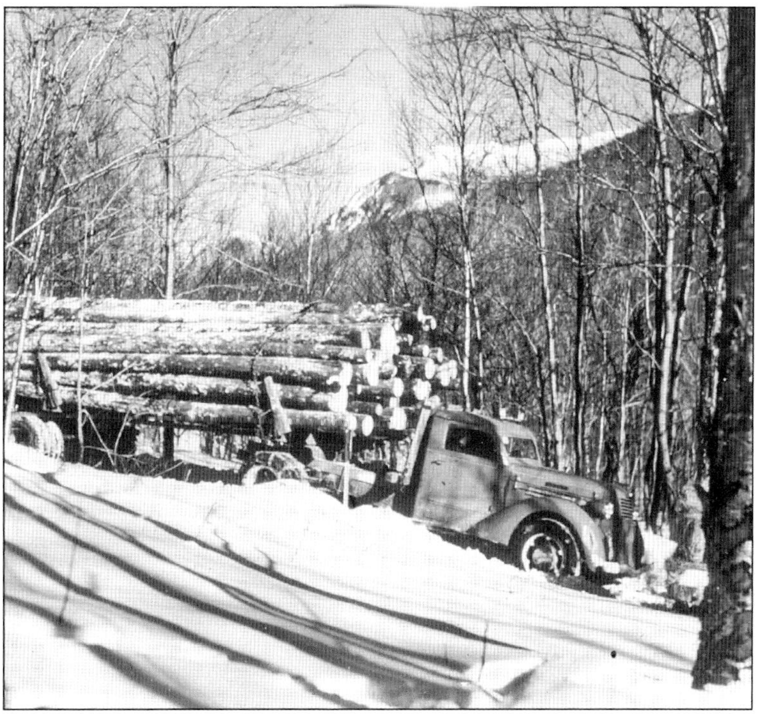

A logging truck went off the road into the woods beyond Eastern Corners. This winter accident occurred along the railroad line that paralleled the Beebe River. The load was probably on its way to a railroad siding for further transport to one of Campton's many lumber mills.

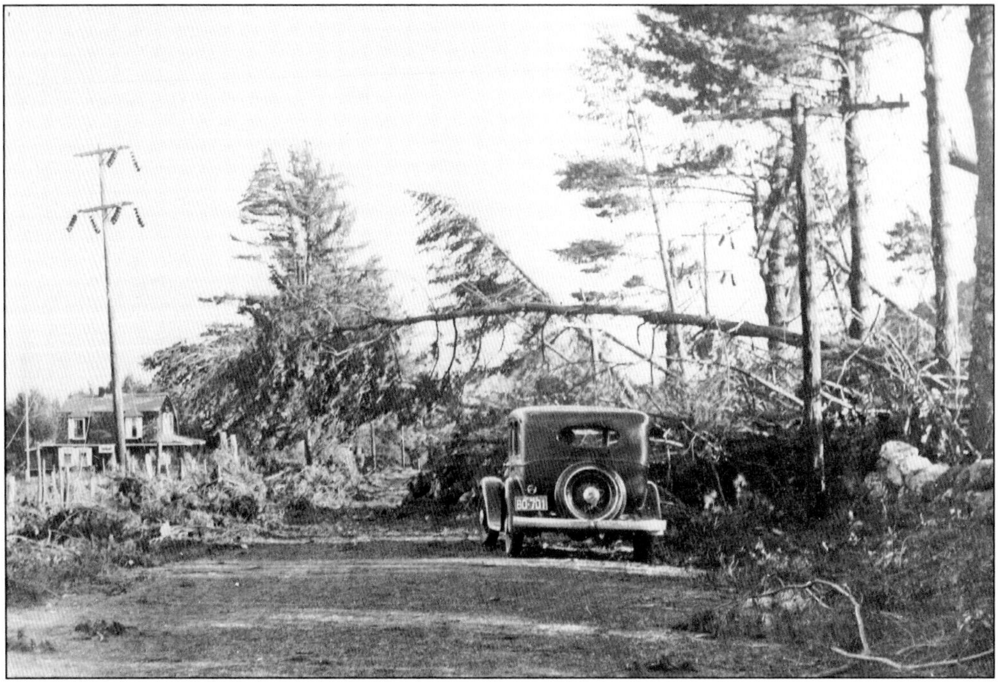

The 1938 hurricane did damage throughout the town. This scene shows destruction at the top of Wishman's Hill, on Route 175 in Campton Hollow.

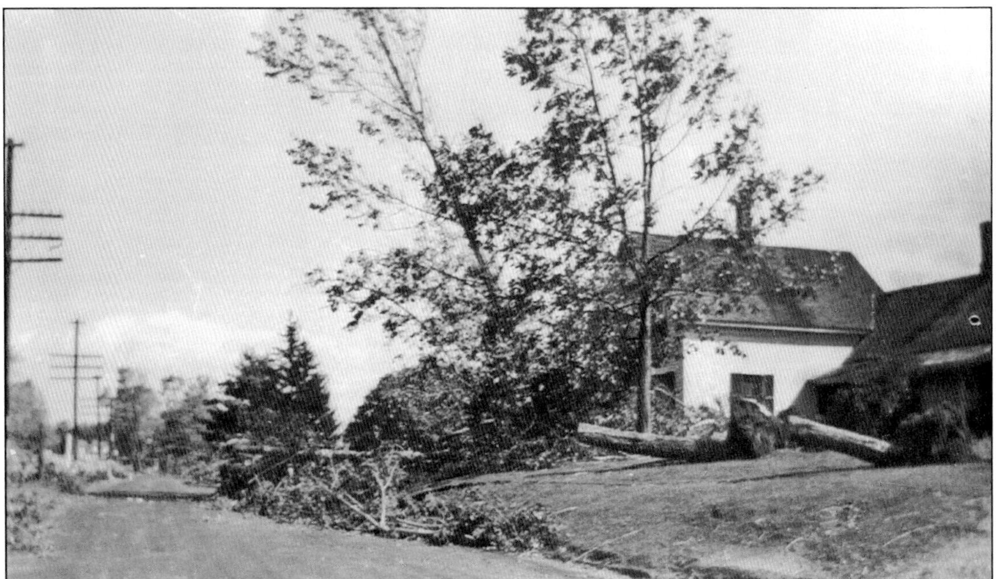

The Fred and Amy Hill Farm, on Route 3 in the Blair section of town, also sustained damage during the 1938 hurricane. Four of the large trees in the front yard were blown over, but all fell away from the buildings.

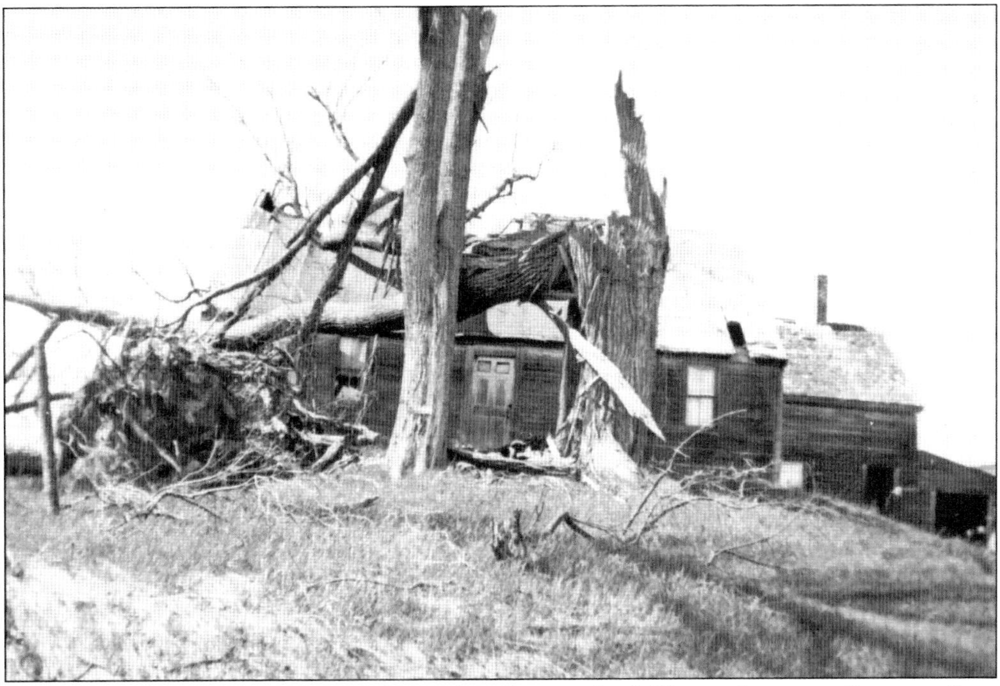

This old center-chimney Cape Cod was the Thomas Cook House. It was in Campton Bog, beyond the Mitchell Farm, on what many now call Hurricane Hill. The house was destroyed by the 1938 hurricane.

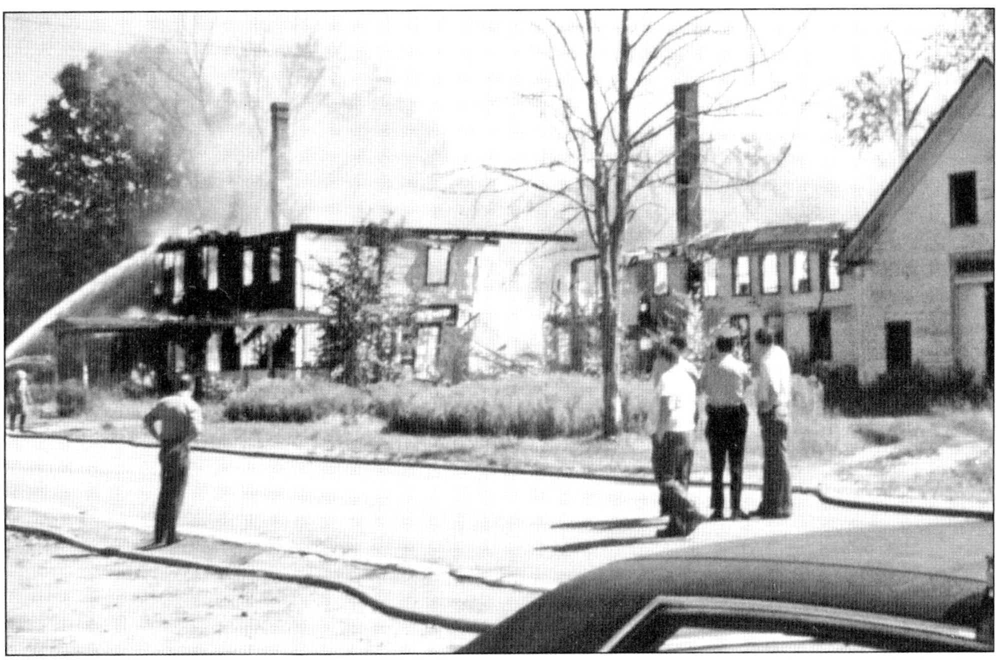

In the 1950s, after the Sceva Speare Hospital opened in Plymouth, the former Emily Balch Soldiers and Sailors Memorial Hospital became a patent museum. In 1974, it burned to the ground. This fire marked the end of the historic Little-Livermore Homestead. The barn was saved, but it too succumbed to fire some years later.

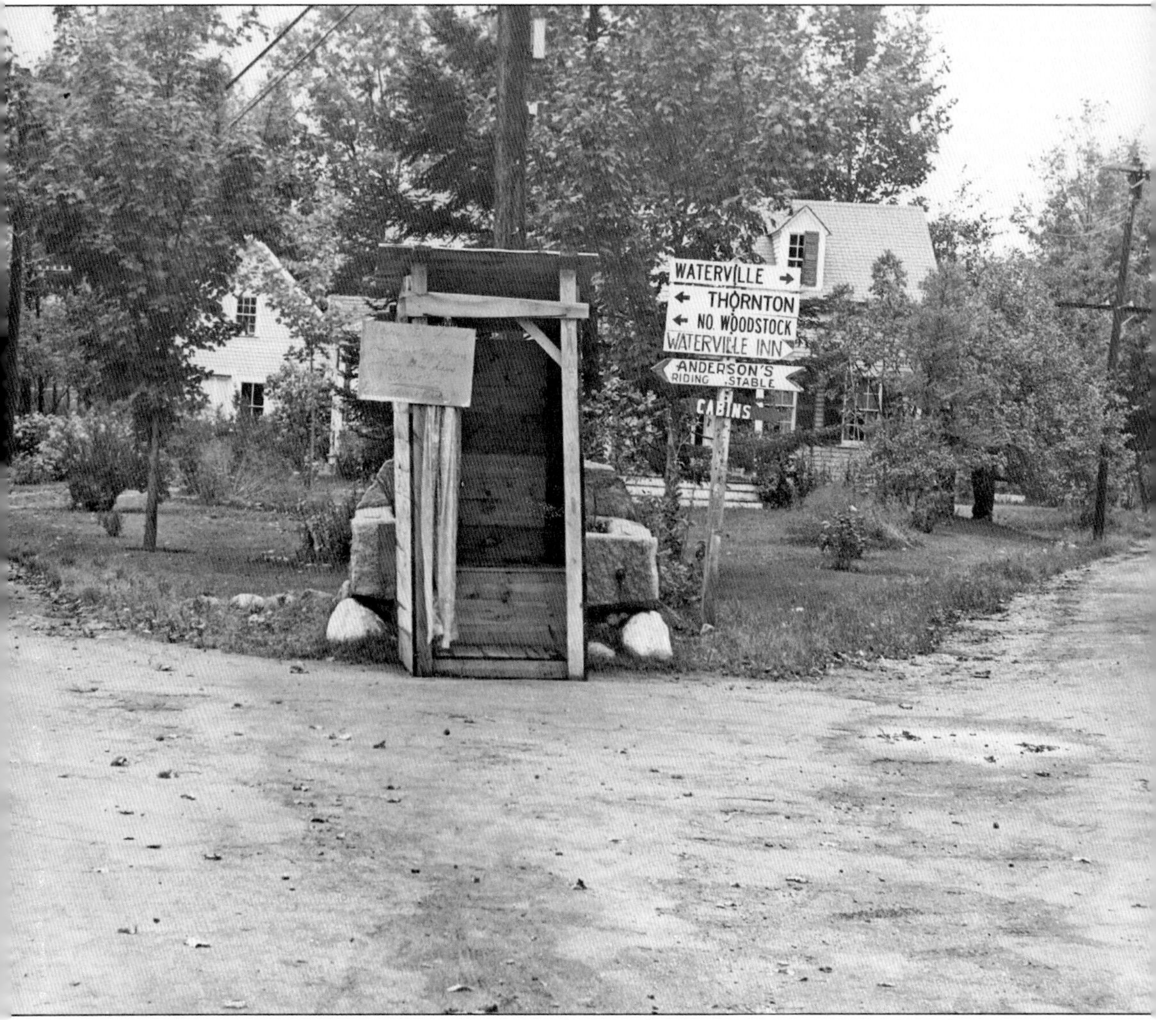

In 1954, an outhouse mysteriously appeared in front of the granite watering trough at the intersection of Mad River and Route 175, and in order to find its owner, the following sign was posted: "If owner is known, please notify him to remove his property within three days. Thank you. $25 cash reward."

Six

Local Folks

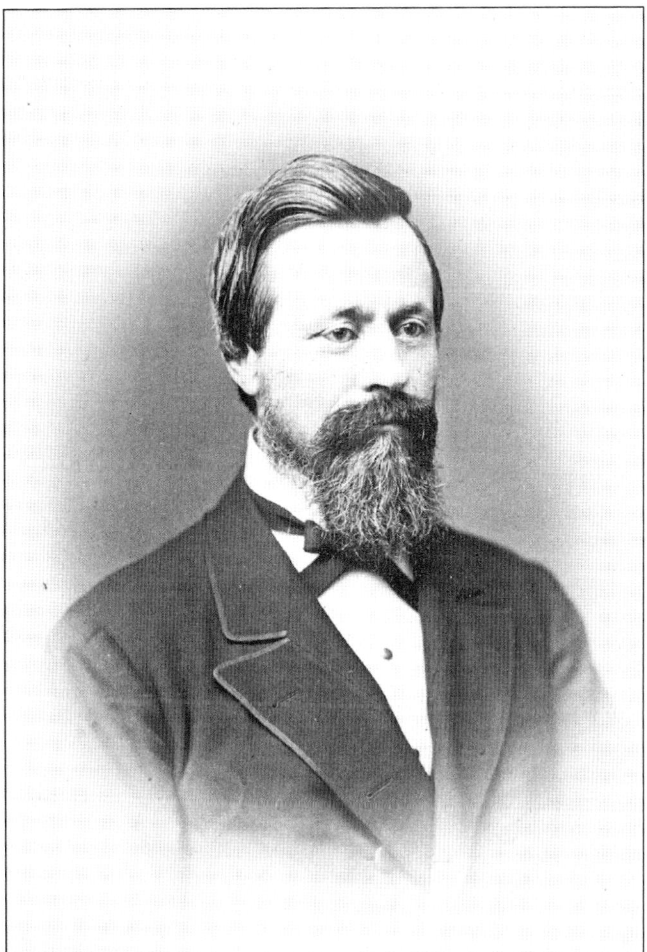

Henry William Blair was born in Campton on December 6, 1834. He served as lieutenant colonel in the 15th New Hampshire Volunteers in the Civil War. He was a member of the state legislature in 1866 and a US representative from 1874 to 1879. Blair was then elected to the US Senate, where he served until 1891. He was years ahead of his time on such matters as public education, racial justice, peace and disarmament, and the rights of women and workers. He died on March 14, 1920, and is interred at Blair Cemetery.

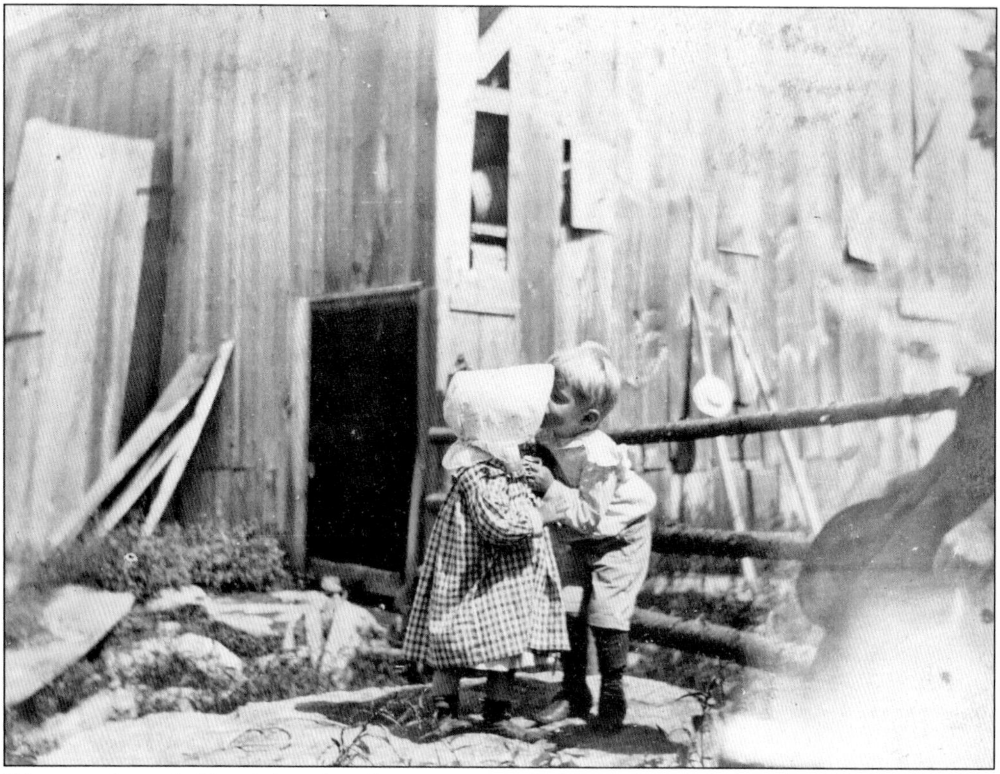

Who are these children? Are they "kissing cousins"? Their identity is a mystery, but there is no question that they are adorable.

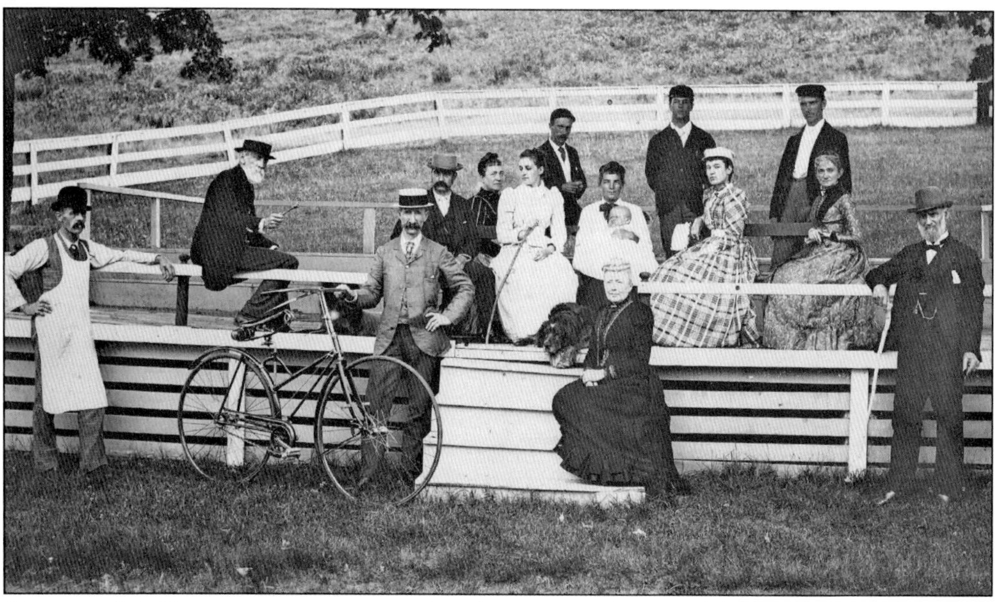

Guests at Blair House are seen enjoying a lovely summer afternoon. Urban dwellers came to the hotel to enjoy quiet, peaceful days, good food, and country living. The Blair Railroad Station was a short distance from the hotel, and coaches from the hotel would pick up guests arriving from cities to the south.

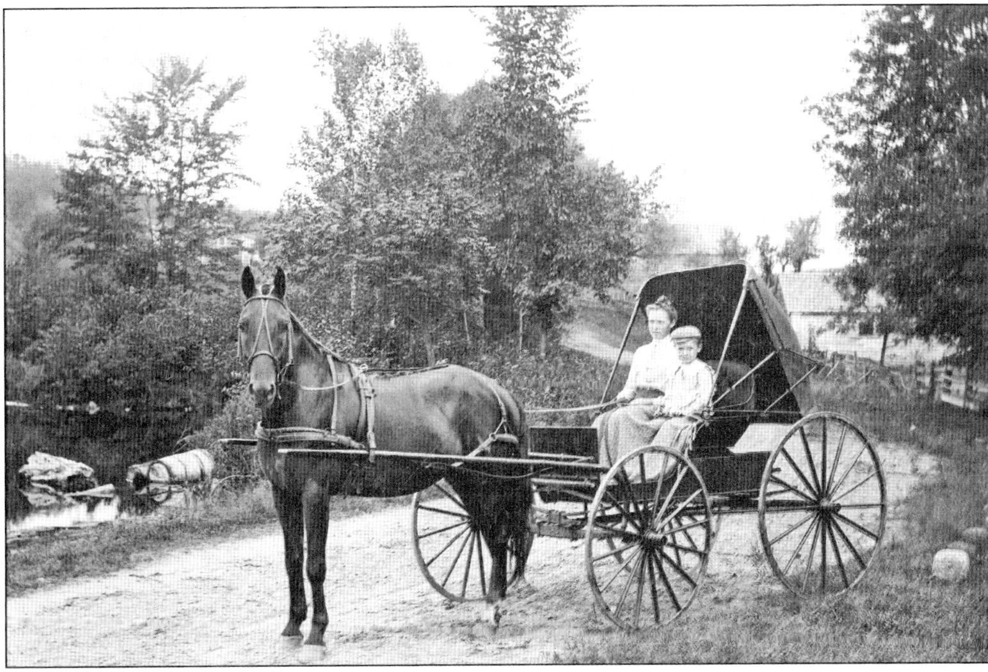

Helen Quimby and son Robert are enjoying a ride in their buggy in the 1890s. Horse-drawn conveyances were the most common means of local transport at this time. Buggies cost as little as $25–$50 and could easily be hitched and drawn by women and children. Helen was born in 1874 and died in 1963 at the age of 89.

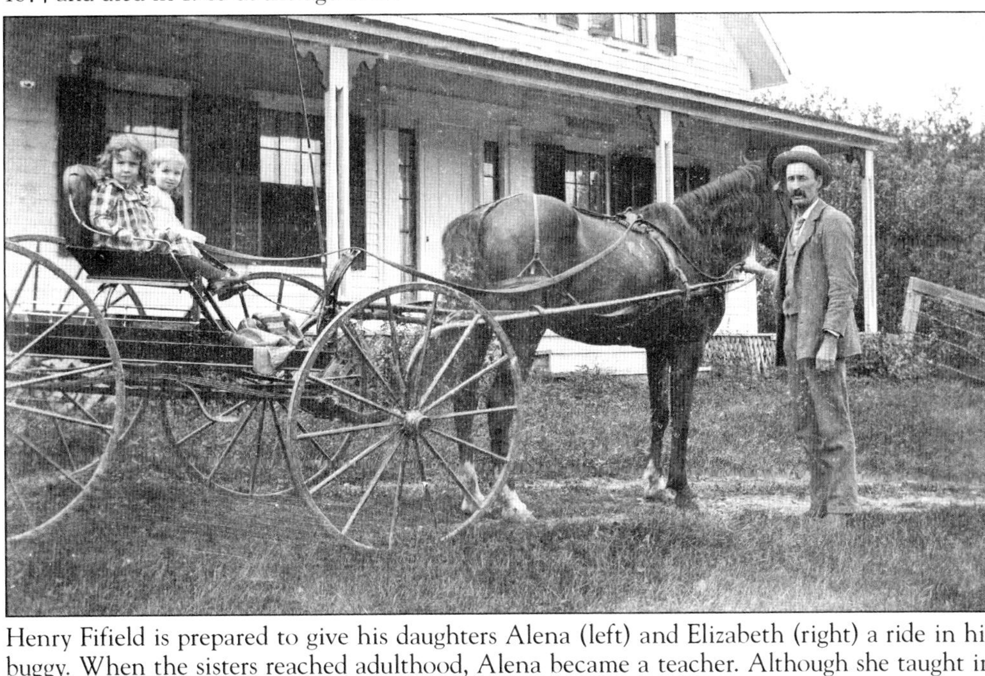

Henry Fifield is prepared to give his daughters Alena (left) and Elizabeth (right) a ride in his buggy. When the sisters reached adulthood, Alena became a teacher. Although she taught in Massachusetts, she returned every summer to her Campton home on Fifield Hill. Elizabeth married Arthur Caldon, and they had five children—Leslie, Winston, Donald, and twins Nancy and Newton.

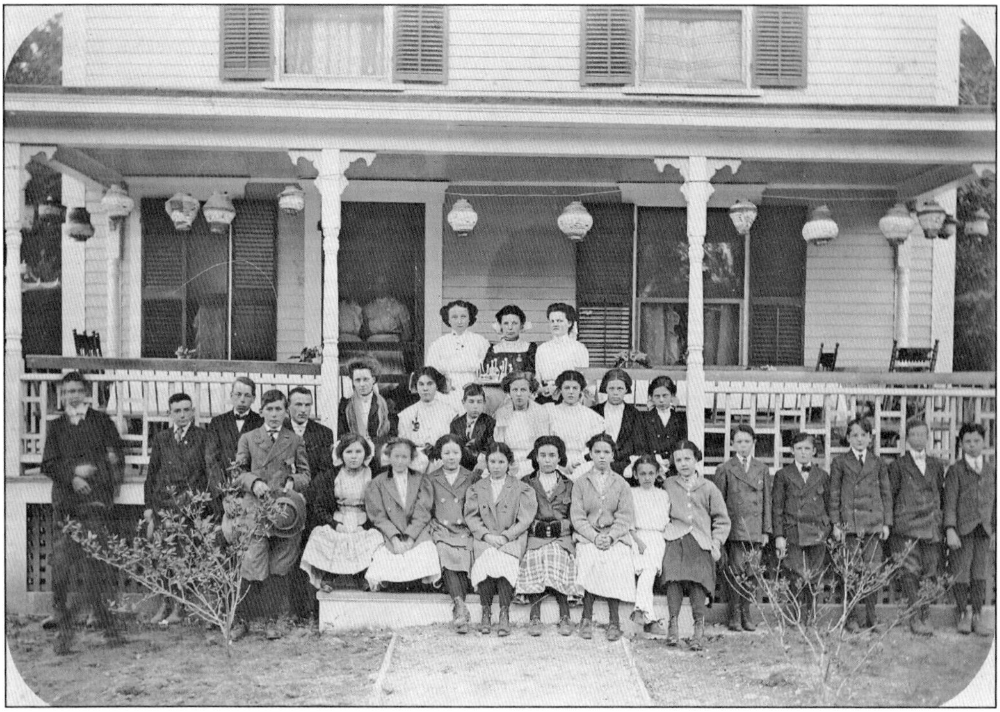

On June 4, 1910, a birthday party was given in honor of Gladys Morrison. Guests included Grace Davis, Bertha Chase, Agnes Downing, Maurice Tasker, Olive Dole, Gladys Chase, Ruth Moulton, Nettie Huckins, Sarah Dole, Blanche Carter, Blanche Caldon, Lorna Tasker, Ora Edgell, Lyle Cheney, Georgia Seeley, Dorothy Lyford, Clarence Hall, Arthur Chase, Sterle Cheney, Lawrence Simpson, Ellison Morrison, Lee McCoy, Charlie Edgell, Herbert Caldon, Ramsey Pettingill, and Oscar Hodgston.

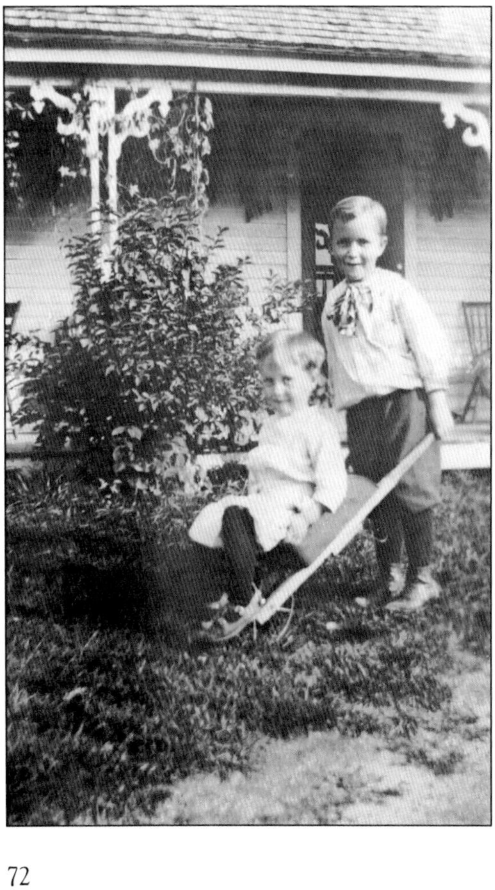

In 1913, six-year-old Maurice Hill is giving his four-year-old brother, Lewis, a ride in a wheelbarrow that had been made by their father, Fred.

Harry Chase operated a furniture factory in the Lower Village that he had purchased from Joel and Nathan Pierce in 1898. Hand-painted bedroom sets, dining room tables, and desks were types of furniture made there (see page 90).

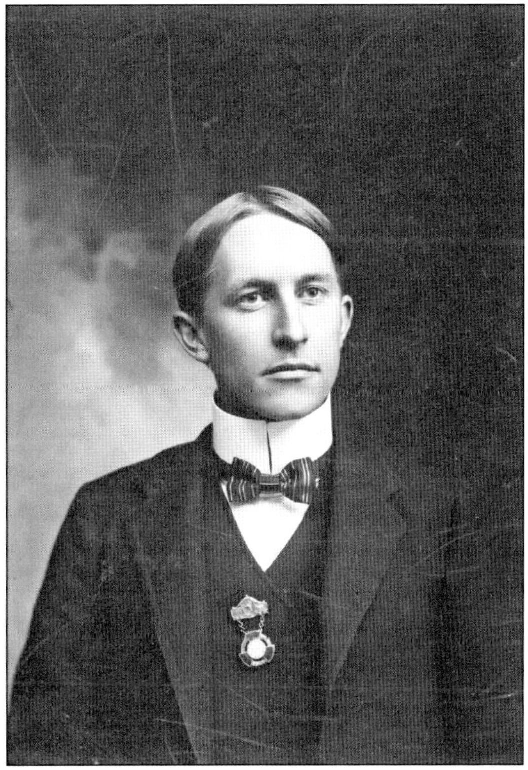

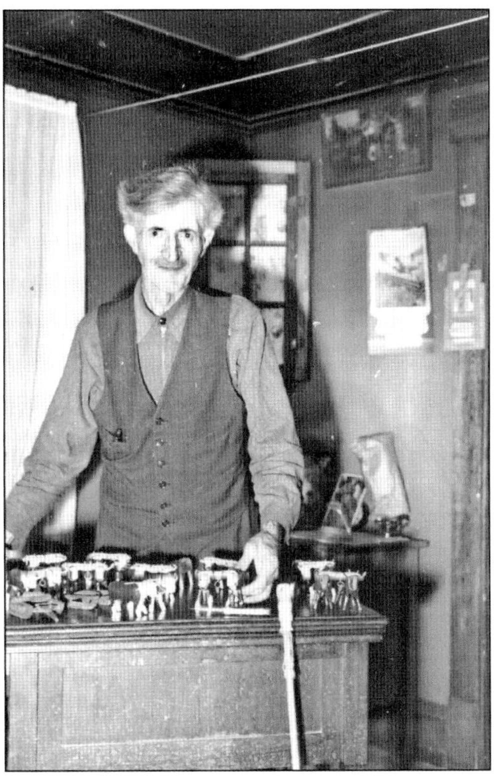

Fisher Ames was a talented local wood carver. In this picture, he is proudly displaying his hand-carved animals. He sold his carvings at fairs, bazaars, and Old Home Day celebrations.

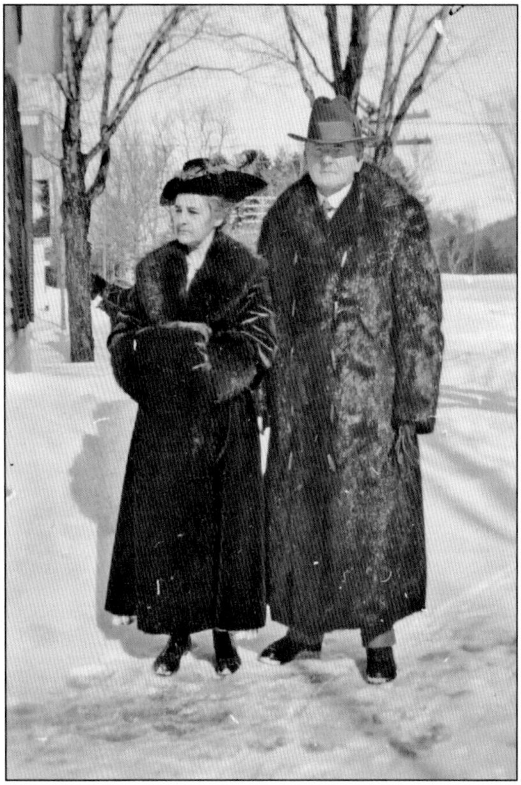

Dr. Harry A. Cheney was a resident doctor in Campton from 1895 until 1946. He remembered that in the days before automobiles were available, his three horses were not too many in a day to make his rounds when grippe was prevalent. He is pictured with his beloved wife, Sarah.

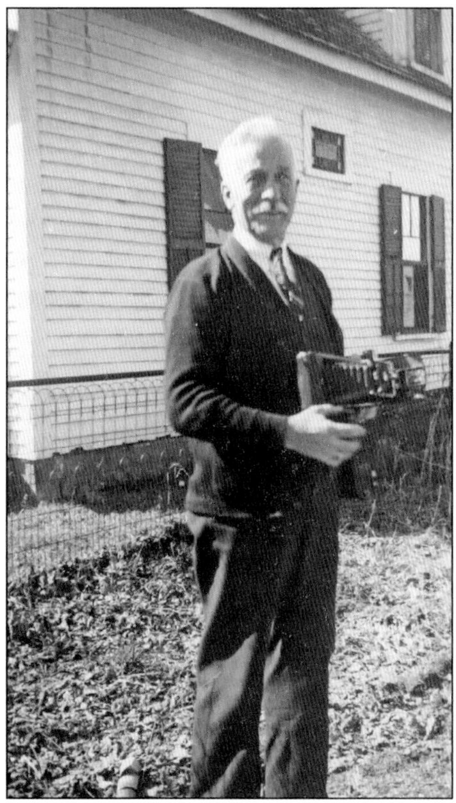

Louis Morrison was proprietor of Morrison's Store in the Upper Village. Louis was the father of Gladys and Ellison. His store later passed to Gladys's husband, George Estabrook, and years later, it is still in operation as the Campton Cupboard.

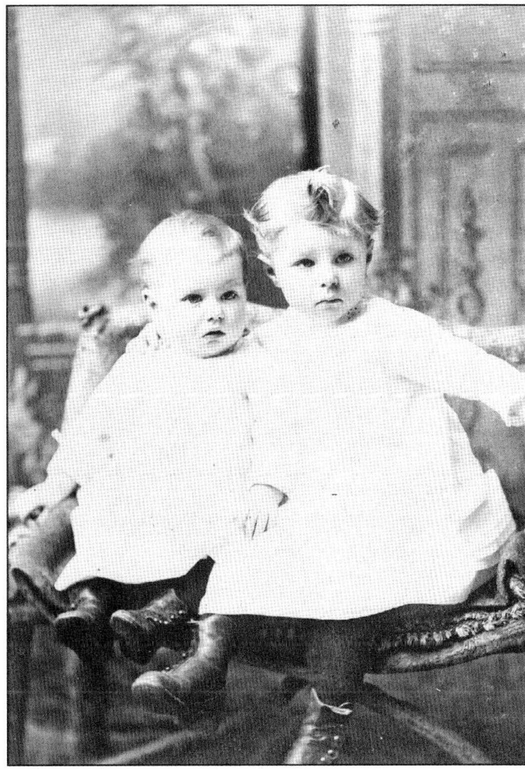

Pictured at right are Webb Little (right) at two and a half years of age and George Little (left) at nine months. Below, they are handsome young men. Webb (below, left) was Campton village postmaster during the Hoover administration, and the post office was located in his home. He was a talented pianist and played for many of the Campton Minstrel Shows. George (below, right) was the father of George I. Little, who sacrificed his life in World War II.

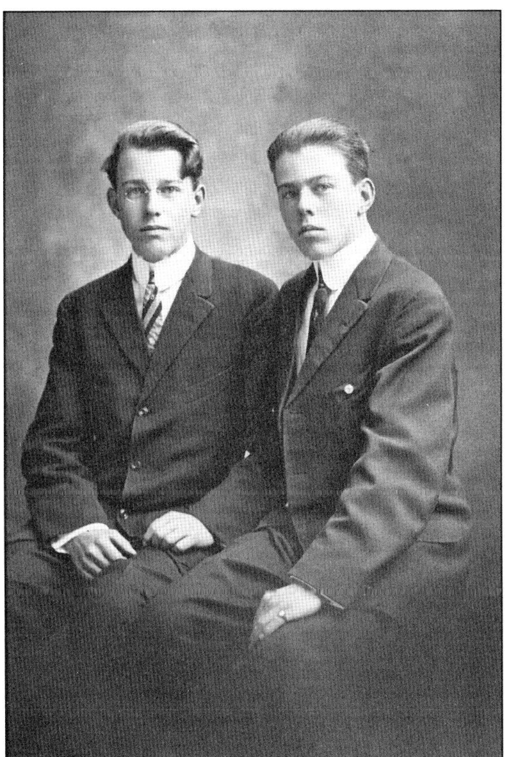

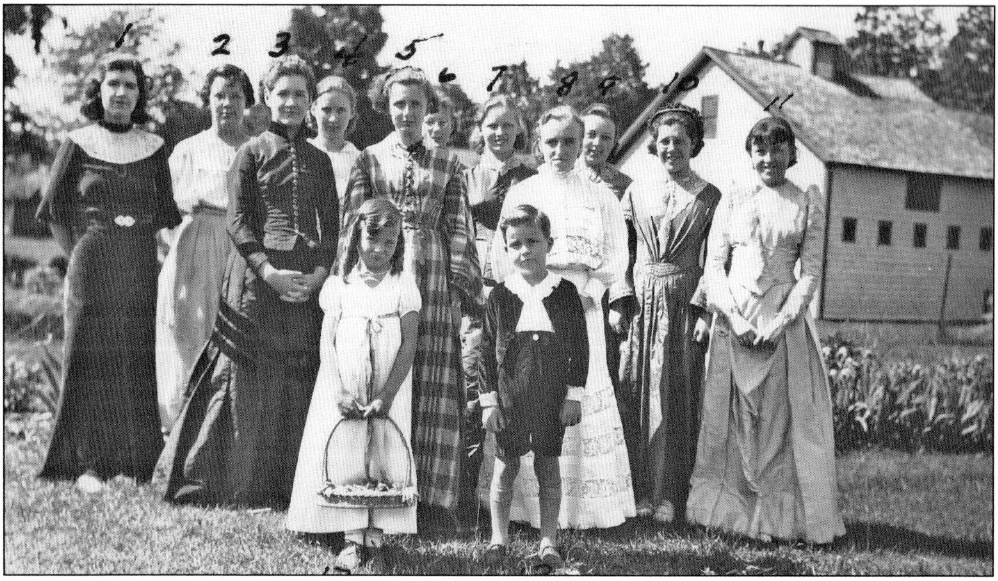

A Parade of Brides was held around 1934. Pictured from left to right are (front row) Aurelia Rodgers, flower girl, and Robert McCoy, ring bearer. Dressed in vintage gowns are, from left to right (second row) Pauline Bangs, Katherine Sargeant, and Marjorie McCoy; (third row) Margery Bangs, Eunice Estabrook, Irmagard Avery, Marge Haartz, Geraldine Avery, Eleanor Estabrook, Charlotte Dole, and Doris McCoy.

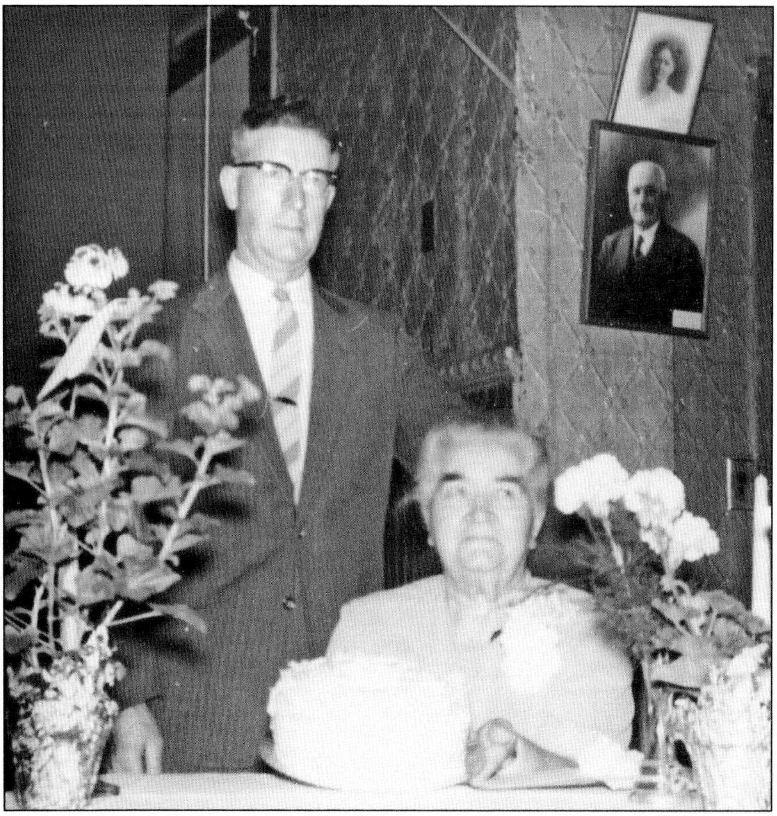

Anna Ouellet celebrates her birthday with her son, Charles. Charles was past master of the Campton Grange.

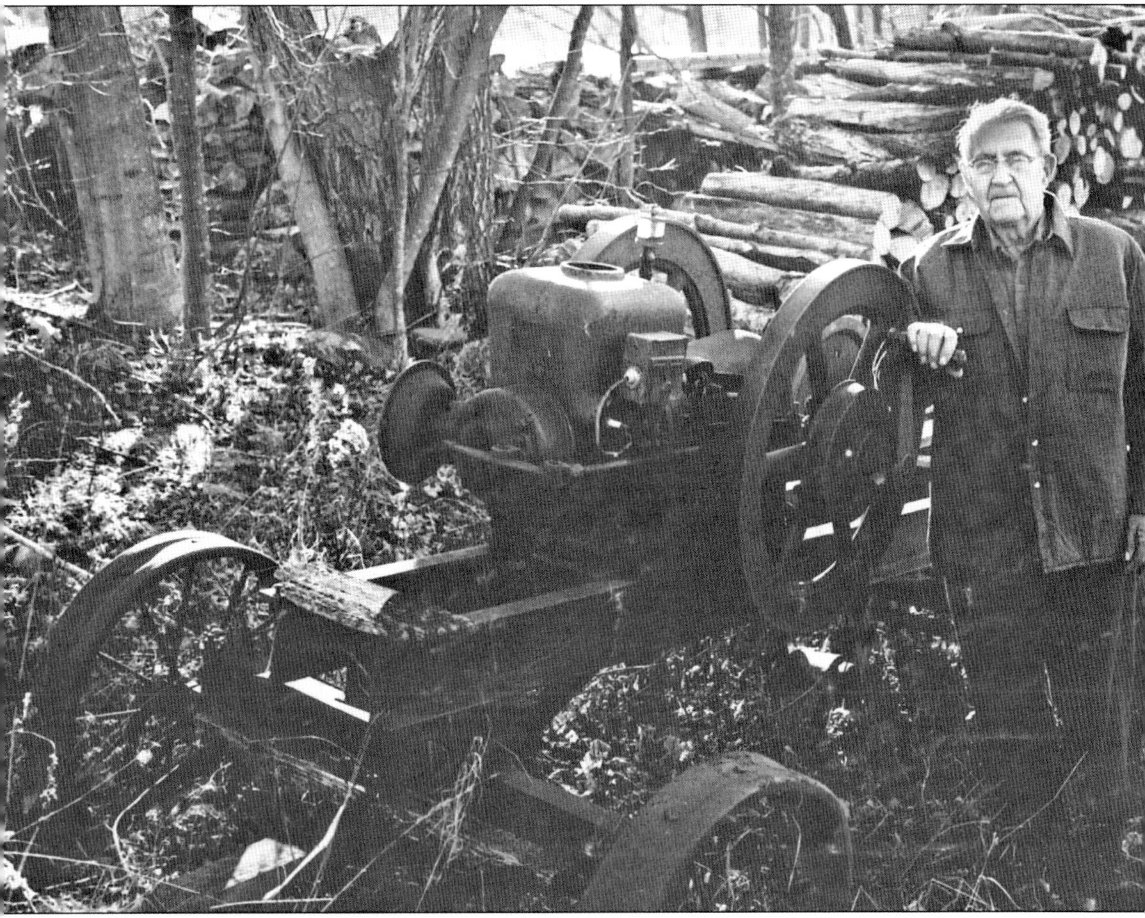

In addition to Bertram "Bert" Pulsifer's professional and community duties, he took great pride in his family and his farm on Pulsifer Hill. With the help of his children, he raised pigs and cattle, produced and sold maple syrup, sold potatoes and blueberries, tended to a large garden, and hayed numerous fields. He cut and planed his own lumber for projects around the farm and still found time to go fishing with his good friends. Bert is pictured here with his favorite wood-sawing machine. When he was 10 years old, he drove by horse cart to the train at Blair Station to pick up the machine for his father. He hauled it home and helped to assemble the machine and kept it in good working order for decades. Bert Pulsifer passed away in 1997 at the age of 91.

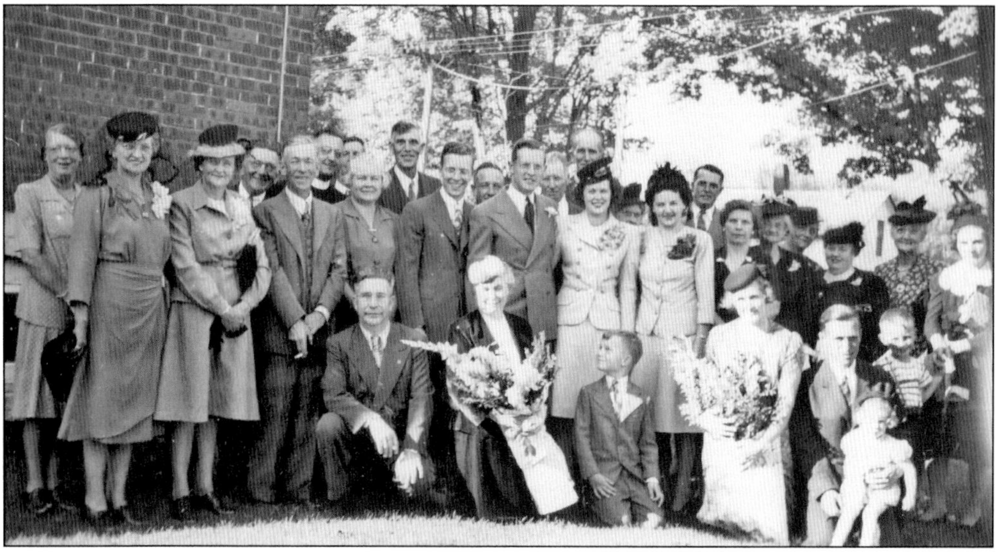

The Brown and Duffy families joined together to celebrate the wedding of Kathleen Duffy and Rupert Brown on October 6, 1946. The bride was the daughter of Nellie and Arnold Duffy, and the groom was the son of Sadie and Irving Brown—all of Campton. Dolores Inkell, standing to the right of the bride, was her matron of honor. Roger Brown, to the left of the groom, was his brother's best man. To the left of Roger are Nellie and Arnold Duffy, parents of the bride. Both Kathleen and Rupert had served their country in World War II.

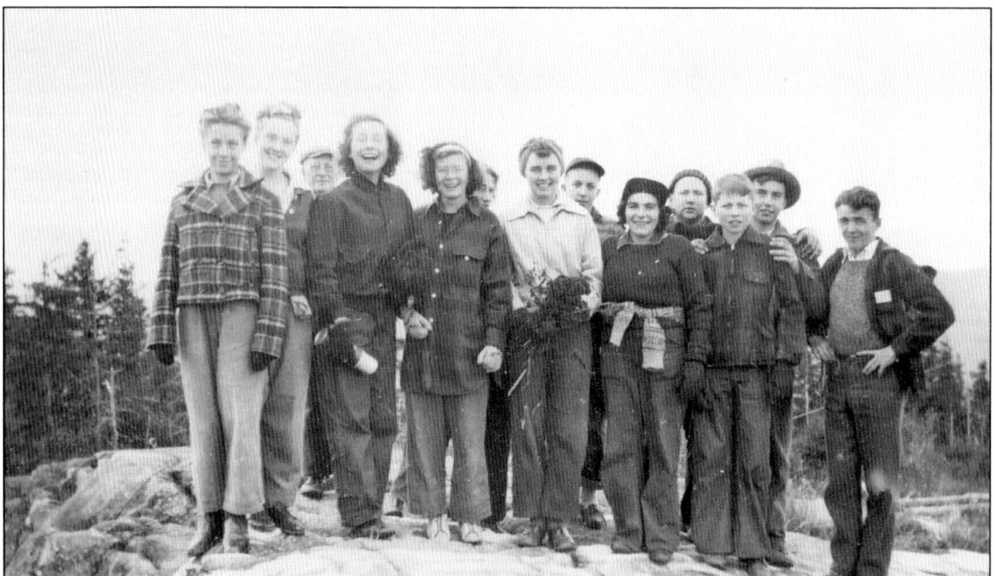

In 1943, the Campton Baptist Church Young People's Group took a hike up Stinson Mountain. Pictured are, from left to right, Eleanor McCoy, Barbara Willey, Frank Fogg, Priscilla Colpitts, Lois Ann Kezer, Joyce Saunders, Beverly Young, Bernard Estabrook, Ruth Morrison, Pastor Raymond Bean, Gutherie Colpitts, Robert McCoy, and Harry Cheney.

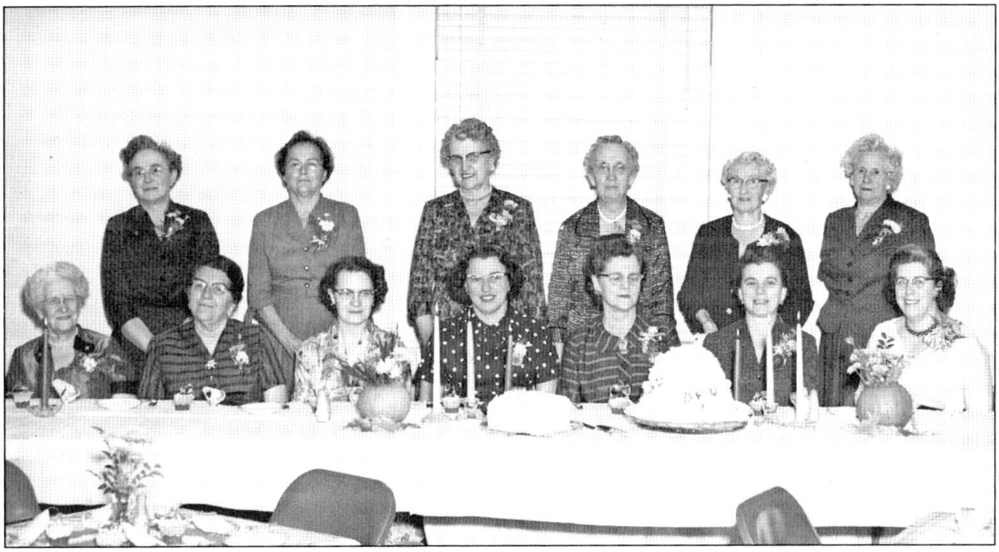

In 1956, the Campton Women's Club held Past Presidents' Night. From left to right are (seated) Grace Dole, Lavinia Dole, Dolores Cheney, Christine Dole, Leta Henderson, Olive Hill, and Charlotte Roberts; (standing) Dorothea Cheney, Gertrude Merrill, Sadie Brown, Nora McCoy, Margaret Little, and Adele Sargeant.

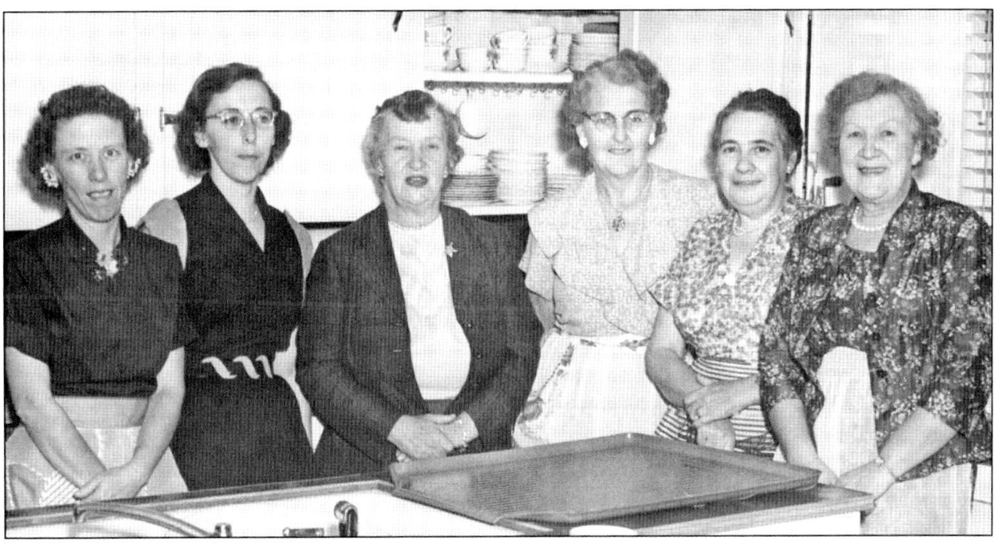

From left to right, Florence McCuin, Teddy Cheney, Margaret Murphy, Florence Silk, Betty Tirey, and Ernestine Hewitt are busy in the kitchen of the Campton Baptist Church.

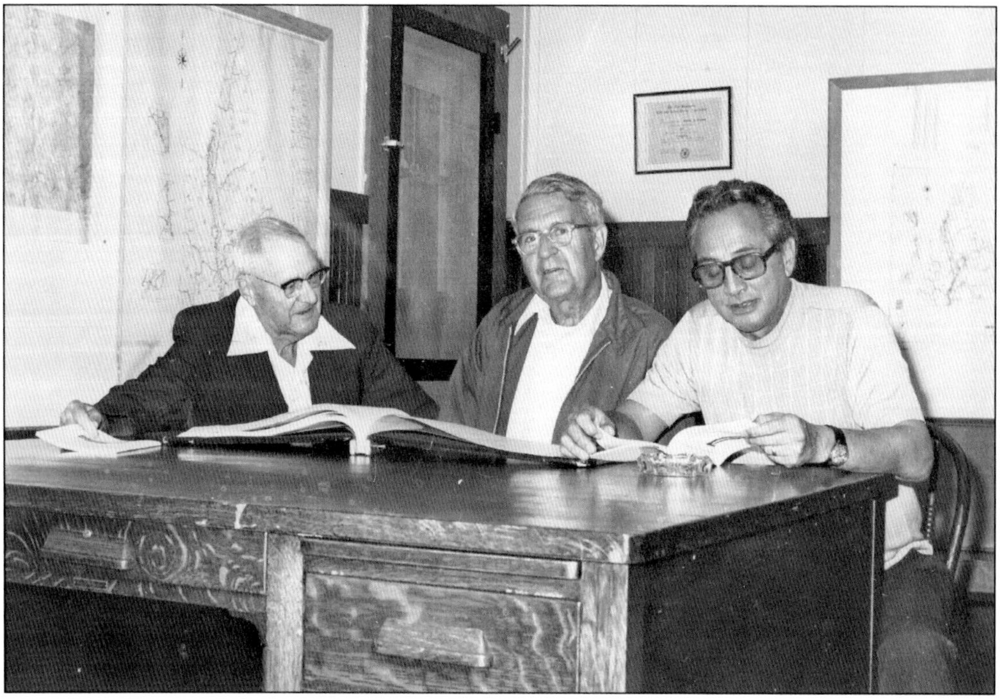

Max Haley, Bertram Pulsifer, and Roger McBride were selectmen for the Town of Campton during the 1970s. Their names are posted on the Bump Covered Bridge, off Perch Pond Road, that was restored during their tenure. Haley served on the board of selectmen for 12 years, Pulsifer for 39 years, and McBride for six years.

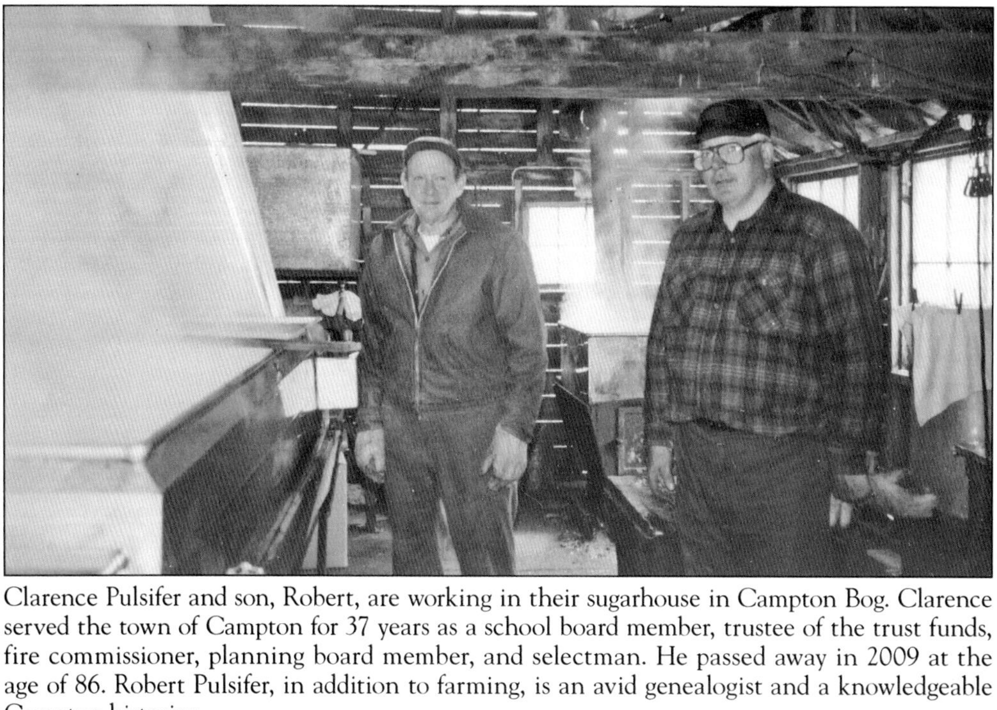

Clarence Pulsifer and son, Robert, are working in their sugarhouse in Campton Bog. Clarence served the town of Campton for 37 years as a school board member, trustee of the trust funds, fire commissioner, planning board member, and selectman. He passed away in 2009 at the age of 86. Robert Pulsifer, in addition to farming, is an avid genealogist and a knowledgeable Campton historian.

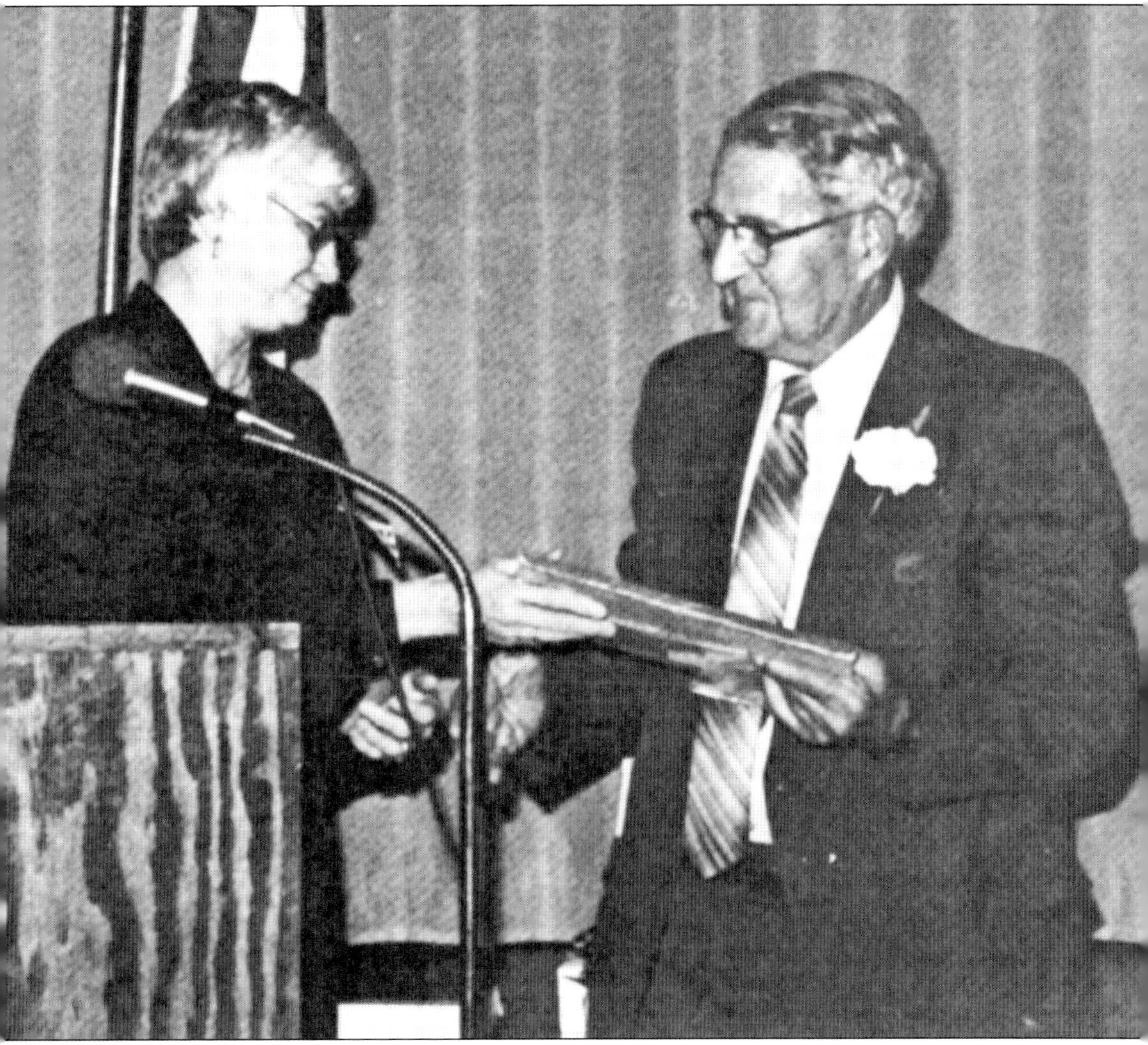

Bertram W. Pulsifer, a selectman of Campton for 39 years, was tendered an appreciation night on October 25, 1980, by his friends. More than 240 turned out to express their thanks. He was presented a wristwatch, a gold Masonic ring, and a book of letters from people who could not attend. Olive McBride, town clerk, presented the gifts. Bertram was also a state representative to the Constitutional Convention, president of the Pemigewasset National Bank, past master of the Campton Grange, treasurer of the Campton Congregational Church, and a farmer.

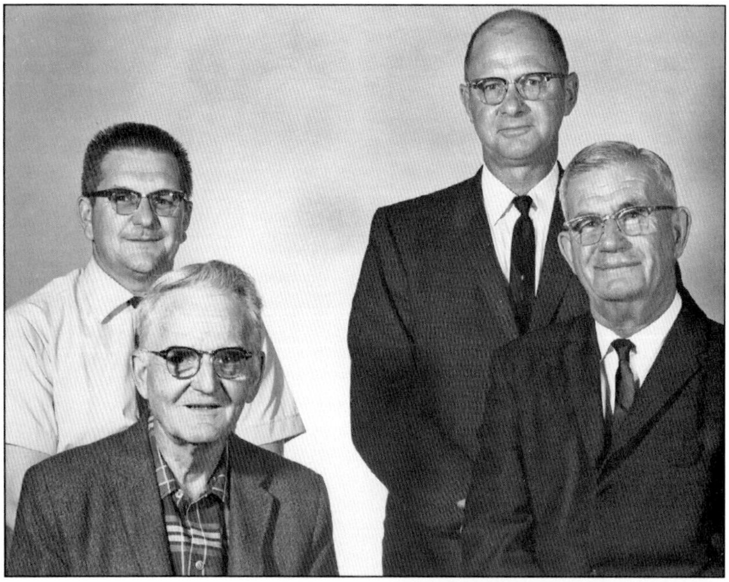

Pictured here in 1967 are members of the Campton Bicentennial Historical Committee. They are, from left to right, (first row) Sterle Cheney and Paul Durgin; (second row) John Dole and Lester Mitchell Jr.

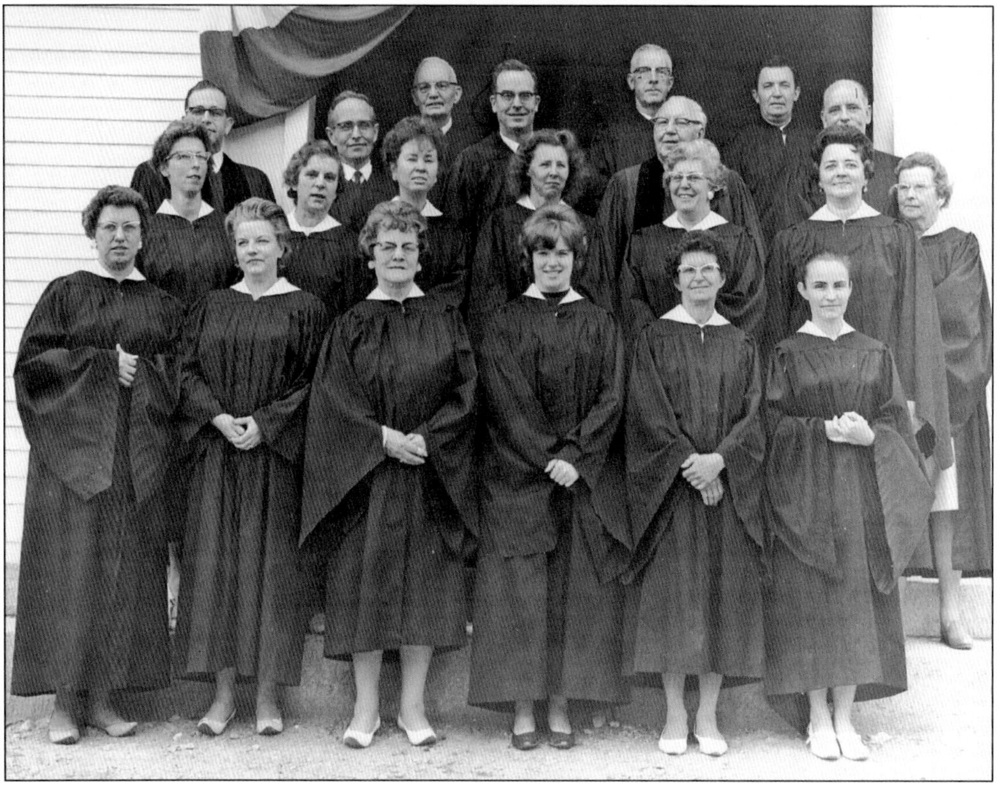

On Bicentennial Sunday, the choirs of the Baptist and Congregational churches joined together. From left to right are (first row) Christine Dole, Priscilla Piper, Leta Henderson, Priscilla Pattee, Alice Piper, and Rose Rosewarne; (second row) Teddy Cheney, Olive Hill, Barrie Saunders, Alice Stickney, Charlotte Roberts, Olive Blake, and Evelyn Ouellet; (third row) unidentified, Lewis Hill, Pascoe Roberts, unidentified, and Burton Pierce; (fourth row) Harold Henderson, Charles Ouellet, and Edward Keeney.

Seven

A Village of Bridges

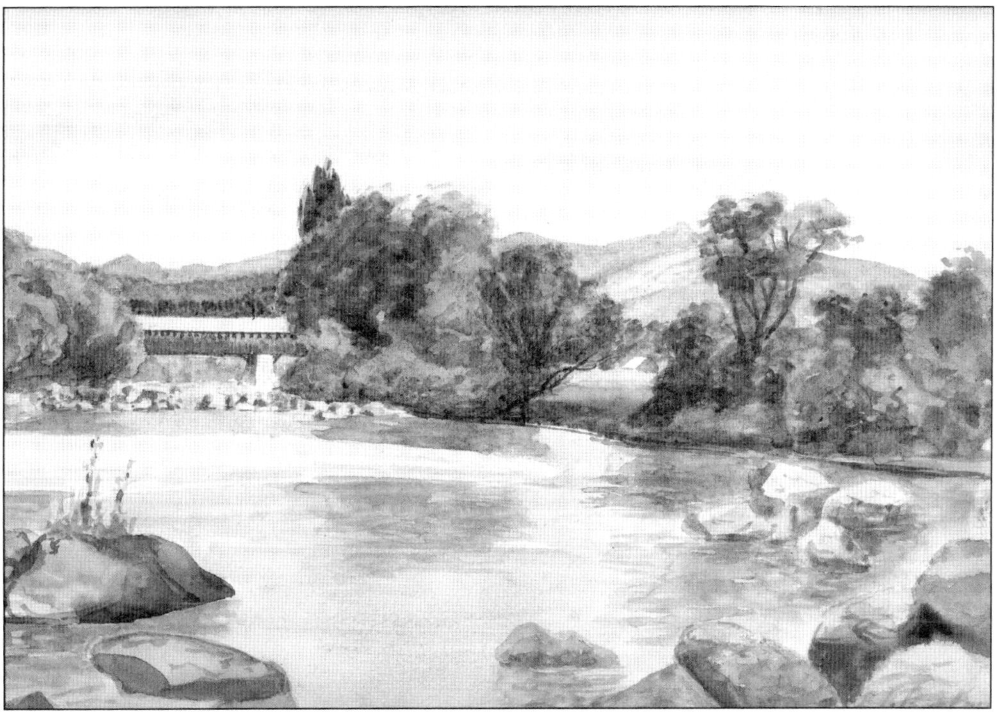

This is a painting by E.L. Proctor of the original Blair Covered Bridge over the Pemigewasset, or the Great River, as it was called. The bridge was built in 1829 and burned in the 1860s. The artist is believed to have been a 19th-century watercolorist.

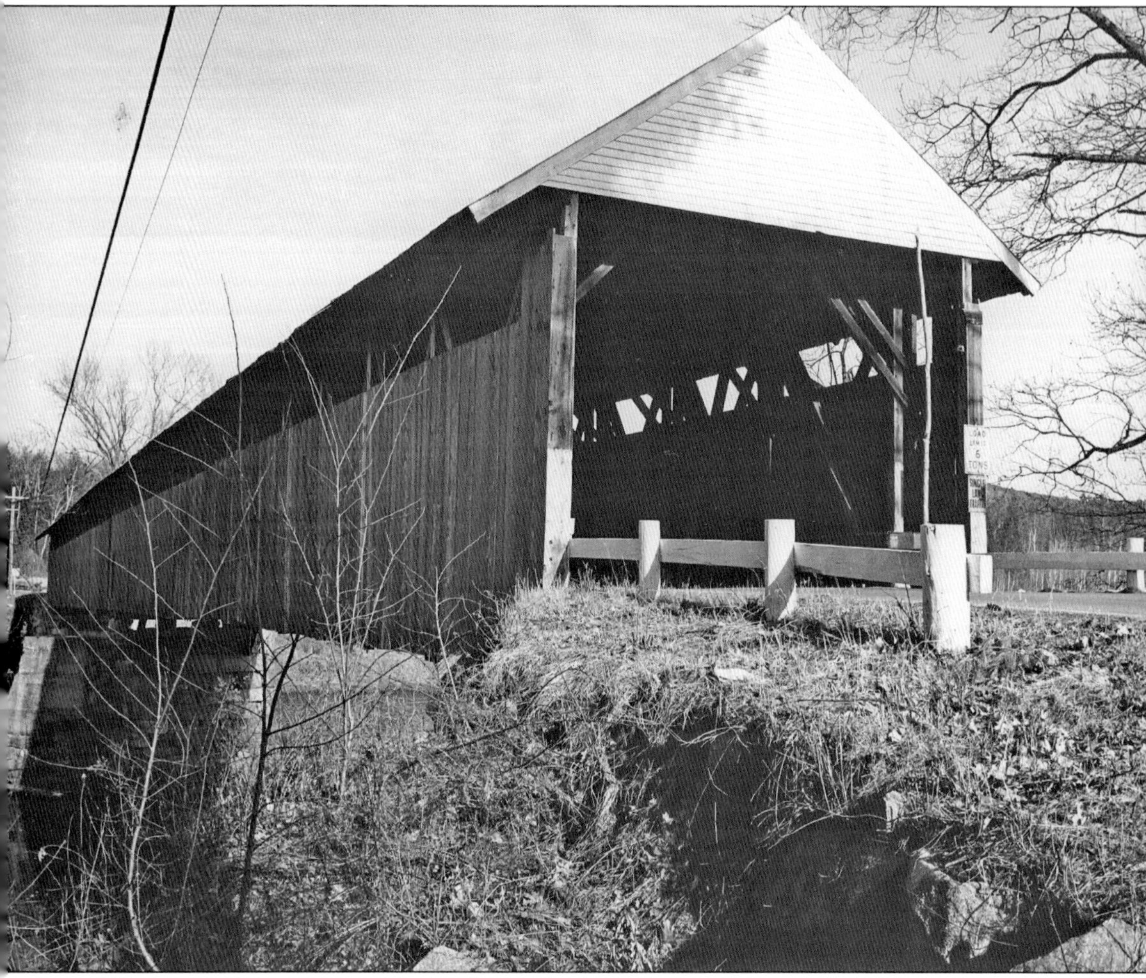

The present Blair Covered Bridge, built in 1870 and pictured in 1950, has undergone several major renovations, the most recent in 2014 by Stanley Graton of Ashland. It is the last remaining covered bridge spanning the Pemigewasset-Merrimack River System.

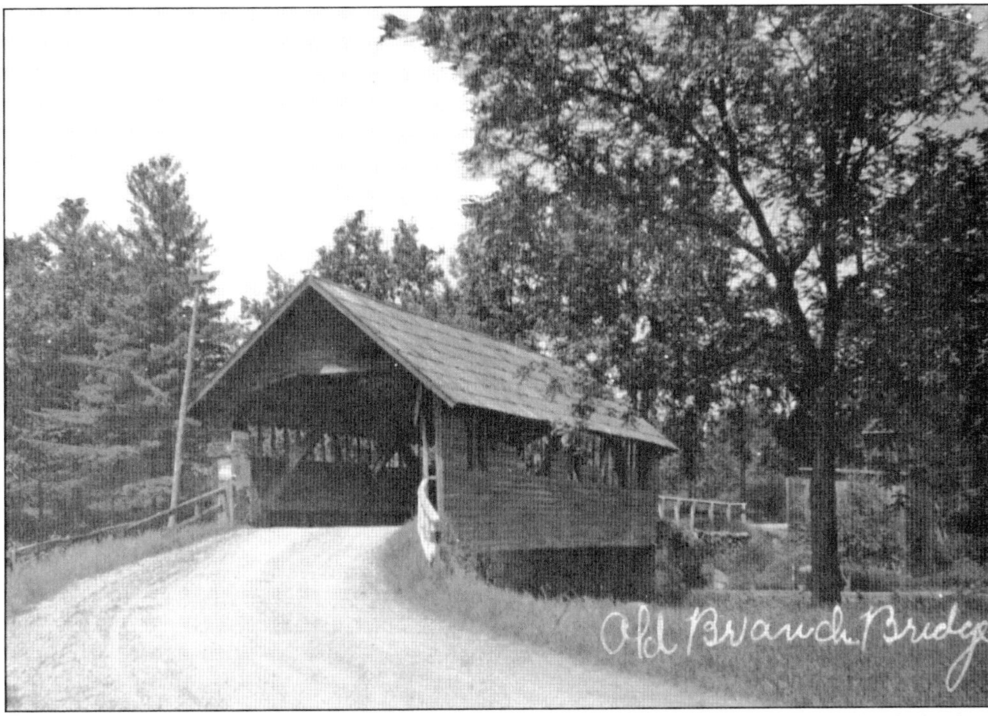

The Old Branch Covered Bridge, in West Campton, was located on Route 3, just north of Chesley's Store and Thornton Collision. It was washed out in the 1927 flood.

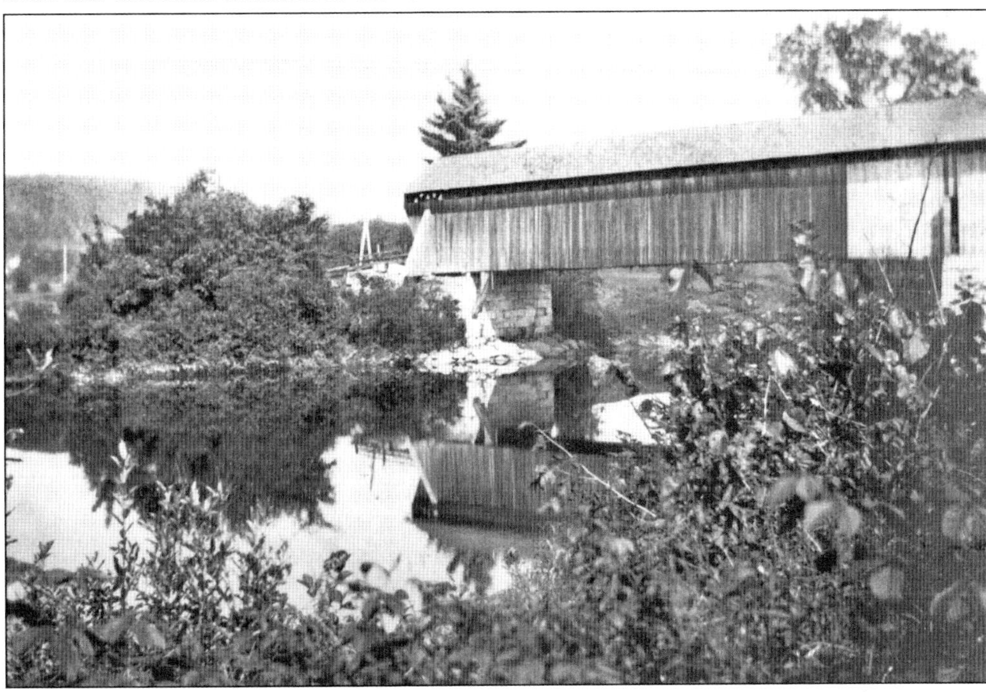
In 1882, the West Campton Bridge was constructed over the Pemi on Route 49. It also was swept off its foundation in the 1927 flood. It was replaced by the current iron-and-cement bridge near Campton Sand and Gravel.

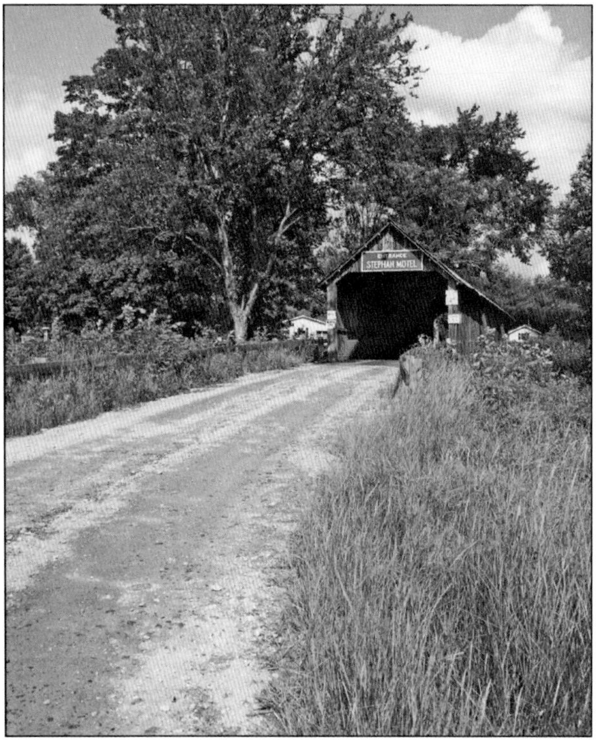

The Turkey Jim Bridge, located in the Branch Brook Campground in West Campton, was named for Jim Cummings, who had raised turkeys on this property. In the 1950s, the property became Stephan's Motel and the bridge became part of the entrance to the lodging facility.

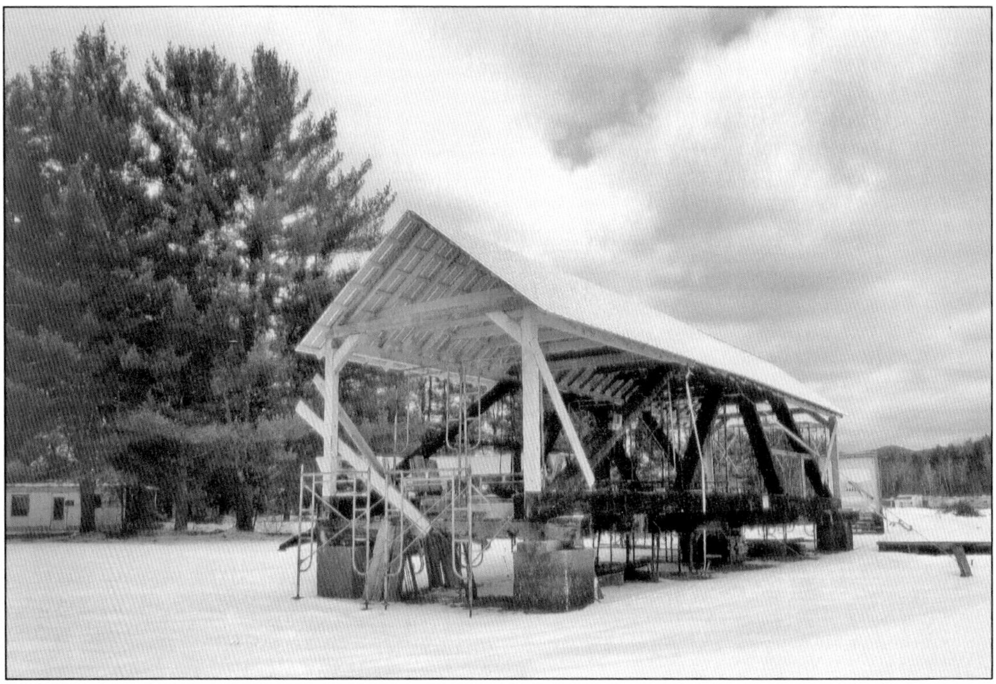

The Turkey Jim Bridge was washed out several times in floods, including in 1927, and then rebuilt. The most recent time was during Hurricane Sandy in October 2012. The picture shows the bridge being reconstructed on dry land in the winter of 2012–2013. It was then moved to the river, just as such construction would have been done generations ago.

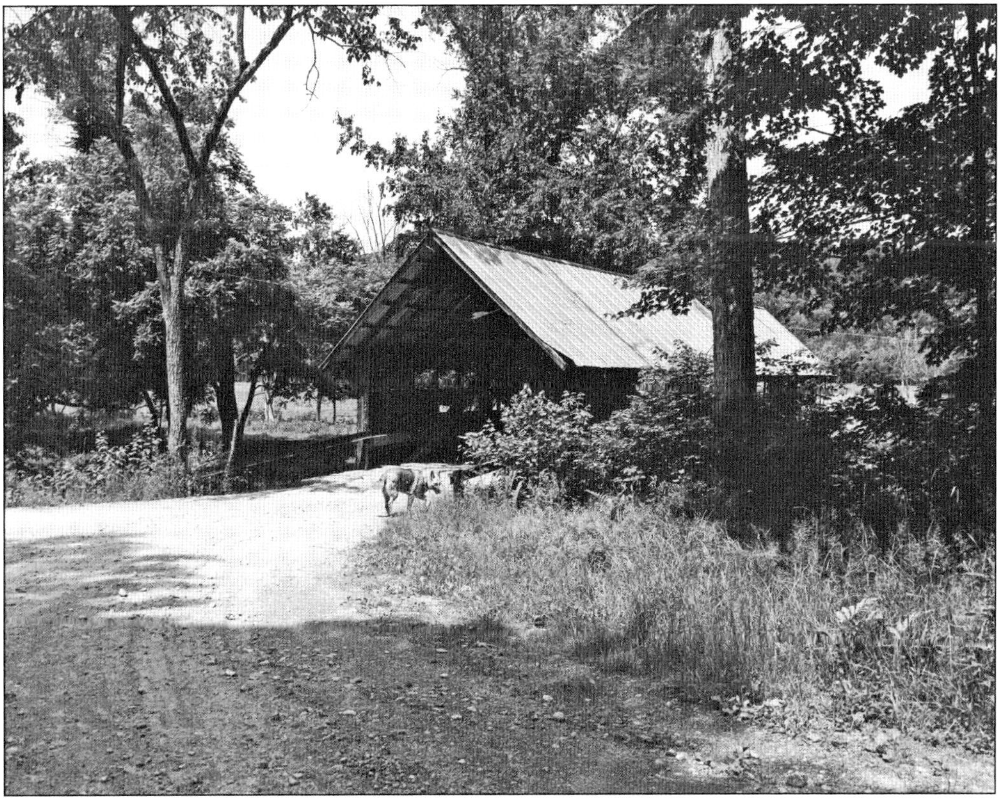

Today's Bump Bridge, at Eastern Corners, was first called the Webber Bridge. It spans the Beebe River from Perch Pond Road to Bump's Intervale.

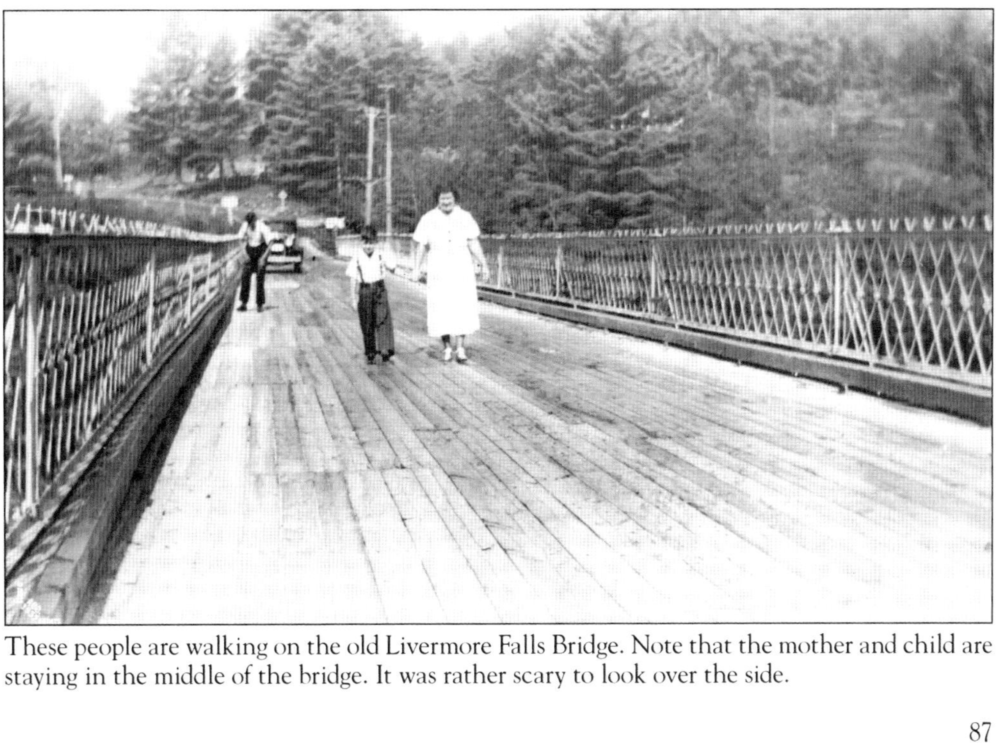

These people are walking on the old Livermore Falls Bridge. Note that the mother and child are staying in the middle of the bridge. It was rather scary to look over the side.

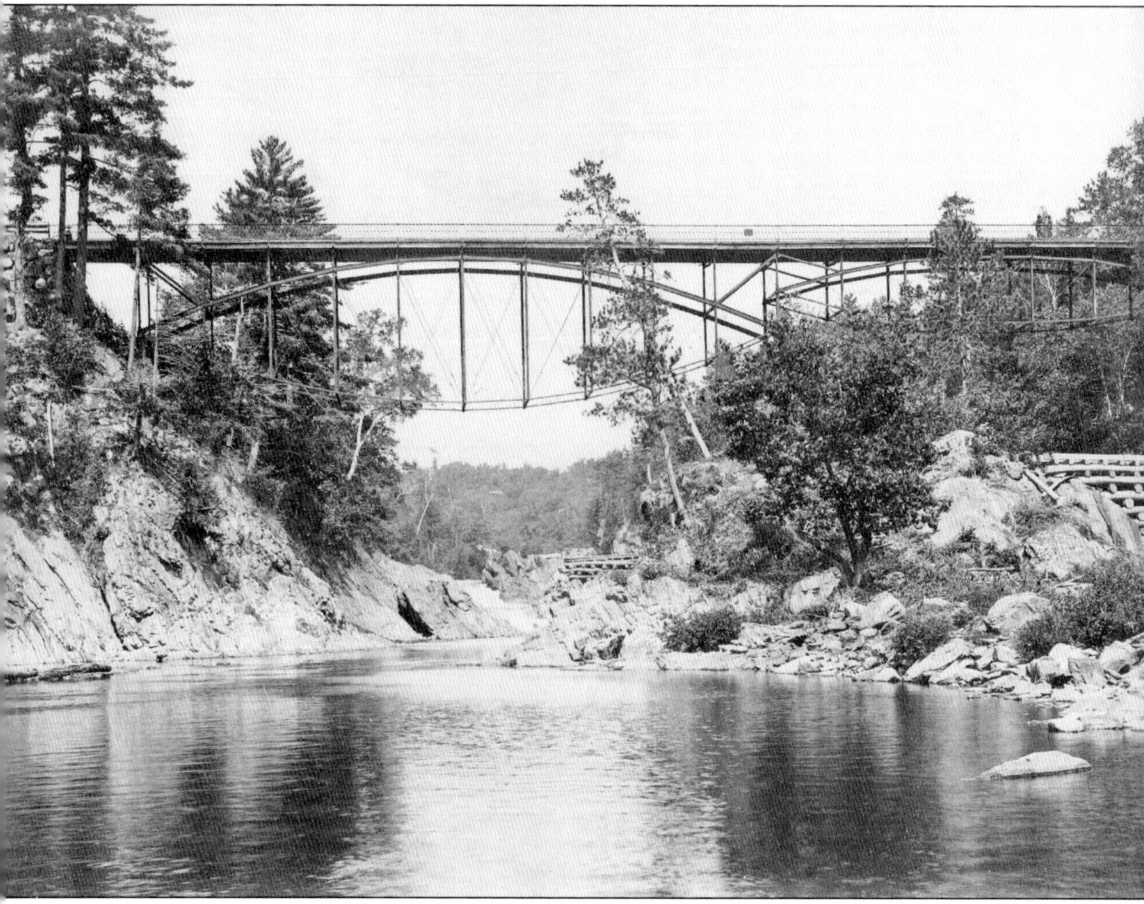

This iron bridge, referred to as the "Pumpkin Seed Bridge" because of its shape, was constructed in 1886; it replaced the two earlier wooden bridges that had spanned the Livermore Falls gorge. Campton, Plymouth, and Holderness all shared ownership and upkeep of the bridge. It was declared unsafe in the 1950s. A portion of the structure is still standing today.

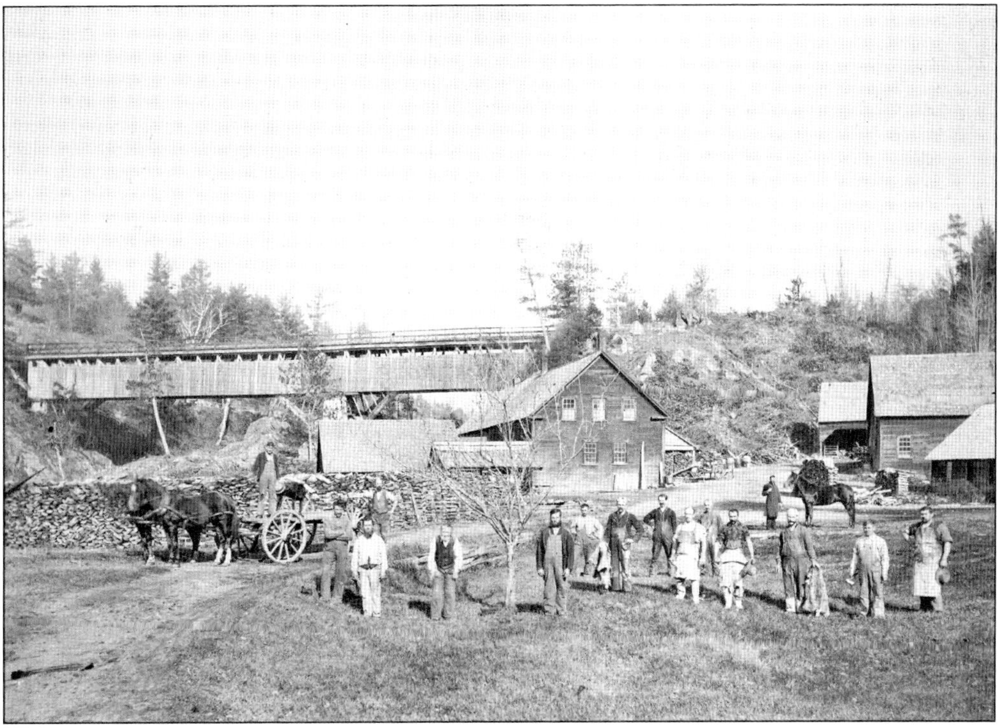

This was the second Little Falls/Livermore Falls Bridge of the 1800s. Horses and horse-drawn carriages traveled on the top of the bridge. The beams supporting the bridge were covered to prevent spray from the falls rotting them; nonetheless, the bridge lasted for only 17 years. The photograph was taken in 1869 from below the falls on the Holderness side of the river.

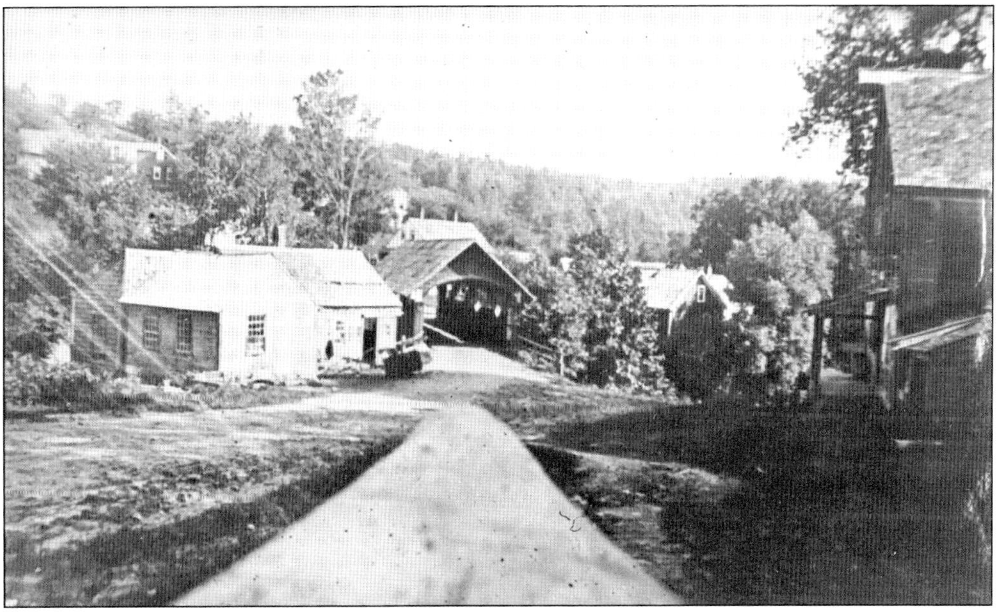

The Campton Hollow Bridge, on Route 175, was the first of three bridges at this location. It was replaced by an iron bridge around 1905, and today a third cement bridge is located here. The bridge is pictured in 1892.

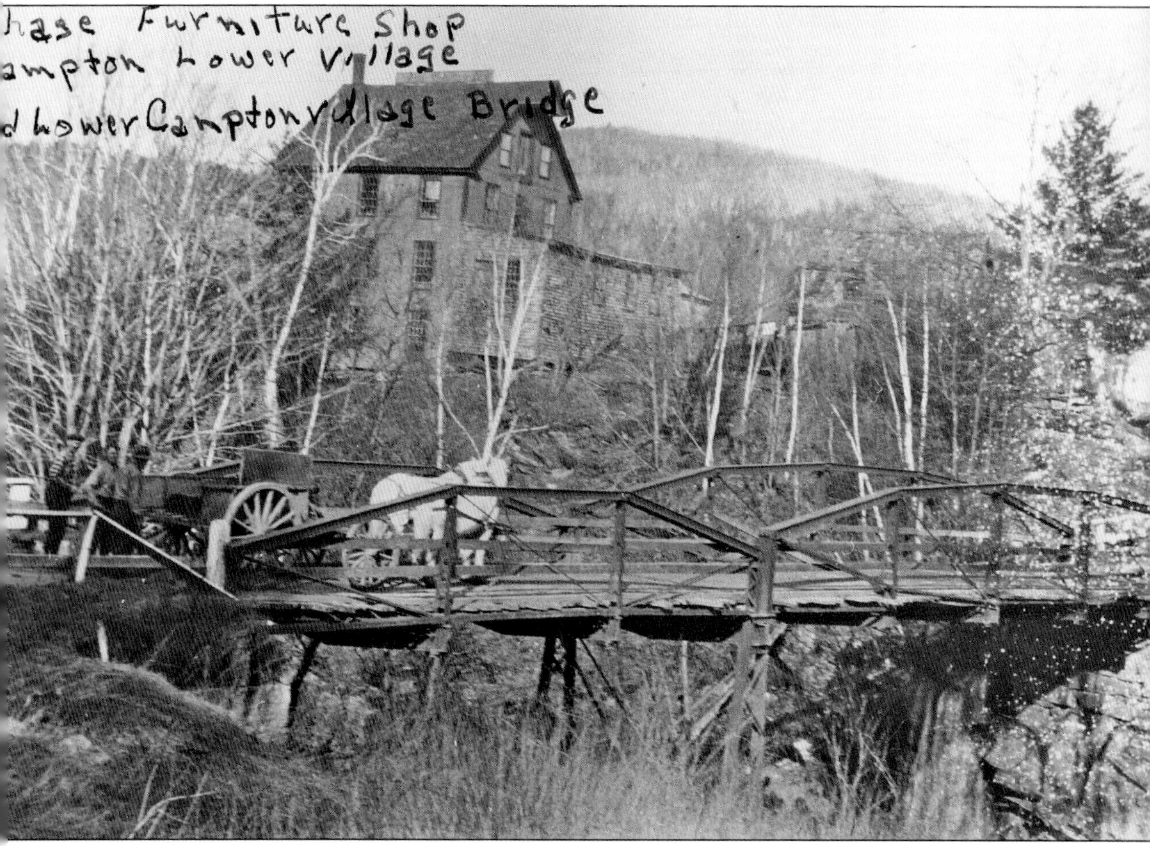

In this mid-1880s view looking south down the Mad River at the Elliott Bridge in the Lower Village, the Chase Furniture Shop can be seen in the background.

Eight

Early Enterprise

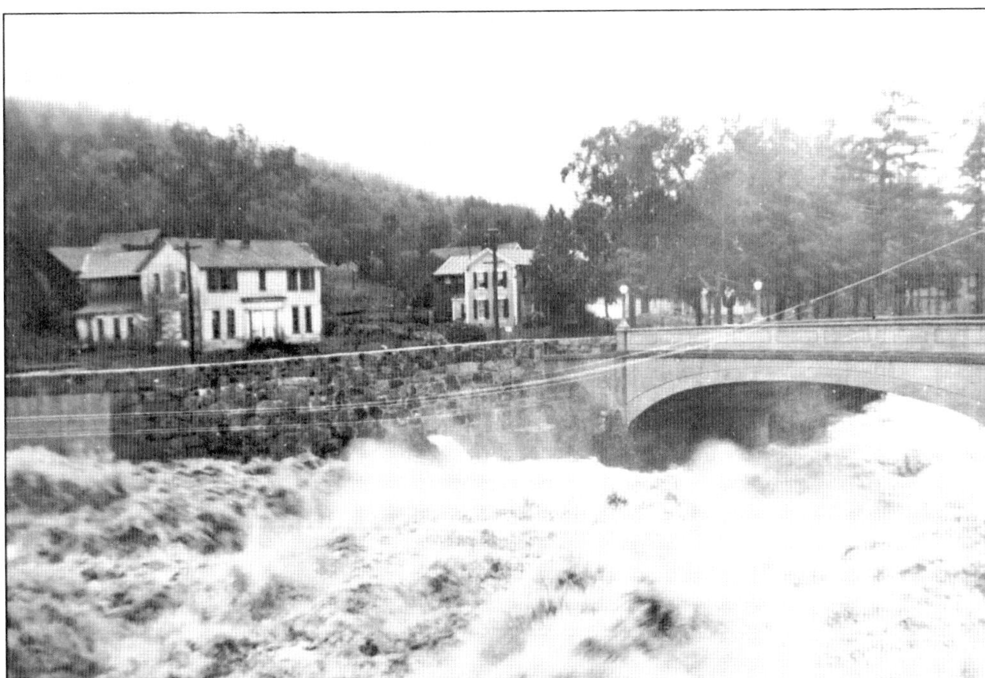

"Why dost thou wildly rush and roar, Mad River, O Mad River?" Henry Wadsworth Longfellow's poem "Mad River" refers to Campton's Mad River, a very busy and hardworking river during the latter half of the 19th century. There were many mills on Mad River, just below the pond—gristmills, a woolen mill, and several mills that manufactured products made from wood.

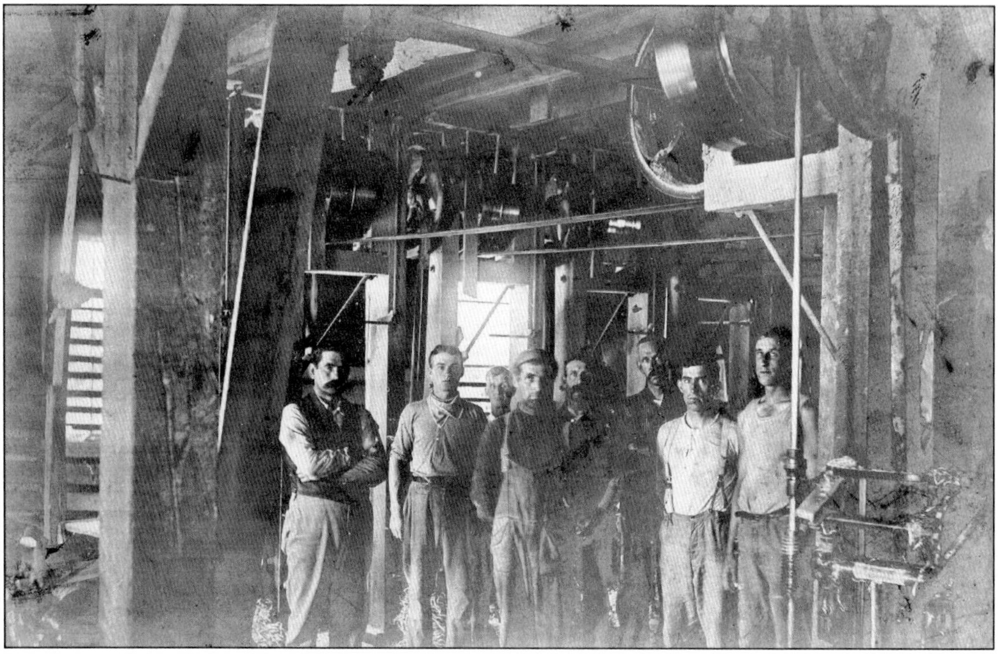

Excelsior Mill workers pause for a photograph in 1890. From left to right are Sam Robie, Harry Cross, James Adams, George Thomson, Will Holmes, Ross Caldon, Archie McCoy, and Henry Morrill Jr. "Wood wool," or excelsior, is a product made of wood slivers cut from logs and mainly used in packaging.

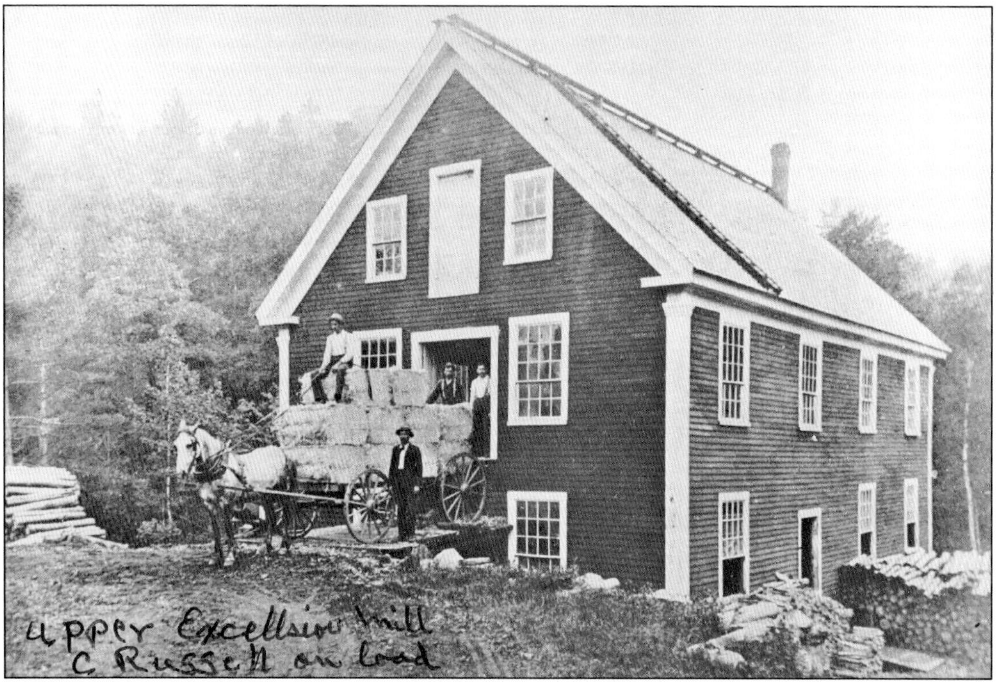

There were two Excelsior mills run by the Tomkinson brothers on the Mad River from 1890 to 1906. Pictured here is the Upper Excelsior Mill. Mill No. 1 produced coarse excelsior, and mill No. 2 produced fine excelsior. Mill No. 2 was sold to Boston Excelsior in 1906 and burned in 1923.

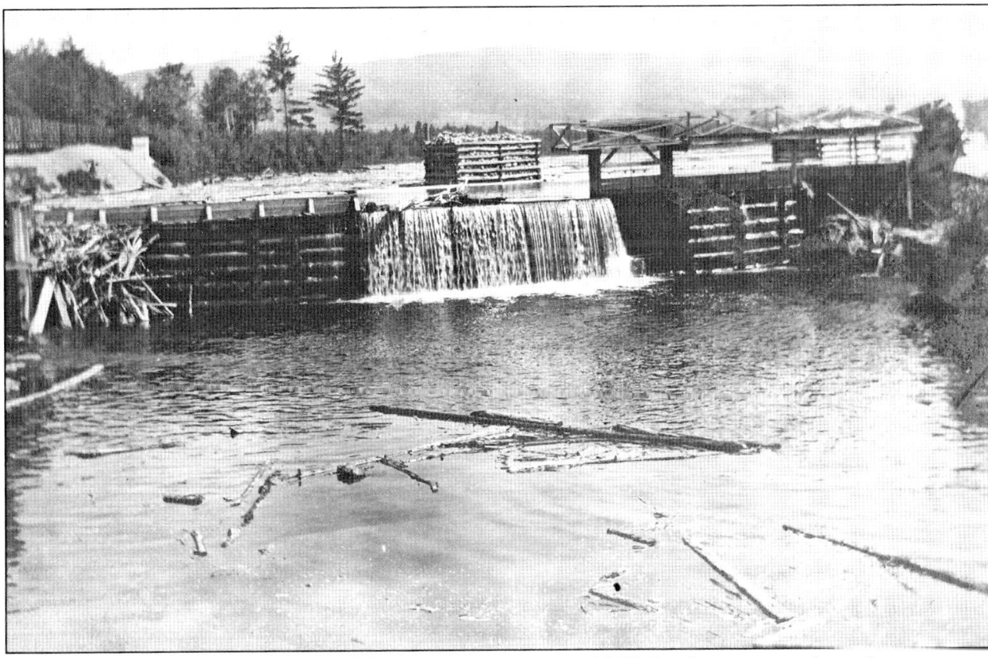

The Campton Dam was the site of logging operations in 1901. In the spring, when the water was high, logs were floated down the river from Waterville Valley. The logs were kept from going over the dam by cribs or boom barriers (seen here) placed in the river to contain them.

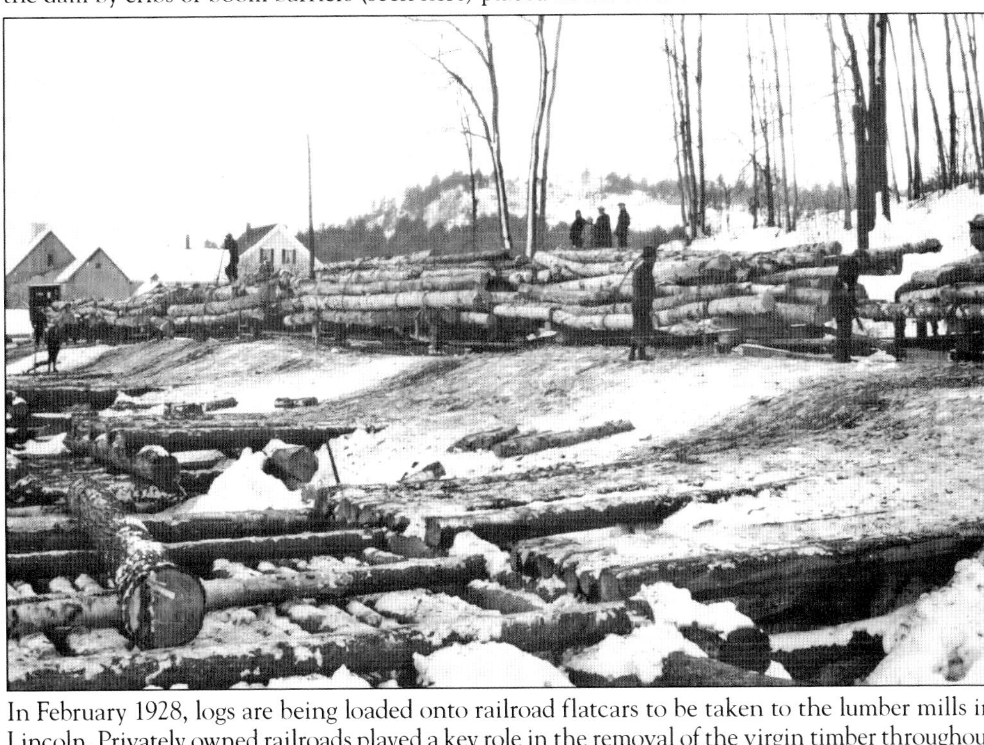

In February 1928, logs are being loaded onto railroad flatcars to be taken to the lumber mills in Lincoln. Privately owned railroads played a key role in the removal of the virgin timber throughout the White Mountains and areas farther north. J.E. Henry is thought to have been the owner of this railroad. The Florence Dole home can be seen in the background.

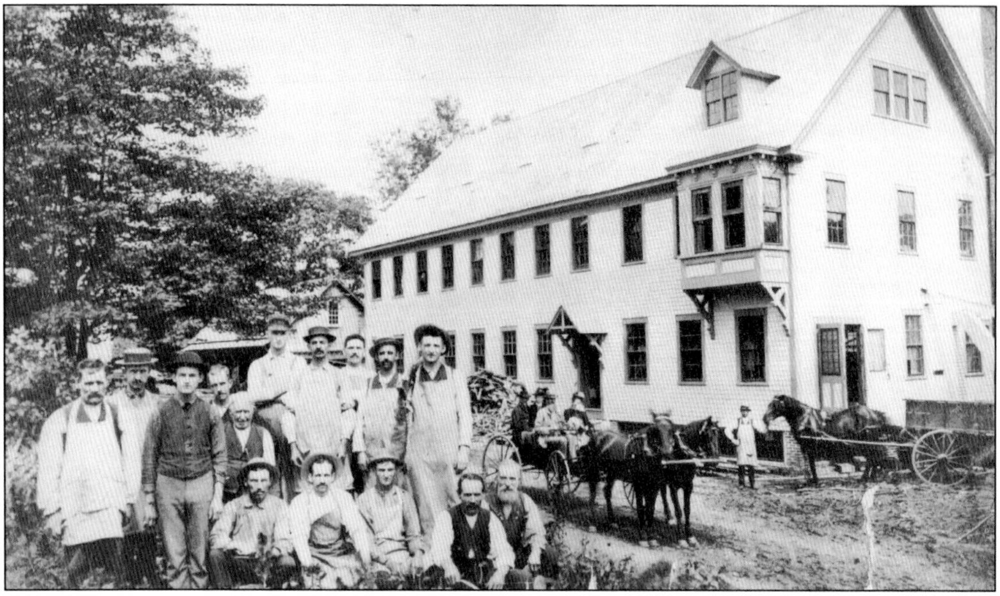

Located on Route 49 in the Lower Village, the Emerson Mill made sashes, blinds, caskets, and coffins. It was destroyed by fire in 1897. From left to right are George Cawley, Will Emerson, Cal Russell, Tom Flanders, Moses Holmes, Dan Morrill, Austin Simpson, Jim Cheney, Rawson Caldon, Deacon Goodhue, unidentified, Ed Bagley, Will Bigelow, and two unidentified.

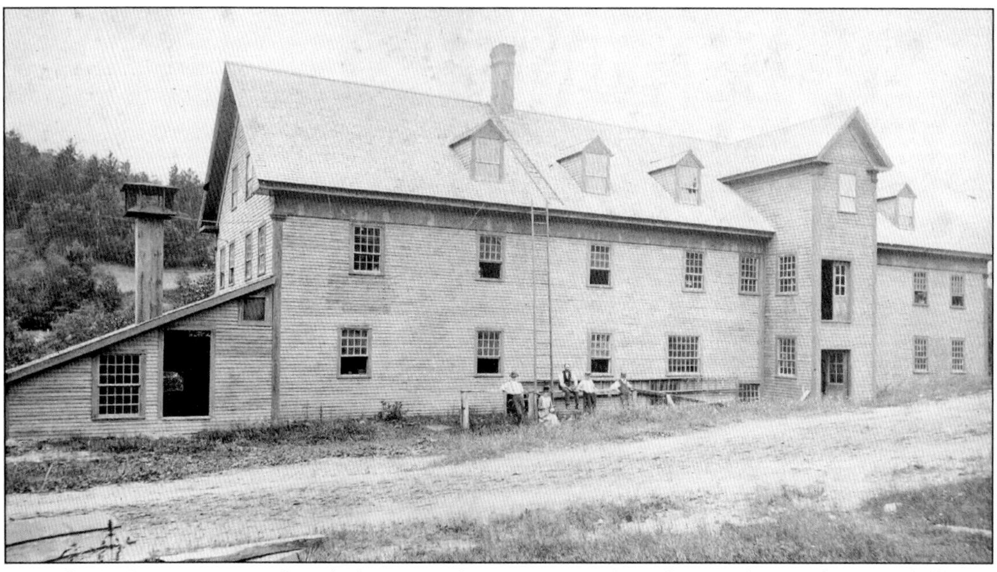

E. Dole & Company was founded in 1820 by Moses Cook and manufactured many different woolen products. Its famous product was Campton Pants, heavy woolen woodsman's pants that "just never would wear out." During World War II, the company made woolen socks, and from that time until the mill closed in 1965, the main product was carpet yarns.

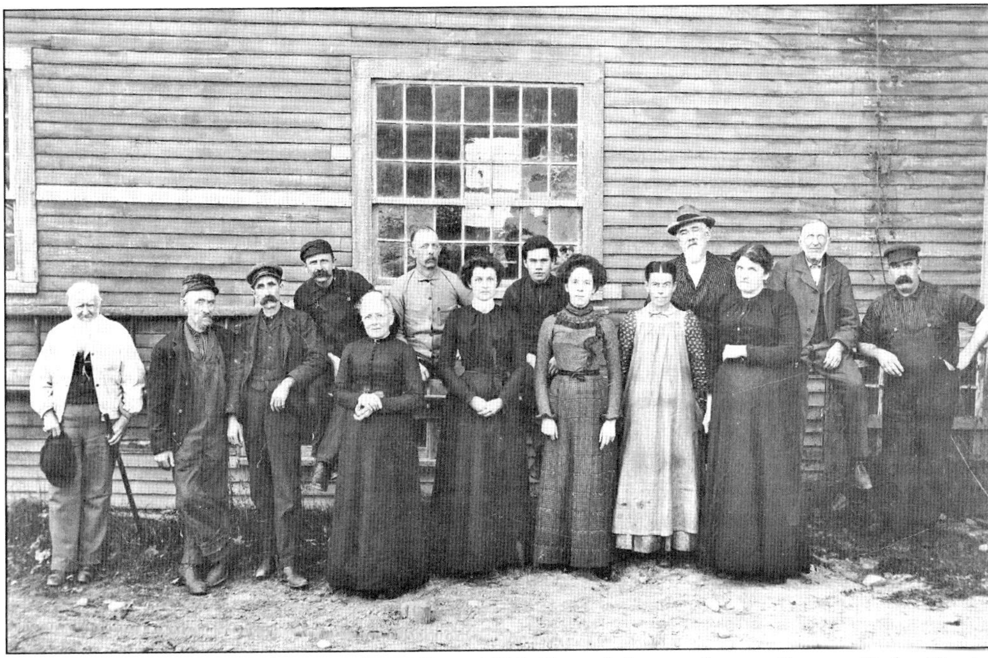

Pictured are workers at the E. Dole Mill in 1890. From left to right are Erastus Dole, Daniel Southmayd, Clarence Ferrin, Bob Cummins, Mary Ann Carlton, Albert Elliott, Nora Webster, Bob ?, Bessie Caldon, Jane Robie, John Hargroues, Minnie Smith, Moses Dole, and Will Bowin.

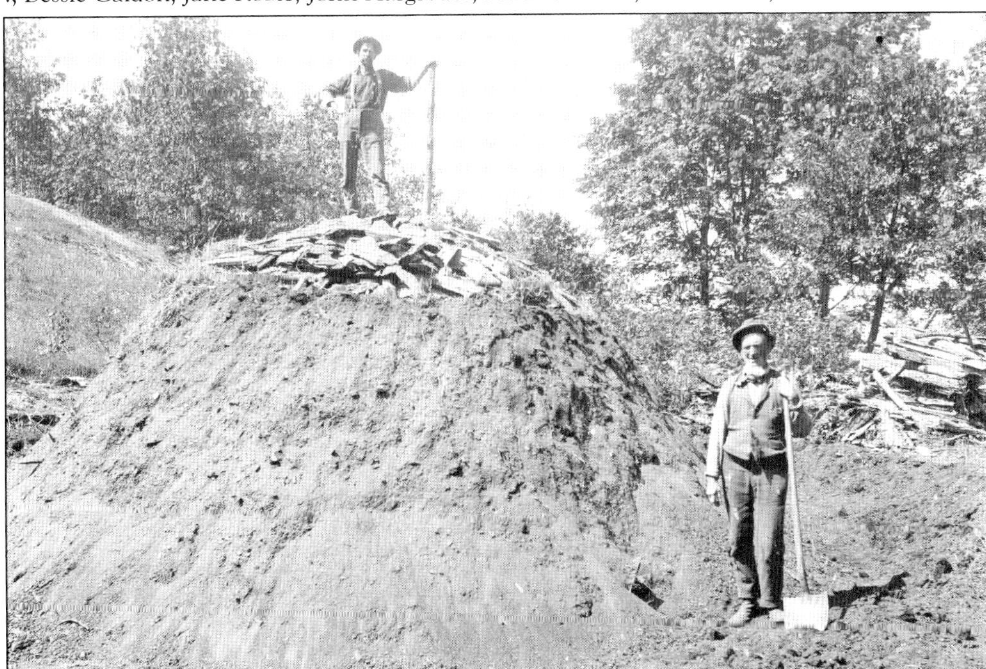

The operation of making charcoal is so delicate that it was generally left to colliers (professional charcoal burners). The burning operation consists of piling billets of wood on their ends to form a conical pile, with openings at the bottom to admit air and a central shaft to serve as a flue. Pictured are two of Campton's colliers around 1890.

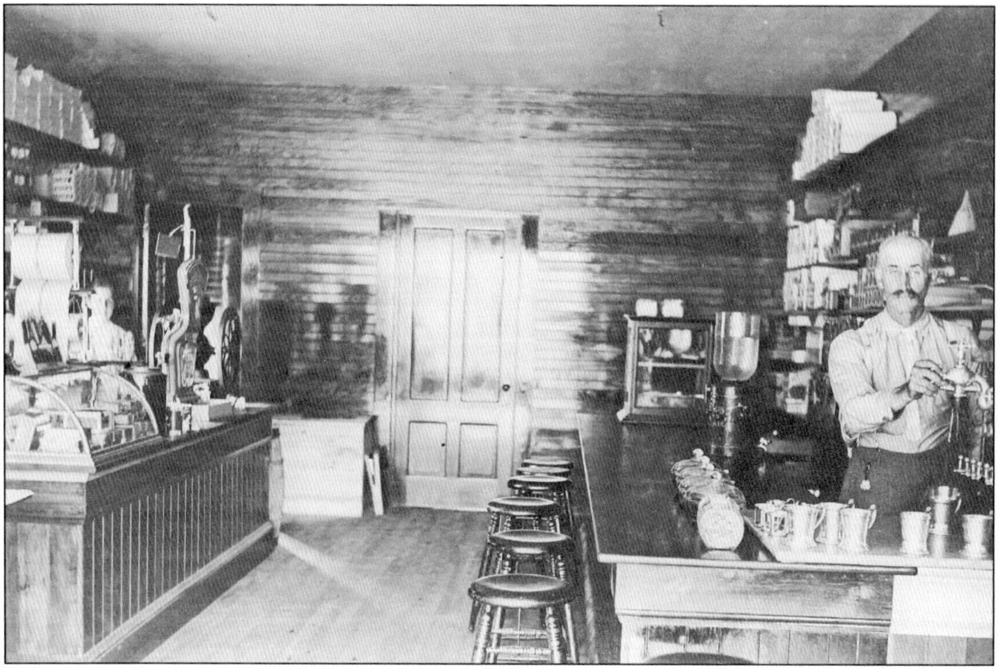

Henry Fifield's store was conveniently located at the corner of Route 175 and Mad River Road and carried all manner of food and household supplies. It was also a place to meet friends and enjoy an ice-cream soda. Henry Fifield is seen here in 1909 working at the soda fountain.

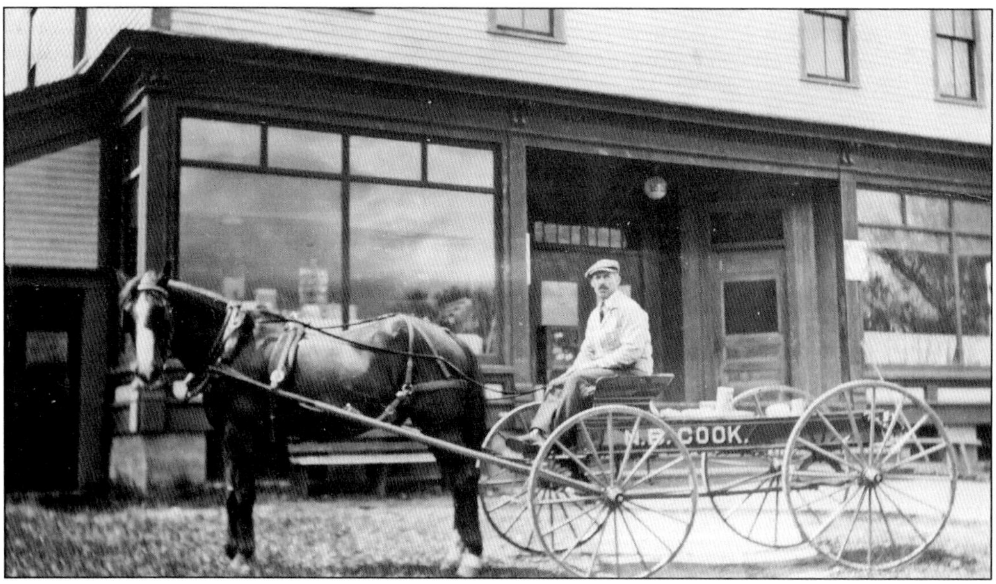

Nelson Cook is sitting in his buggy in front of Cook's General Store, which was in the Odd Fellows Building. The building, constructed in 1911, housed the store, the central telephone office, a kitchen, and a dining room on the first floor. The second floor was meeting rooms, and the third floor featured a large hall with a stage where three-act plays, dances, and other entertainment were presented. After World War II, White Mountain Industries, an apparel maker, used the building. Today, it houses apartments.

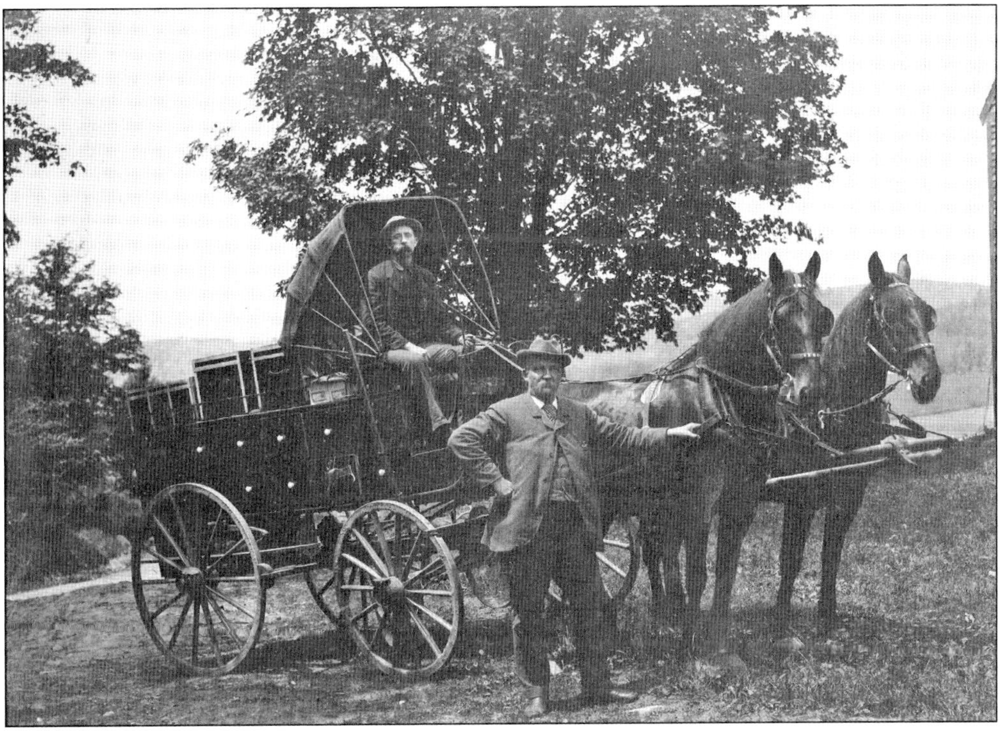

Ben Sanborn drove from house to house selling shoes. It is believed that he made shoes as well as repaired them for his customers. By the late 19th century, he may also have sold ready-made shoes. Pictured in 1915 are Sanborn (standing) and William Rowe (driving the cart).

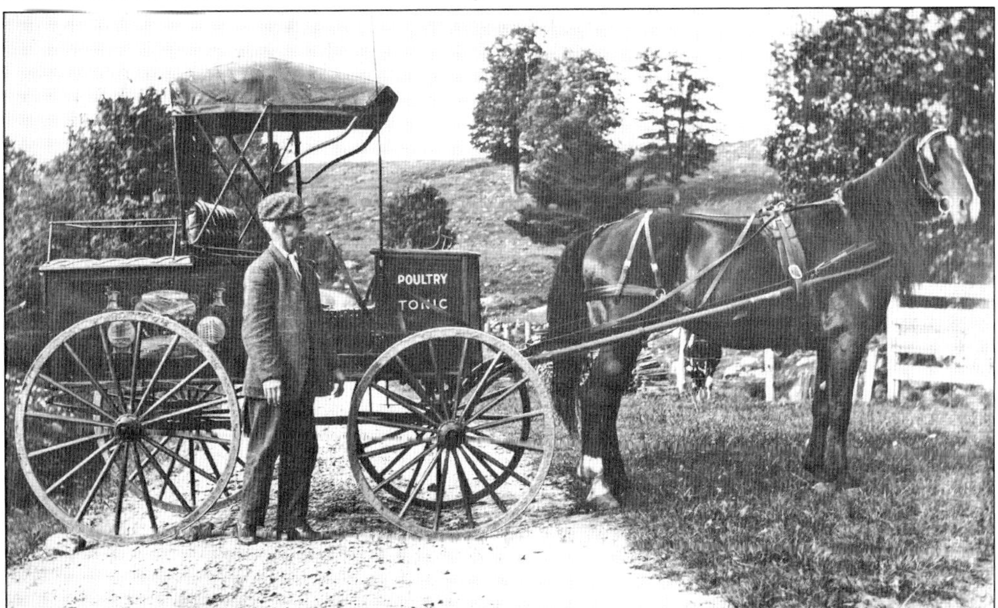

James Adams is standing beside his Poultry Tonic wagon, in 1915. Tonics, or pick-me-ups, were big sellers in the early 1900s. Traveling salesmen went from farm to farm selling bottled energizers for animals and people alike. Adams specialized in tonics for chickens.

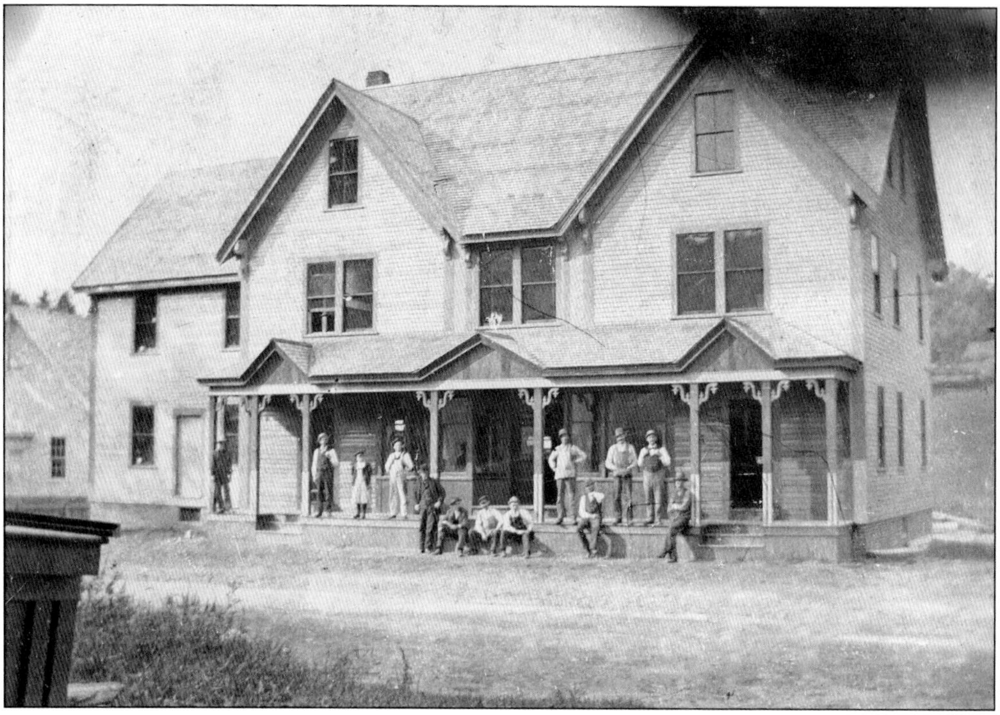

Adams Store, in Campton Village, has a long history of successful ownership, starting with William Adams in the 1890s. Shown here is Adams (second from left) standing in front of his store. The Morrisons owned the store after Adams.

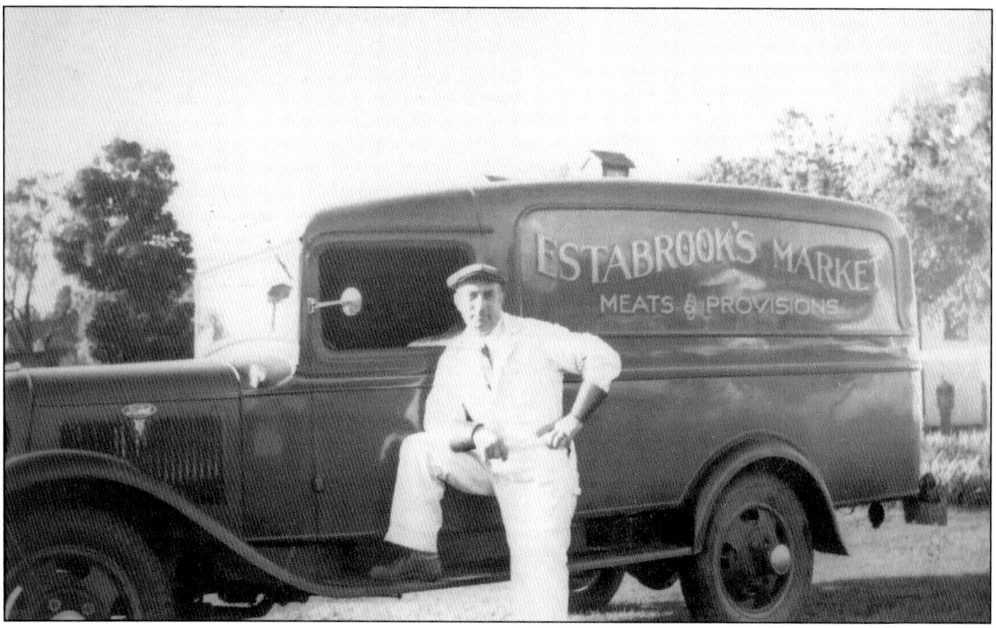

George Estabrook, shown here by his delivery van, had a meat store in his home in the Upper Village and wanted more space. George bought the Morrison Store (in the previous image), which later became McCoy's Store and, after several more owners, the Campton Cupboard. The small-town store has been in business for an impressive 126 years.

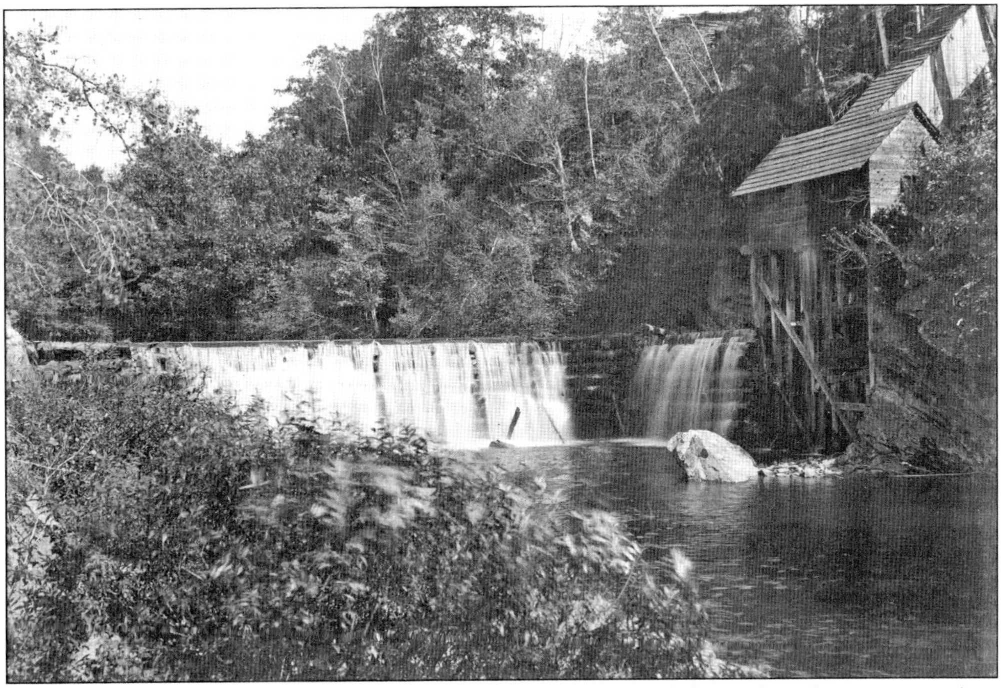

Harry Chase ran this furniture factory in 1898. It was conveniently located on the river, providing easy access to lumber. The factory turned out beautiful, handcrafted pieces, many hand-painted with flowers, trees, and mountain scenes. A few fortunate Campton families still own furniture made in this Lower Village factory.

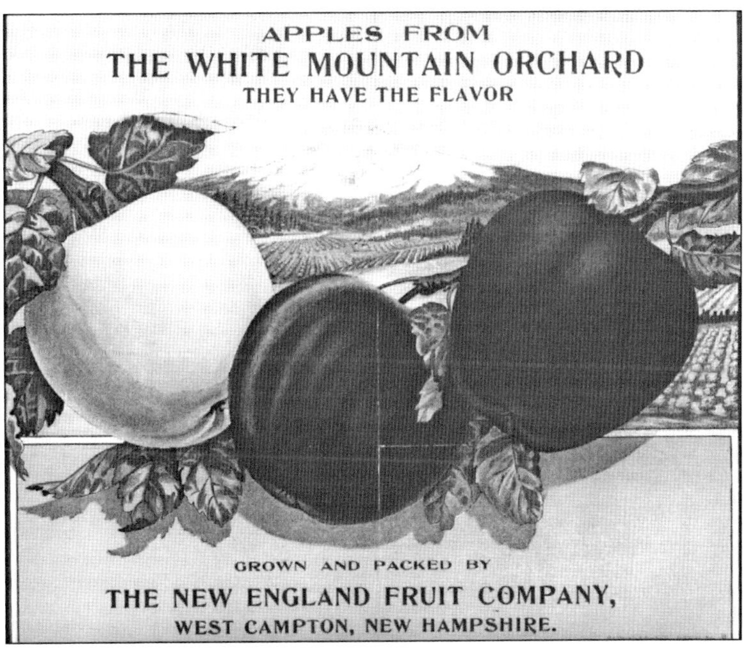

The White Mountain Orchard in West Campton was originally owned and operated by Kent Pearly. Robert Kelly purchased the orchard in 1945, and the Kelly family ran it until 1985.

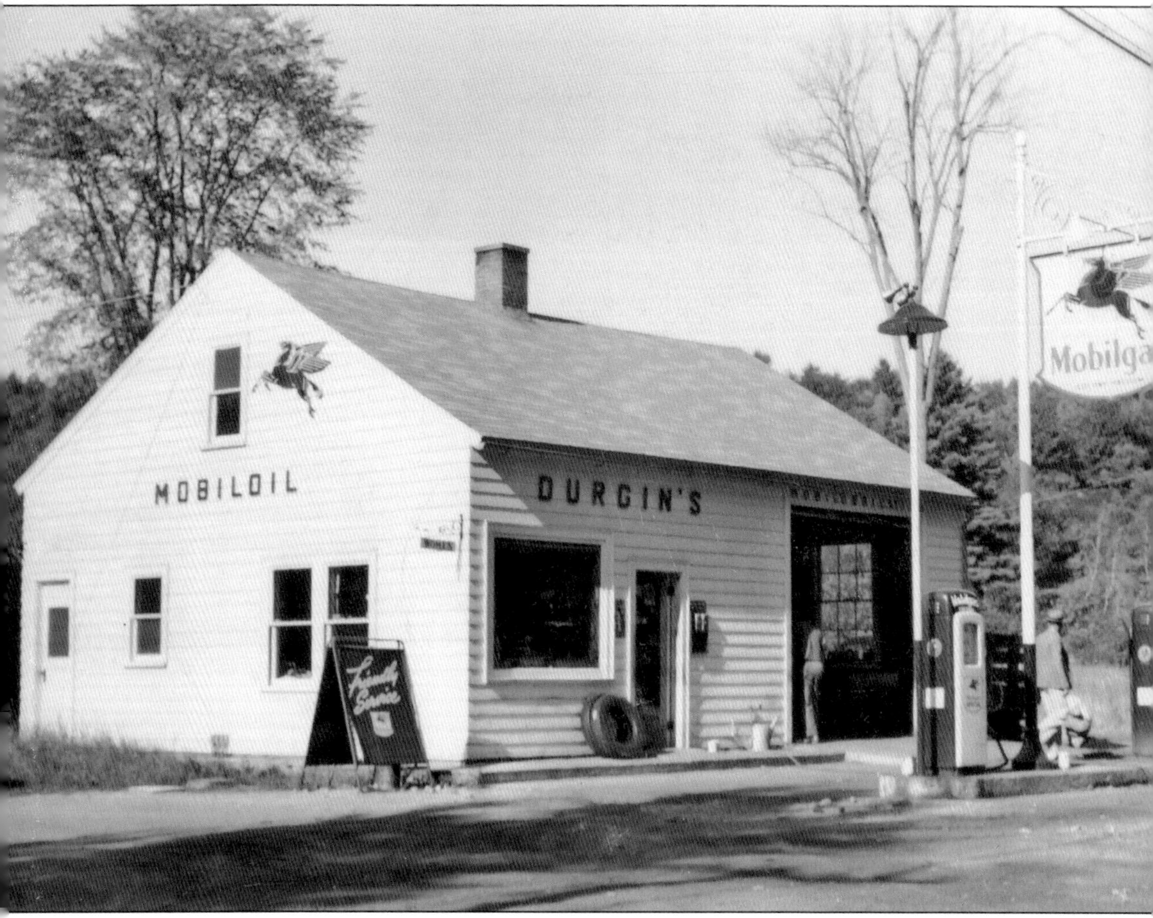

Durgin's Garage is a landmark on Route 3. Gas was sold here long before 1941, when the garage was built by Paul Durgin. Paul and his wife, Gladys, and their children ran the garage until 1975. It was a family business, so one would see all the Durgins, including their daughter, Mary, pumping gas. The business located here is now owned and operated by Mark Schultz as J&M Imports.

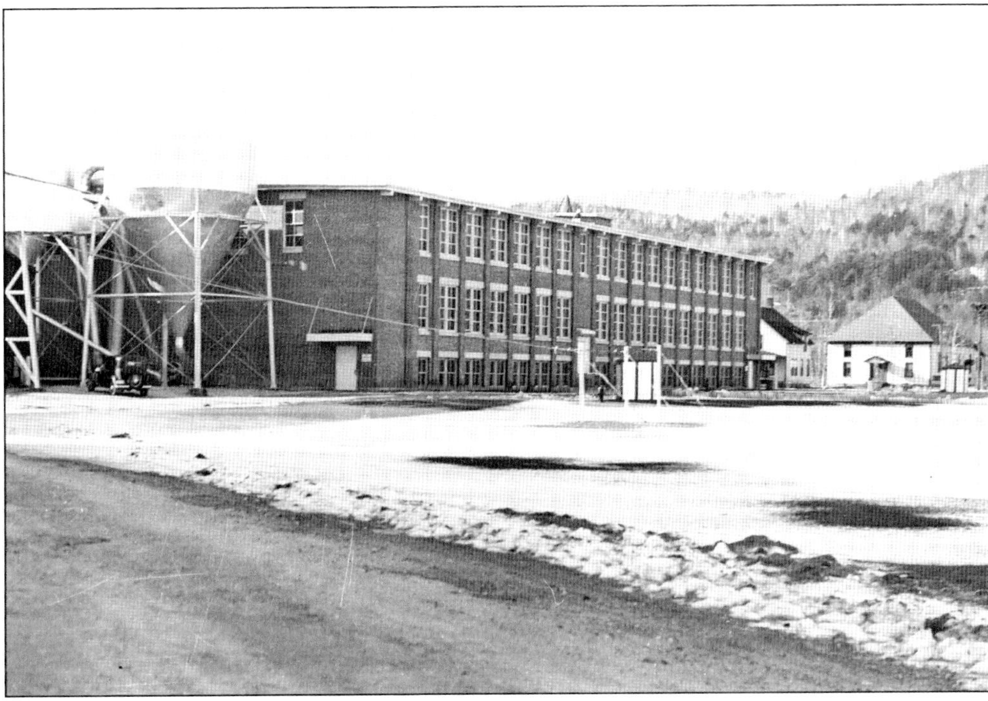

One of the area's largest employers was the Beebe River Mill, built in 1917 by the Woodstock Lumber Company and Parker Young to harvest area timber. In addition to the mill, an entire town was built, complete with houses for the workers, a company store, a boardinghouse, and even a movie theater. In 1926, the mill complex was bought by Draper Corporation to be used for the production of bobbins for Draper's textile mills. Beebe River was the world's largest bobbin producer. Shown here are two views of the bobbin finishing mill; the one below shows the convenience of the railroad.

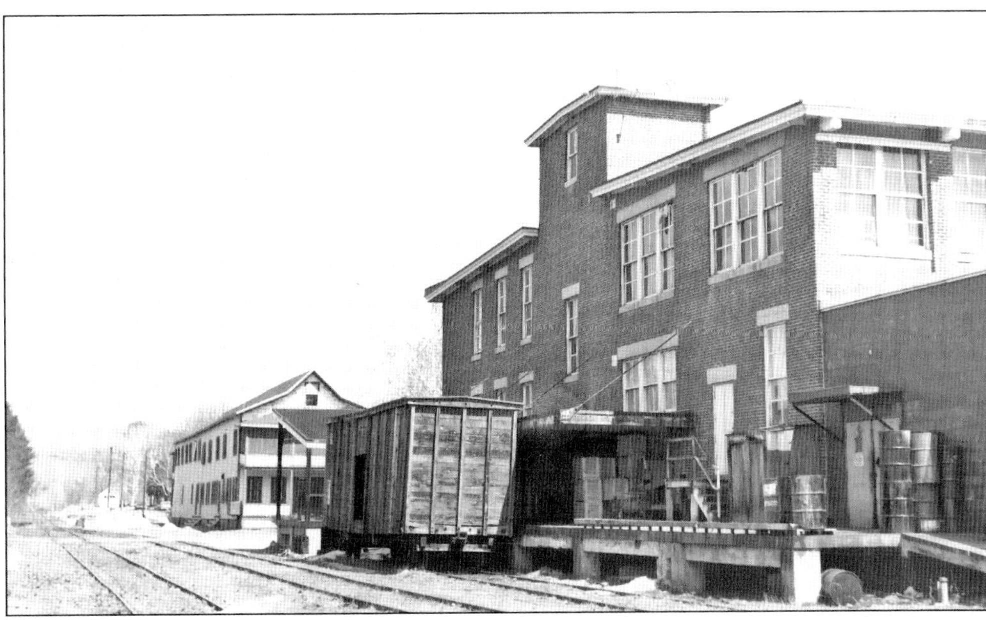

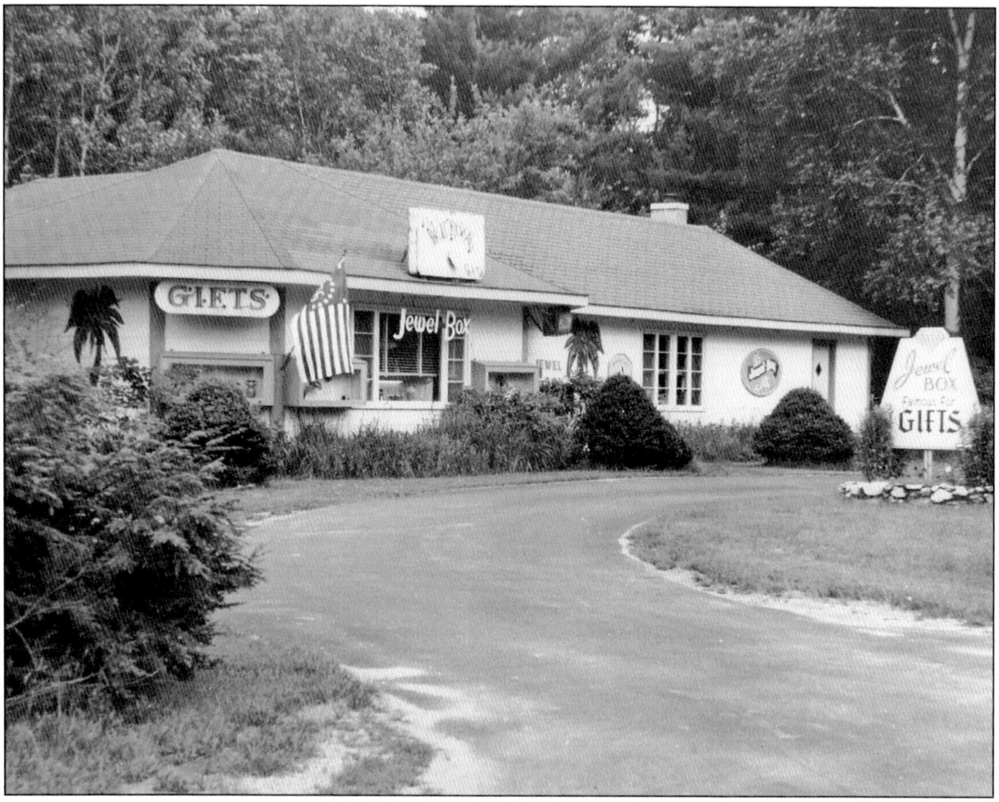

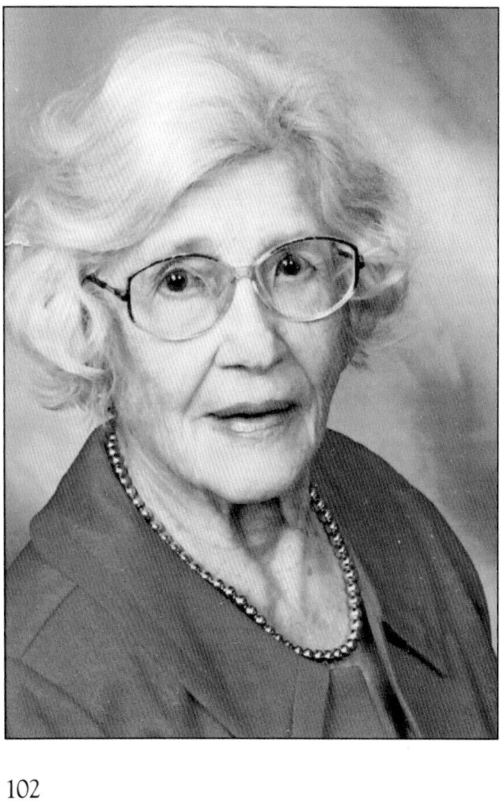

The Jewel Box, run by Edna and William O'Brien, opened around 1955 and continued until the early 1990s. It is still a point of reference on Route 3. Edna (pictured) was active in her church and community affairs, serving on the school board for many years and also as the leader of her church ladies guild. Over the years, Edna was an avid and knowledgeable gardener and was always giving plants and flowers to help others complete their gardens. She also supplied flowers to her church every Sunday. Edna, beloved by all who knew her, also enjoyed painting and painted many handcrafted items for the Jewel Box. As the oldest Campton resident, Edna held the Boston Post Cane until her death in 2017 at age 98.

Nine

Recreation and Celebration

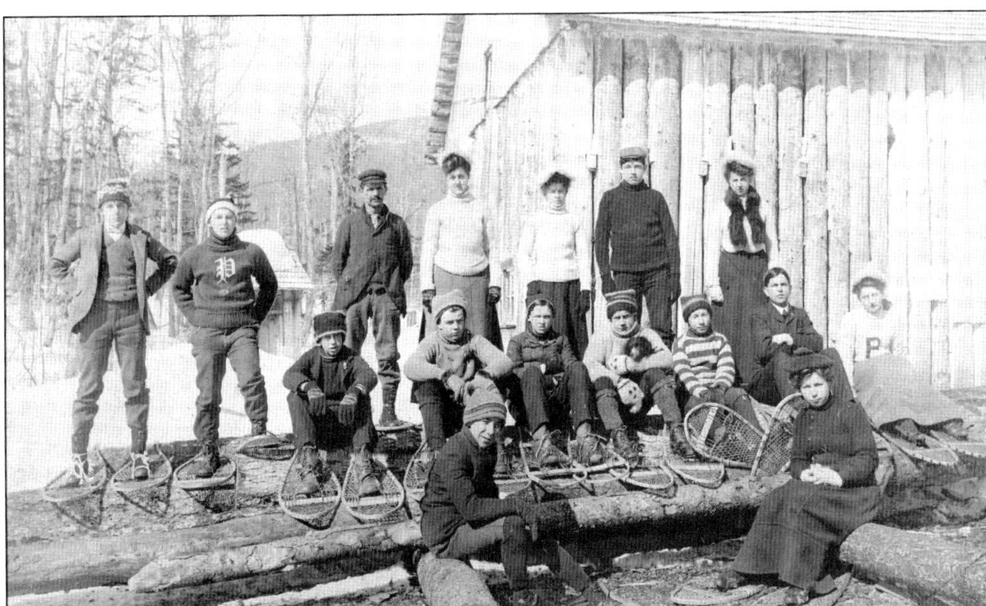

Campton snowshoers in 1904 are wearing the popular bear paw type of snowshoe. From left to right are (first row) Charles Pettingill and Ella Nath; (second row) Irving Sanborn, Erastus Dole, John Saunders, George Little, Carl Smith, Ray McCoy, and Mildred Adams; (third row) Lynn Bowles, Webb Little, John Broch, Marian Adams, Grace Green, Ola Smith, and Dell Simpson.

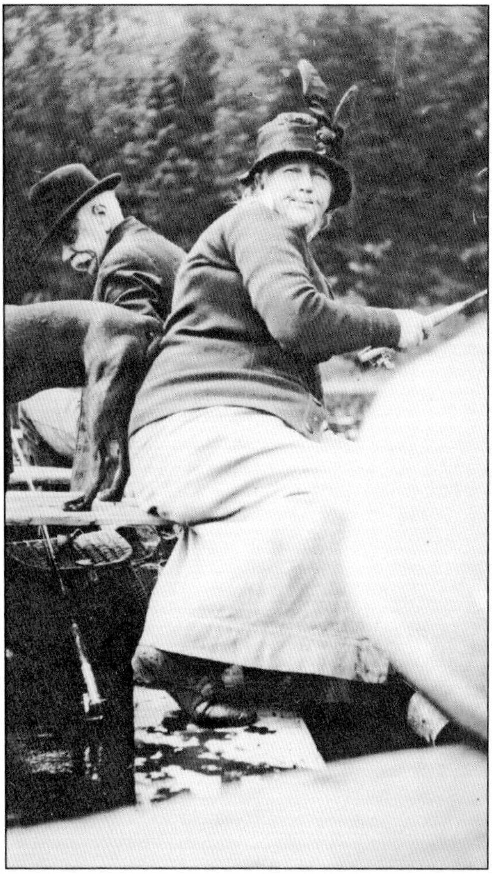

Moody and Lillian Dole were avid fishermen, and they caught many big fish. They owned a log cabin, a boat, and a boathouse on the Sandwich Notch Road on Hall Pond where they spent many of their leisure hours. They are shown here fishing in the middle of the pond with the support of their canine companion.

Riding bicycles was a popular sport in 1885. Standing are, from left to right, Austin Simpson, William H. Adams, Moody Dole, John Merrill, and Will Emerson.

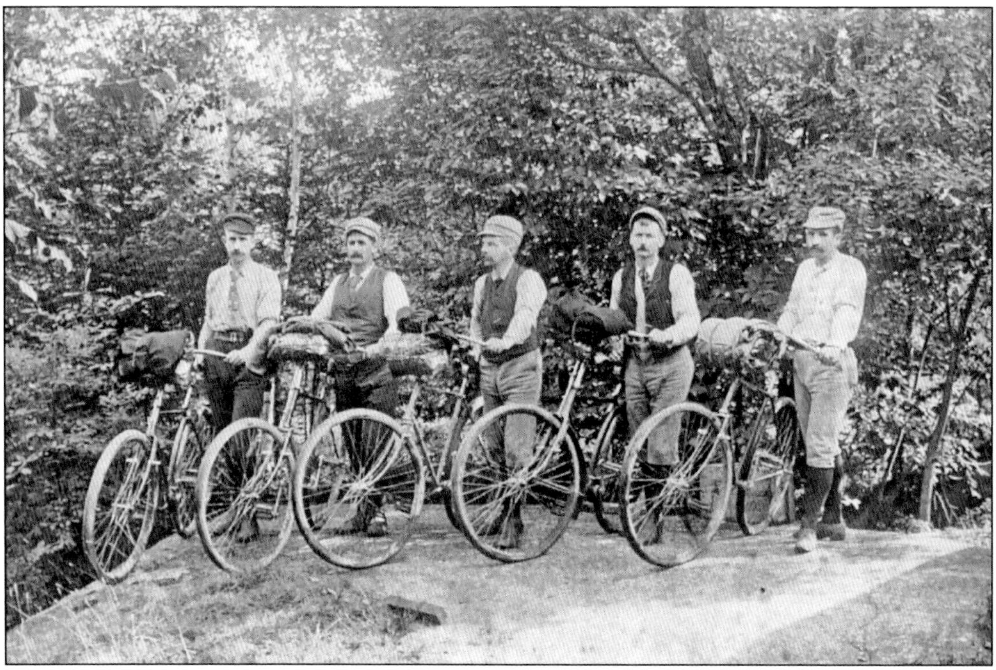

Daniel Cook is prepared to go hunting with his faithful dog companions. As well as a form of recreation, hunting was an important means of providing food for the family table. Venison was an especially popular supplement to the family diet. Daniel owned a sawmill and also took in guests at his farm.

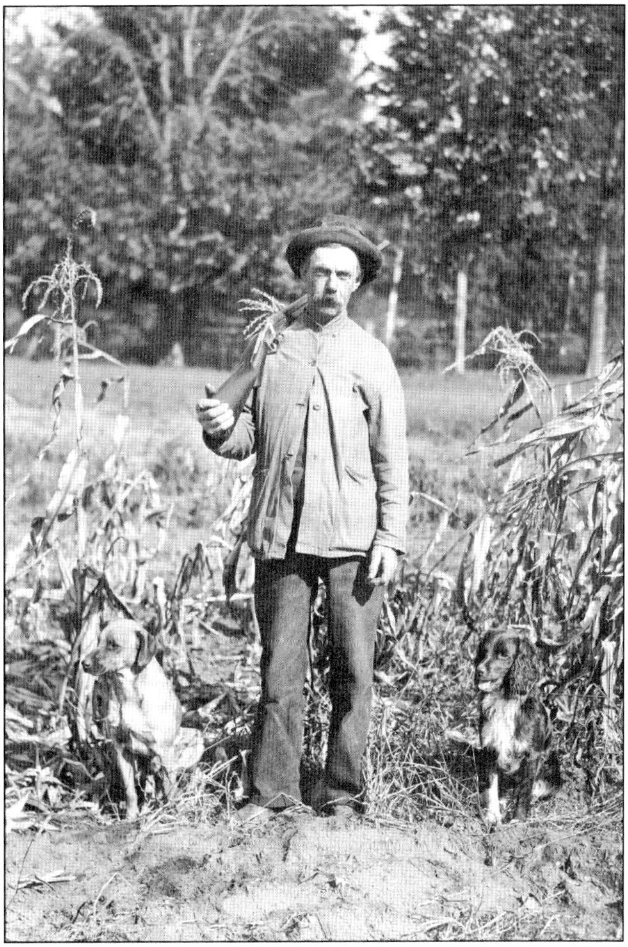

Members of this hunting party are standing next to a converted Ford Model T on the Beebe River Railroad tracks in 1926. They are near Camp 12, about a half mile from the end of the railroad.

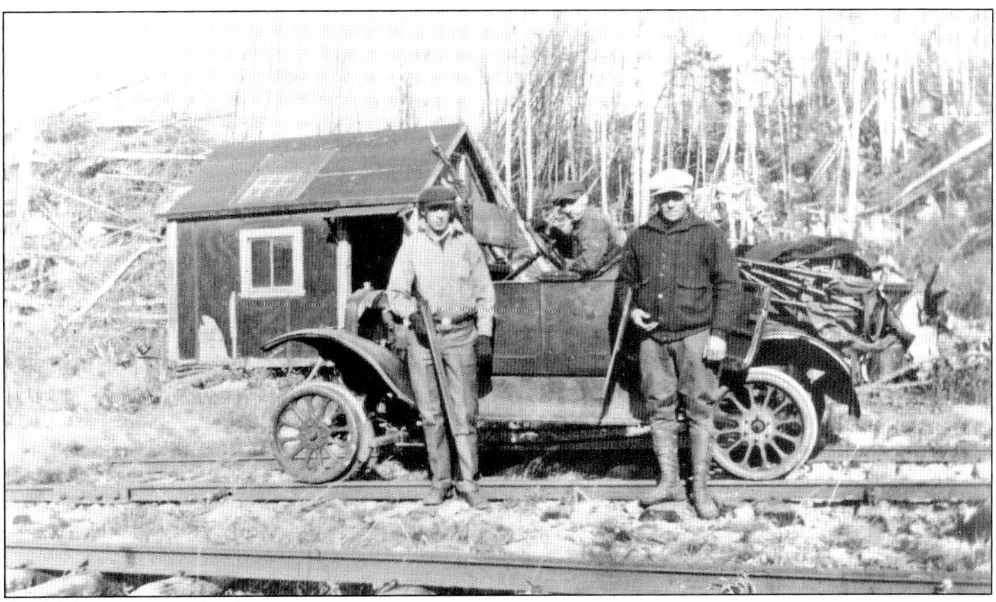

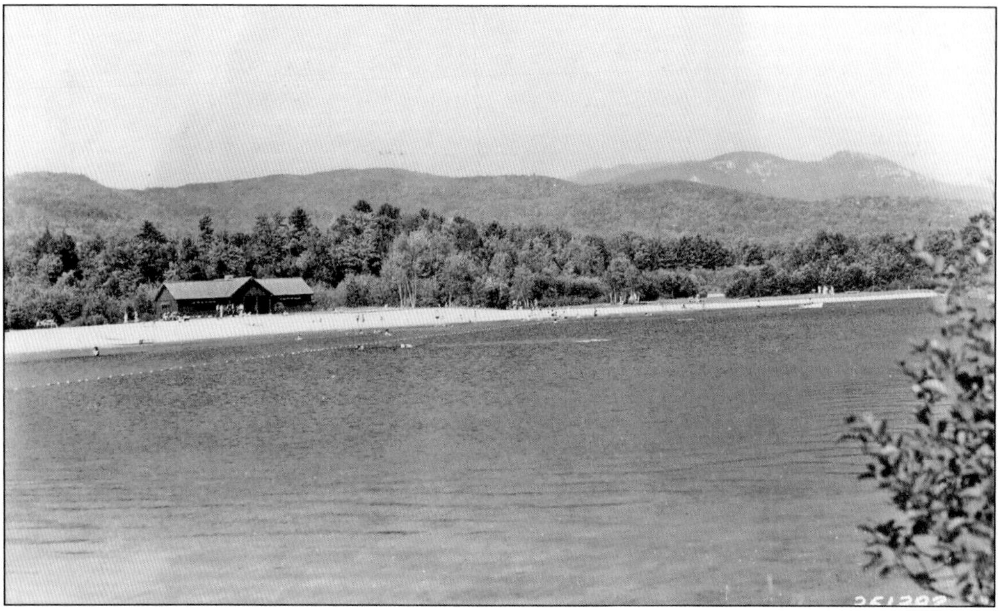

The Forest Camp and Beach at Campton were established in 1936. They were built by the Civilian Conservation Corps as was the bathhouse. In addition, there were picnic facilities with fireplaces and running water. From left to right, Welch, Dickey, and Tripyramid Mountains are seen in the background. (Used with permission of the Forest History Society.)

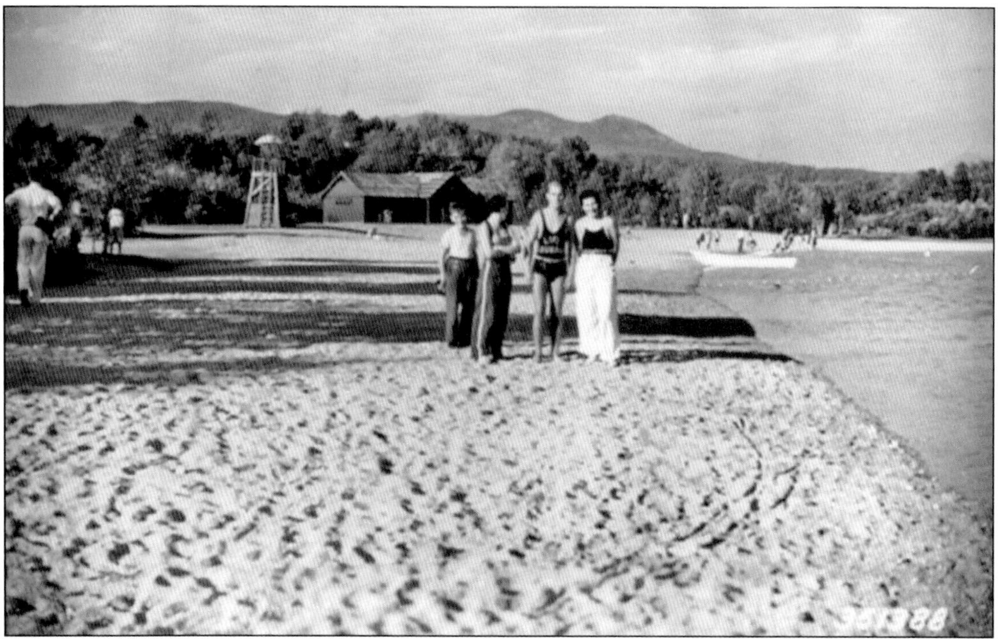

The pond and beach were enjoyed by campers and locals. The beach was destroyed by a flood in 1959. One of the benches from the bathhouse is currently located in the Grange Hall of the Campton Historical Society. It was a gift from Marolyn Fillion, whose father, Frank Broad, helped dismantle the bathhouse after the flood. The Campton Pond Forest Camp is owned by the US Forest Service as part of the White Mountain National Forest and is still maintained for camping. (Used with permission of the Forest History Society.)

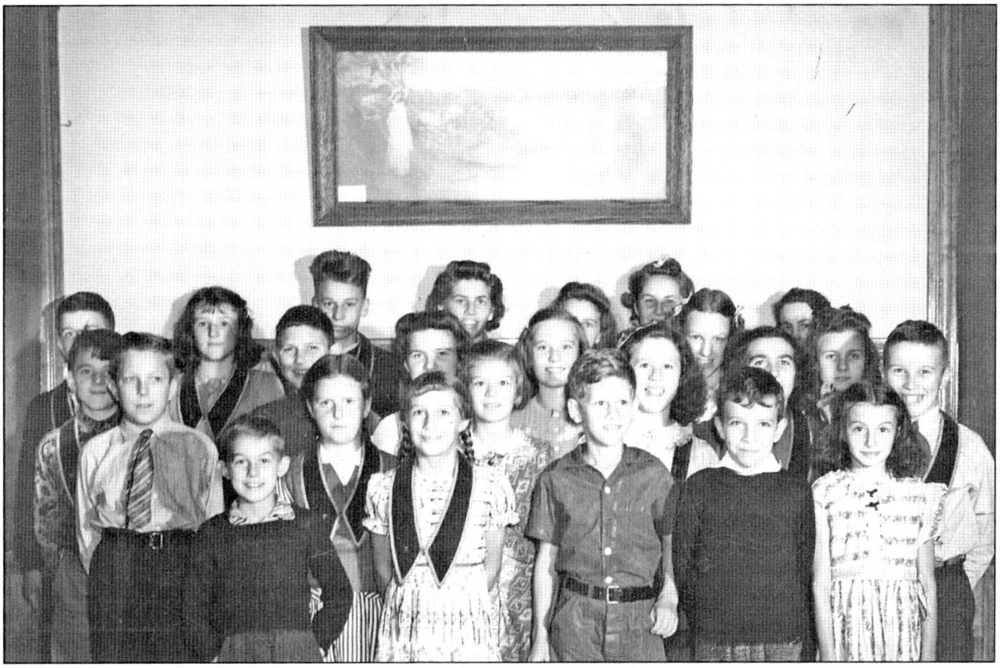

Osceola Juvenile Grange was organized in 1928. These children were members in 1938. From left to right are (first row) Ray Sellingham, Eleanor McCoy, Willis Merrill, Darwin McCoy, and Marie Laduc; (second row) Bernard Estabrook, unidentified, Lois Kezer, Marilyn Moulton, Ruth Morrison, and Britain Potter; (third row) Harry Cheney, unidentified, Myrtle Downing, Barbara Willey, Joyce Saunders, and Aurelia Rodgers: (fourth row) unidentified, Nancy Curtis, Horace Croft, Betty O'Hearn, unidentified, Beverly Sellingham, and unidentified. Meetings were held in the hall over the store, now known as the Campton Cupboard.

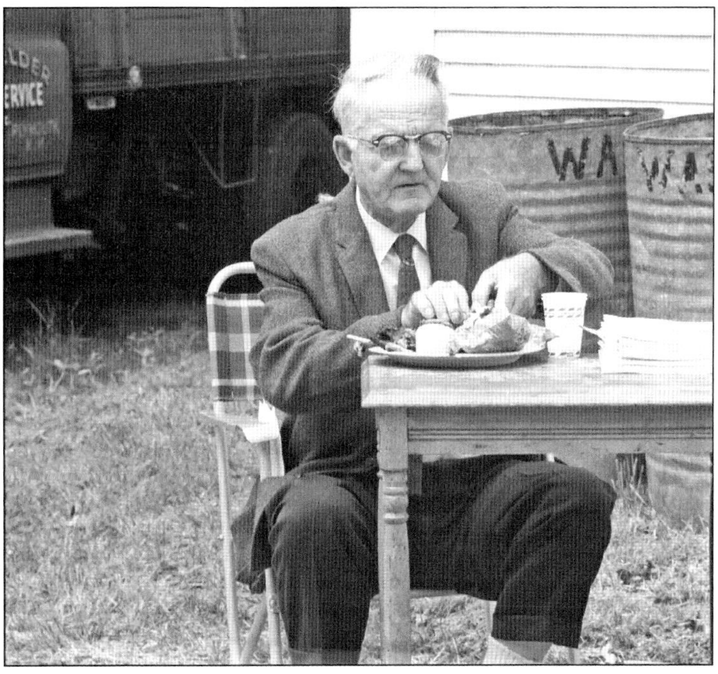

Sterle Cheney served as town clerk from 1956 through 1977 and also served as town treasurer from 1954 until 1980. His humor and genial personality lightened the atmosphere of many a town meeting. An appreciation night was held for Sterle on May 12, 1976, in the Campton Baptist Church vestry. Here, he is seen enjoying lunch at the 1967 Campton Bicentennial.

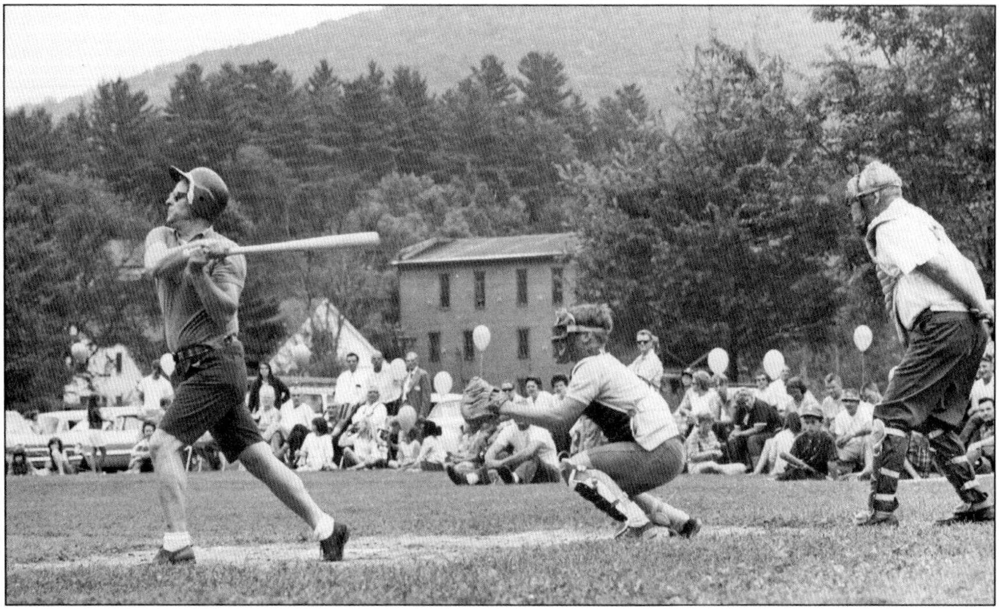

Baseball was a popular sport in Campton and Beebe River for both players and spectators. Roger Brown is at bat, Brad McCormack is the catcher, and Grant Chayer is the umpire in this photograph.

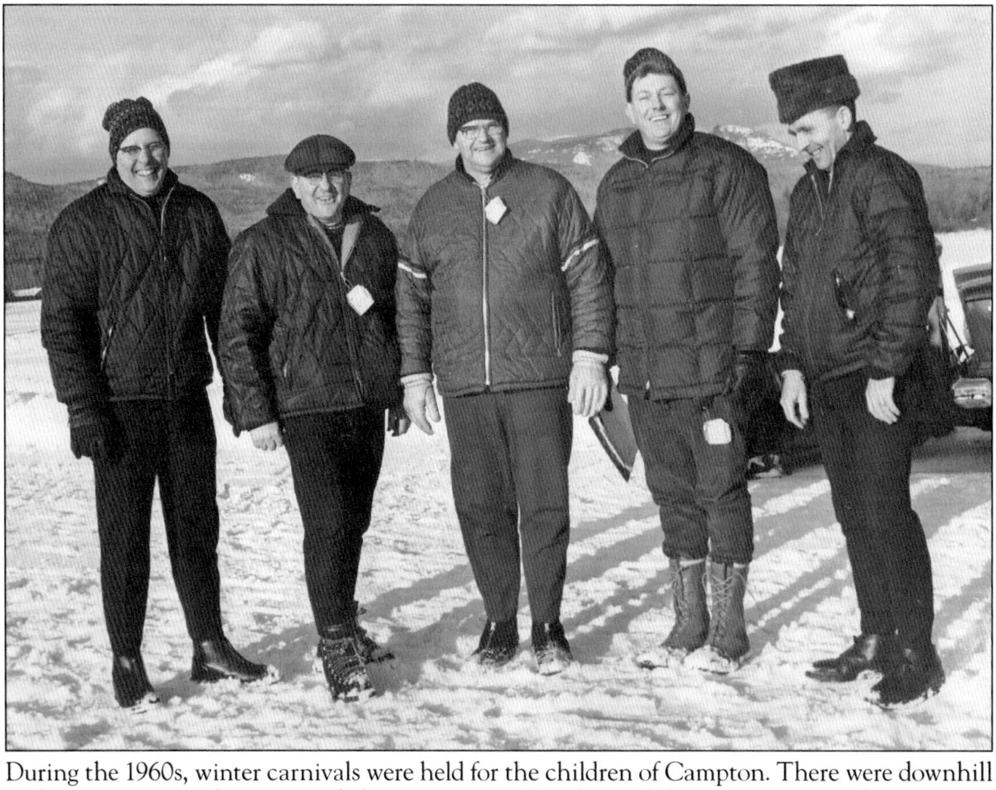

During the 1960s, winter carnivals were held for the children of Campton. There were downhill and cross-country ski races and skating events. Members of the winter carnival committee seen here are, from left to right, Roger Brown, John Dole, Dan Downey, John Mayhew, and Harry Cheney.

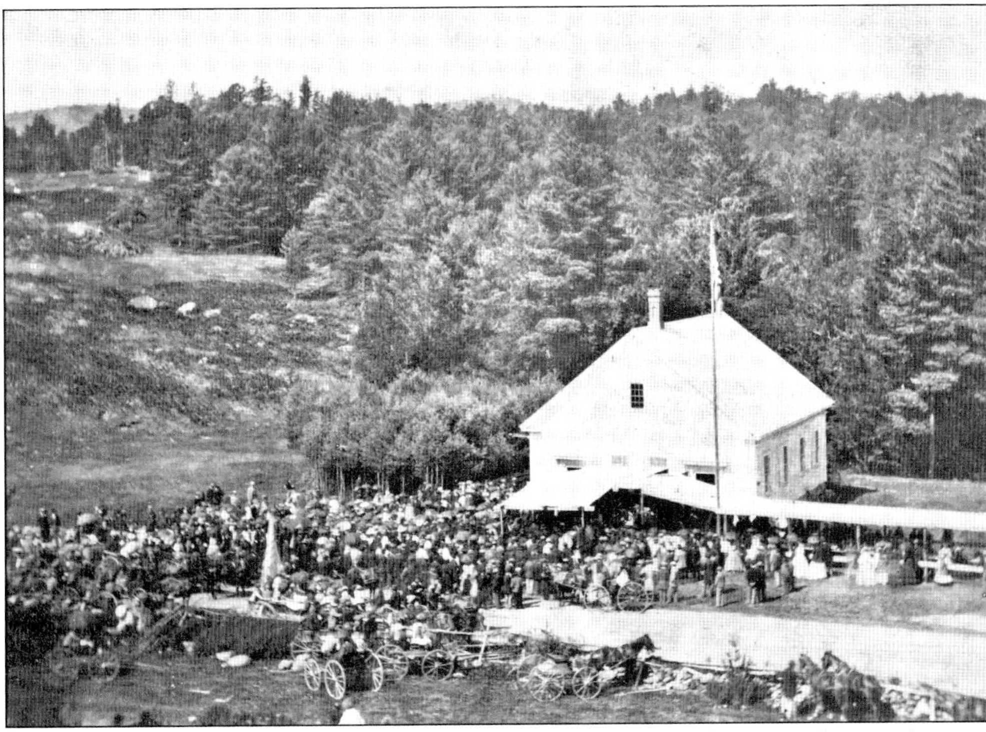

The 1867 Centennial Celebration shows the people of Campton gathering at the town house to celebrate 100 years of incorporation.

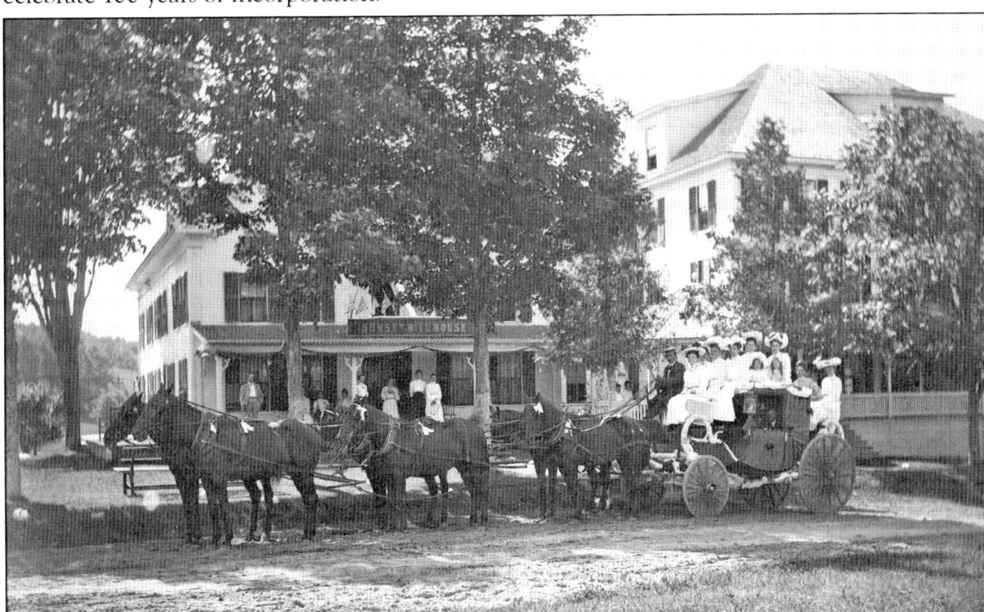

A stagecoach and six ready horses rest in front of the Sunset Hill House in Campton, waiting to take part in a parade in celebration of Old Home Week in 1905. Old Home Week is best described as a Campton reunion that honors its history and celebrates its citizens past, present, and future.

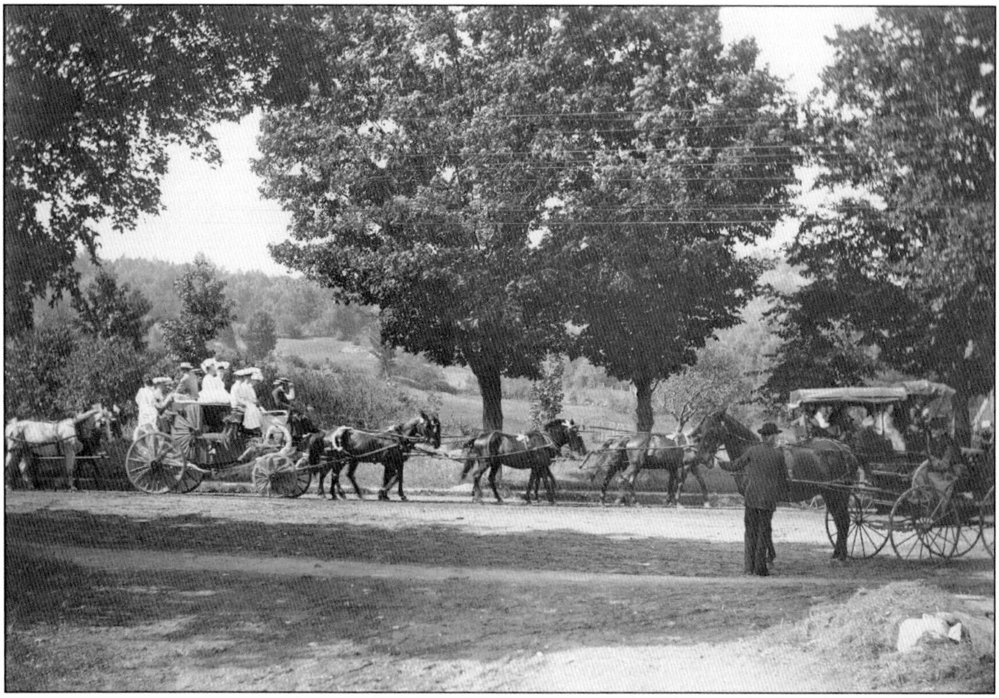

The old stagecoach was originally used as the main mode of transportation between Plymouth and Woodstock before the Pemigewasset Valley Railroad was built. Here, the stagecoach is part of the 1905 Old Home Week celebration.

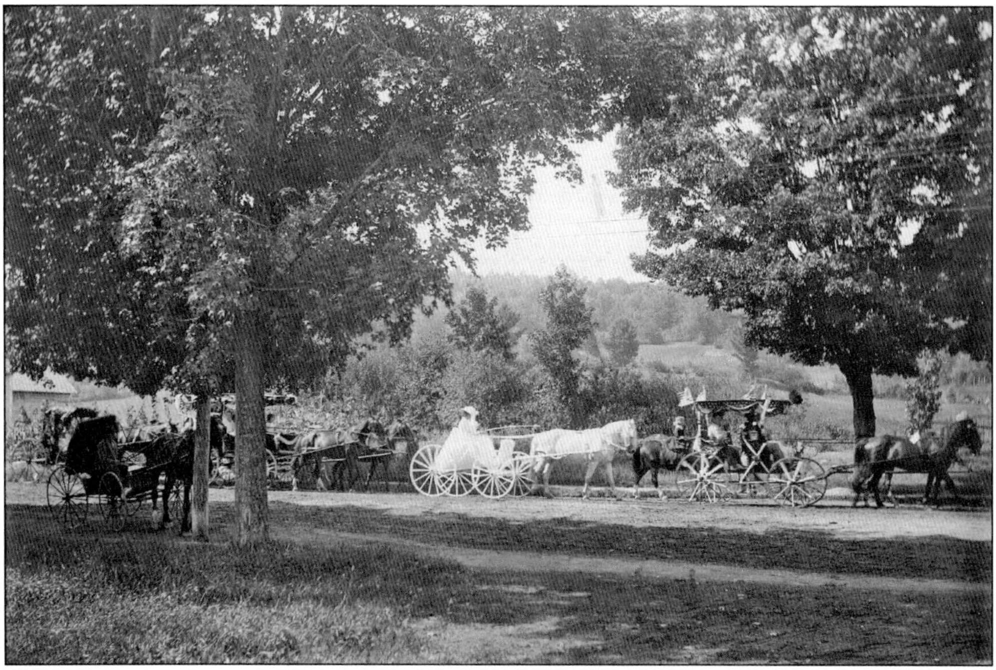

Moody Dole's carriage is in the lead, with horses Millie and Nellie. Olive Dole is riding Old John, a horse belonging to Webb and George Little. The white horse and carriage carrying Florence Russell and Edna Fisher in this 1905 Old Home Week parade appear to be an angelic apparition.

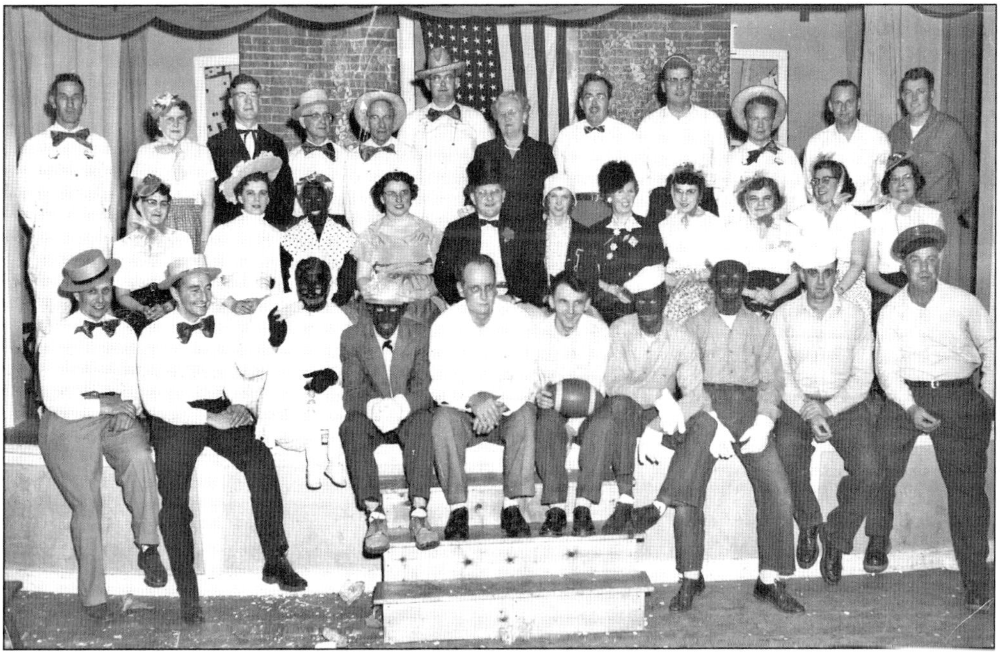

The minstrel shows of the 1950s were great fun for all. Today, minstrel shows are considered racially insensitive and offensive, but they are part of American history. From left to right are (first row) Lewis Hill, Bob Little, Roger Brown, Larry Thompson, Burt Pierce, Harry Cheney, Russell Sargeant, Larry Chayer, Chet Amos, and Holly Willard; (second row) Simone Little, Olive Hill, Joyce Mayhew, Christine Dole, John Dole, Shirley Downey, Mildred Uhlman, Veronica Cate, Alice Willard, Charlotte Roberts, and Jane Pierce; (third row) Mort Uhlman, Evelyn Ouellet, Charles Ouellet, Irving Brown, Dick Bean, Tubby Steele, Mayma Pierce, Phil Roberts, Pascoe Roberts, Red Anderson, Danny Downey, and John Mayhew.

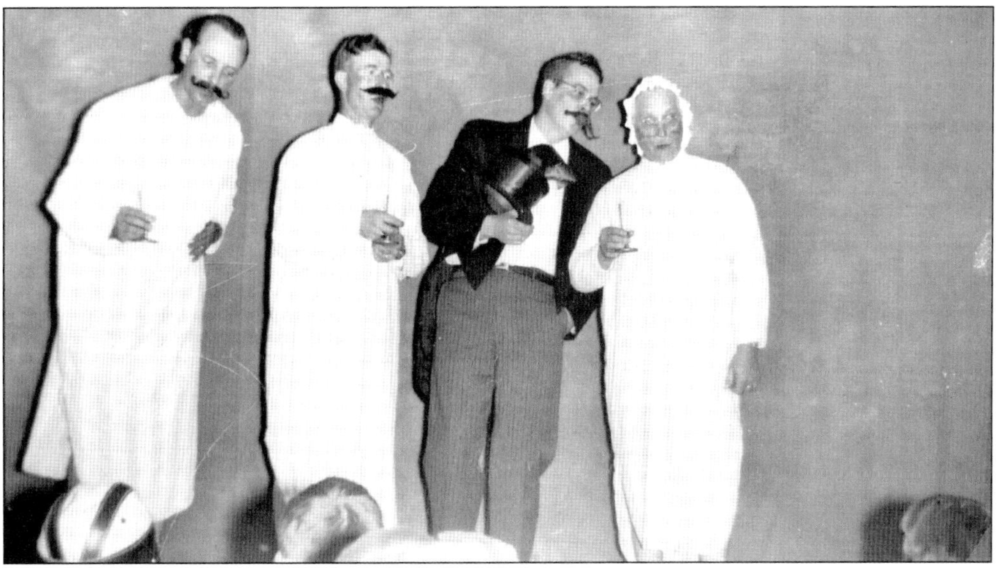

Burt Pierce, who was the main spark plug behind the organization and production of the minstrel shows, always enjoyed hamming it up with his fellow players. Shown here are, from left to right, Pierce, Charlie Ouellet, Pascoe Roberts, and Irving Brown.

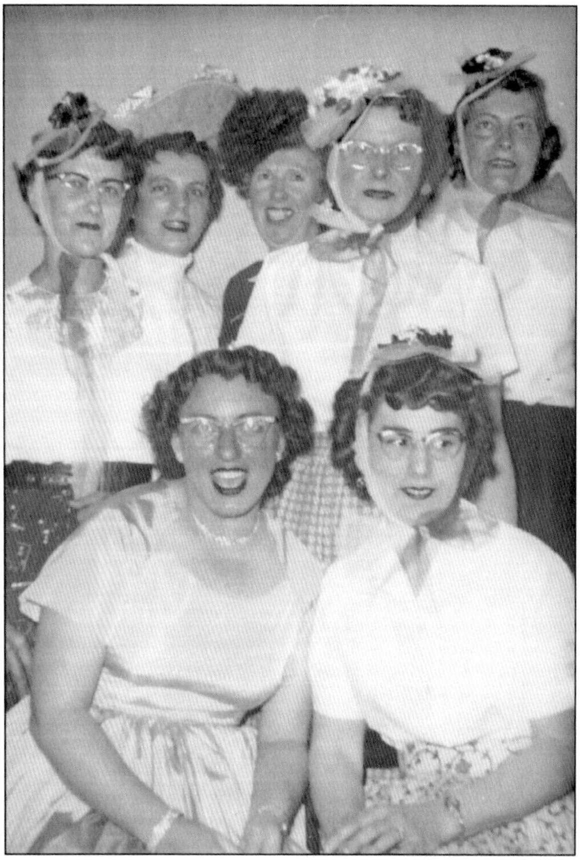

There was never a shortage of talented ladies to sing and dance in the minstrel shows. Pictured here are, from left to right, (first row) Christine Dole and Veronica Cate; (second row) Simone Little, Olive Hill, Mildred Uhlman, Evelyn Ouellet, and Jane Pierce.

In 1955, Pres. Dwight D. Eisenhower, on his way to Lincoln with his chief of staff, Sherman Adams, was persuaded to cut the ribbon to open the Pemigewasset National Bank and the Plymouth Guarantee Savings Bank. People of Campton lined up along Route 3, near Blair Bridge, to get a glimpse of President Eisenhower.

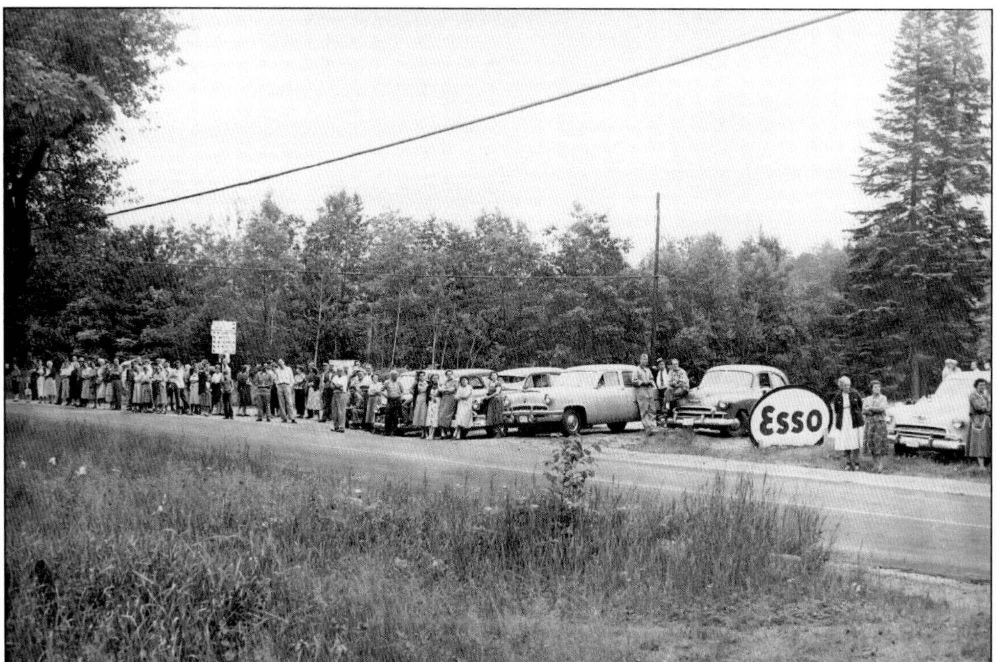

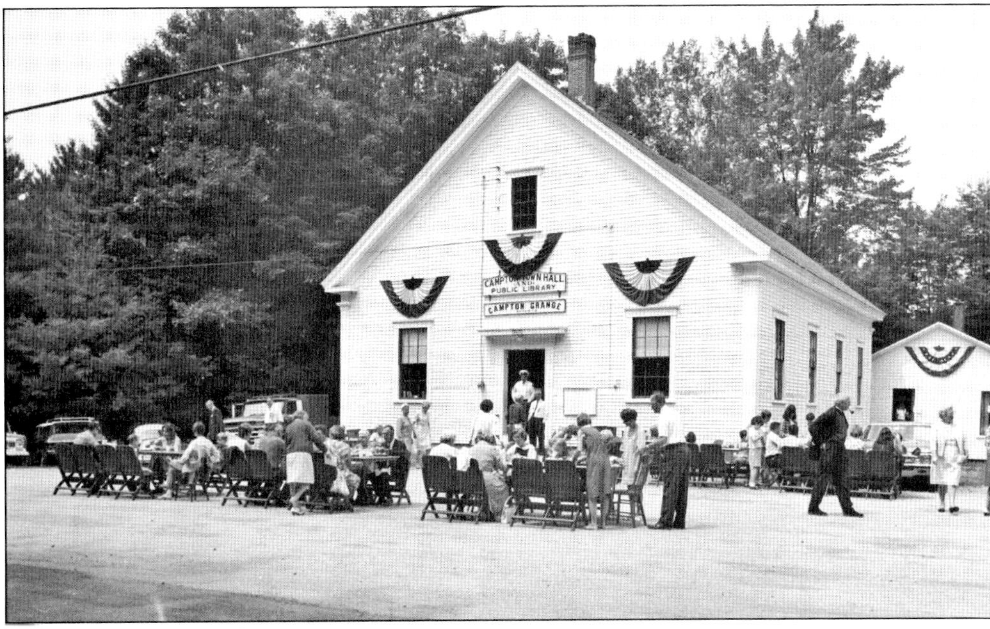

The 1967 Bicentennial Celebration took place at the Campton Town Hall, Public Library, and Grange Hall in Campton Hollow.

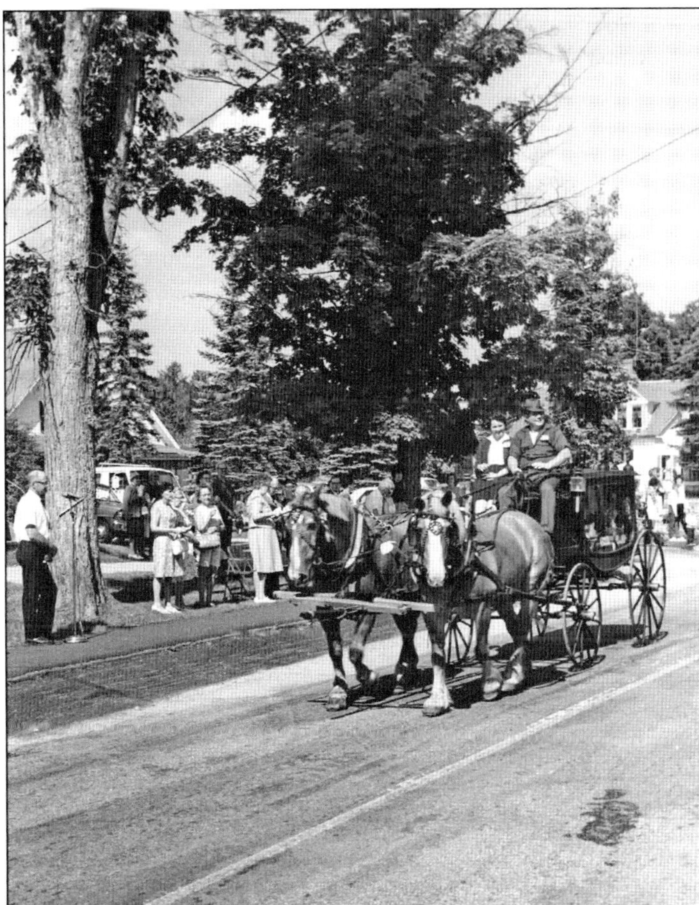

Harold Avery Jr., accompanied by Mildred Avery, drove the Campton Town Funeral Coach in the 1967 Bicentennial Parade.

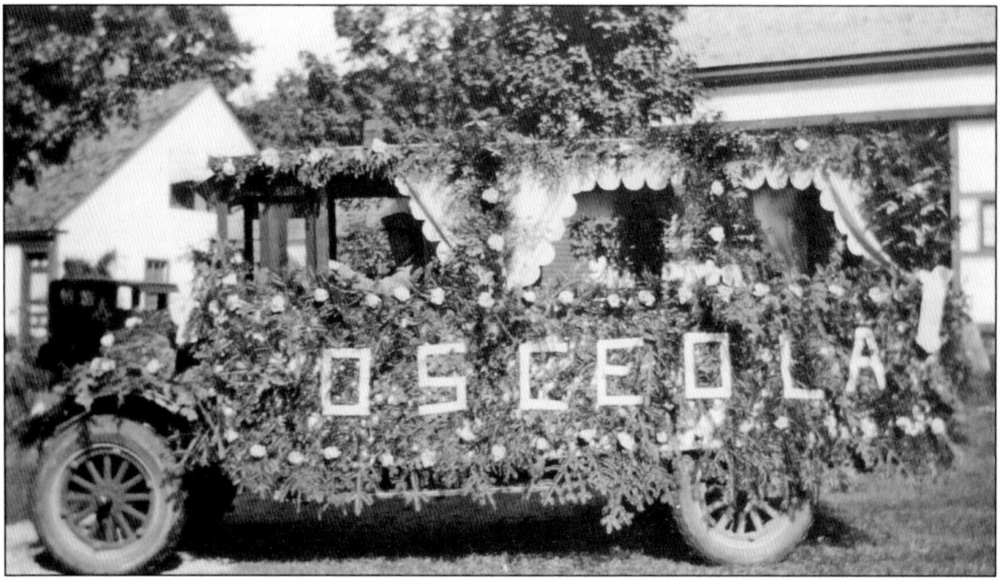

Osceola Grange participated in a parade with this very interesting float pictured around the 1920s and decked out in fir branches and roses.

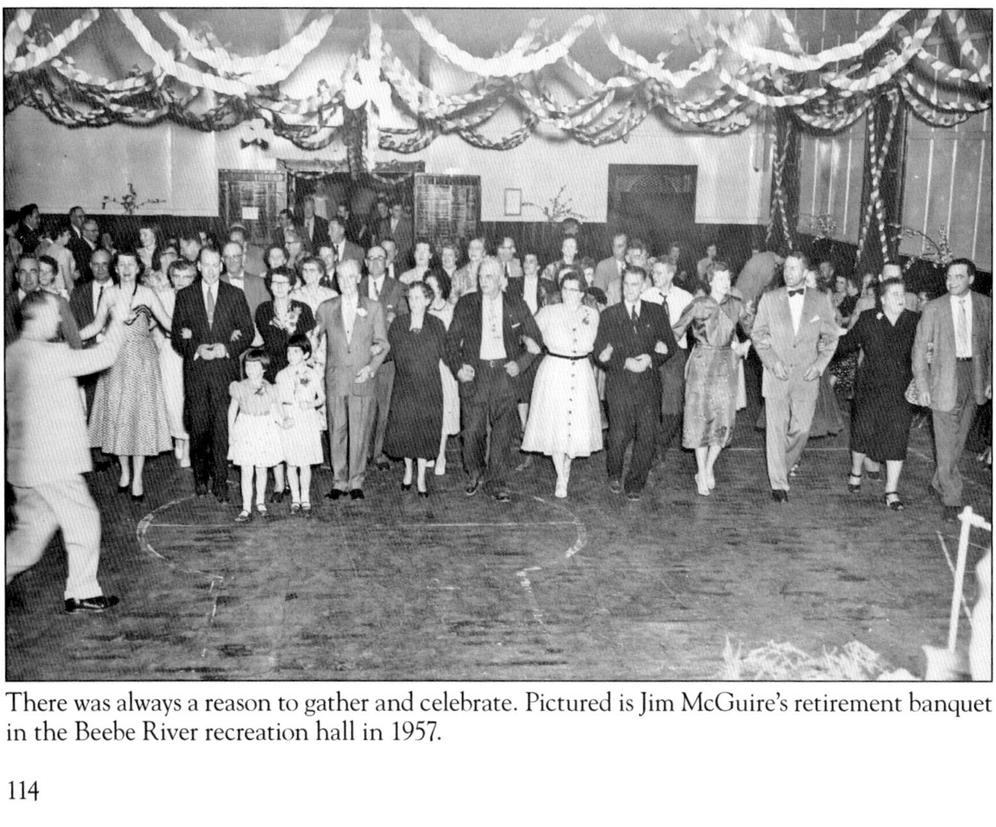

There was always a reason to gather and celebrate. Pictured is Jim McGuire's retirement banquet in the Beebe River recreation hall in 1957.

Ten

Bygone Buildings

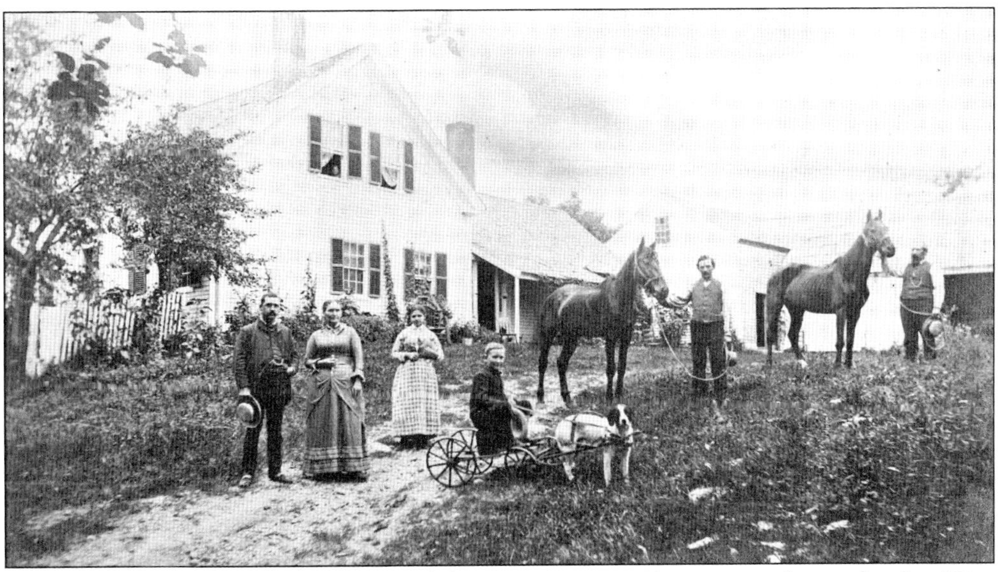

The Cook-Hill Farm, one of several Cook farms in Campton Bog, was on the north side of Bog Road. In 1880, at the time of this picture, it was owned by Samuel French Hill. The house burned down around 1970. From left to right are Henry Smith, Lucy G. Hill, an unidentified summer worker, Fred Hill, an unidentified summer worker, and Samuel F. Hill.

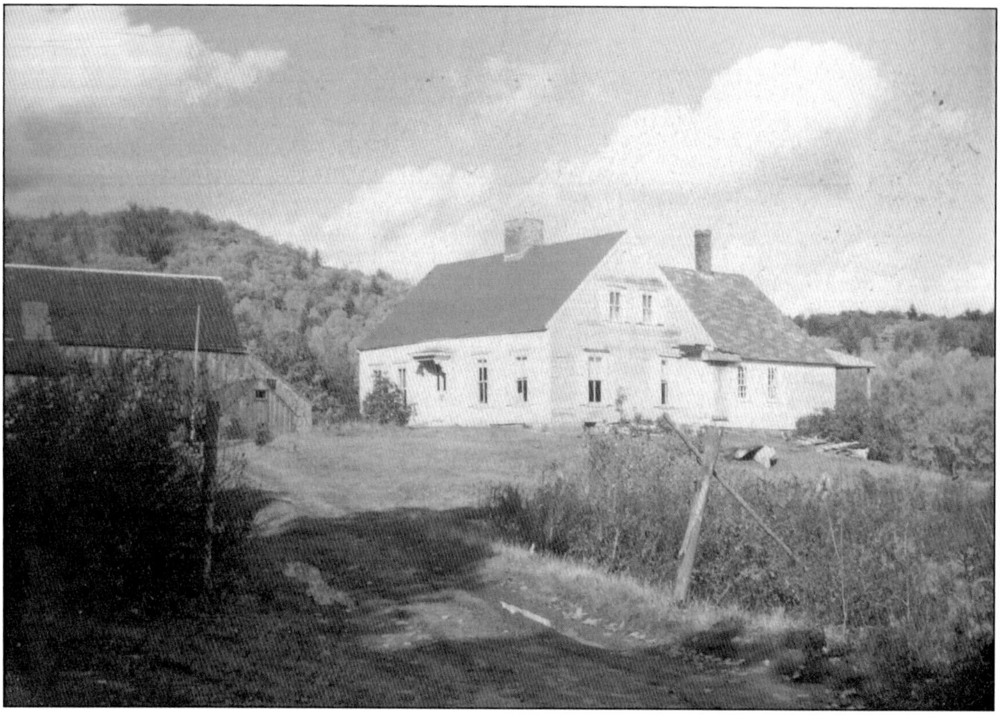

The Marsh-Page House was on Page Road at Eastern Corners. The uncle of Sylvester Marsh, the founder of the Mount Washington Cog Railway, owned this farm in the early 1800s. Sylvester grew up on a nearby farm.

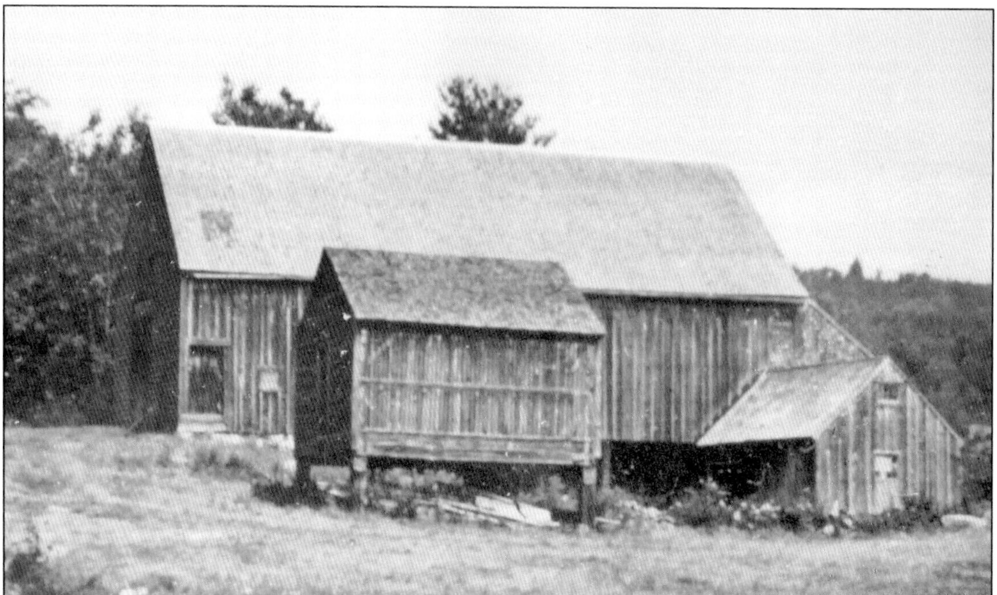

The Marsh-Page Barn (built around 1790) is one of the few remaining hand-hewn timber barns in Campton. In the foreground is the corncrib, sitting on top of four granite posts. The corncrib continued to be an essential farm building well into the 20th century. This corncrib and other outbuildings are no longer standing, but the barn is still standing tall.

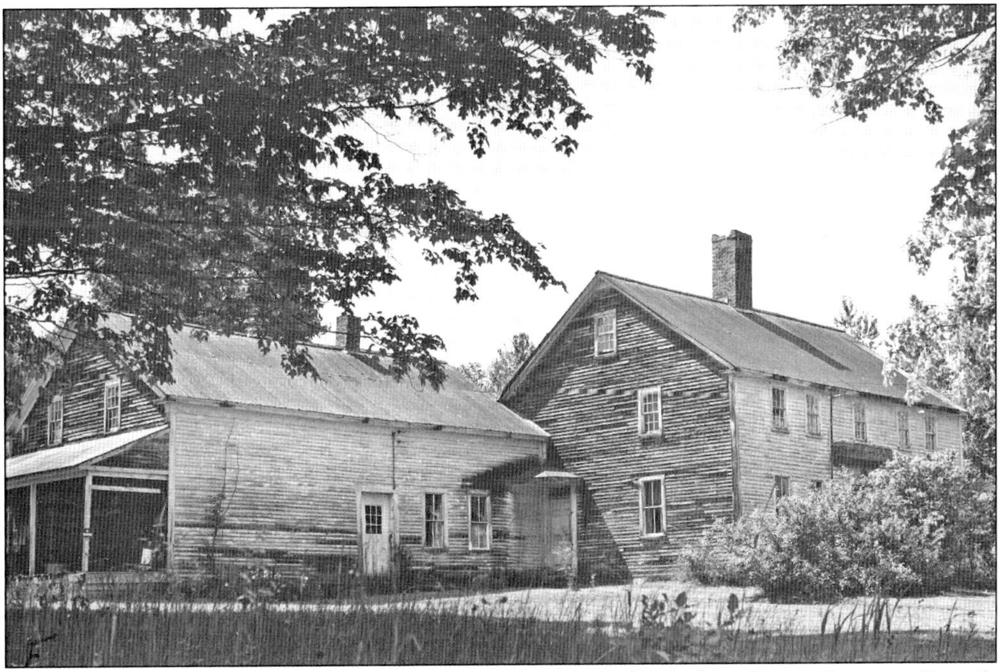

The Spokesfield House, in West Campton, once stood north of where Route 3 crosses Branch Brook, on the west side of the road.

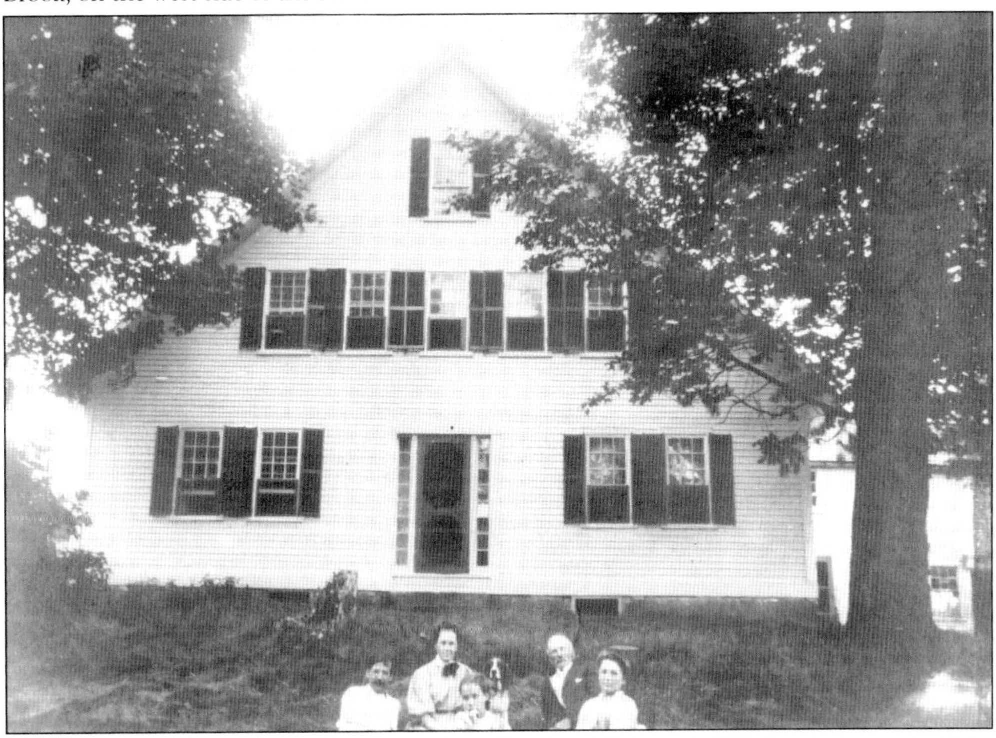

The White Mountain Orchard was on Mason Road, off Ellsworth Hill Road. It was the Kelly family residence when they operated the White Mountain Orchard. The house was torn down in the late 20th century.

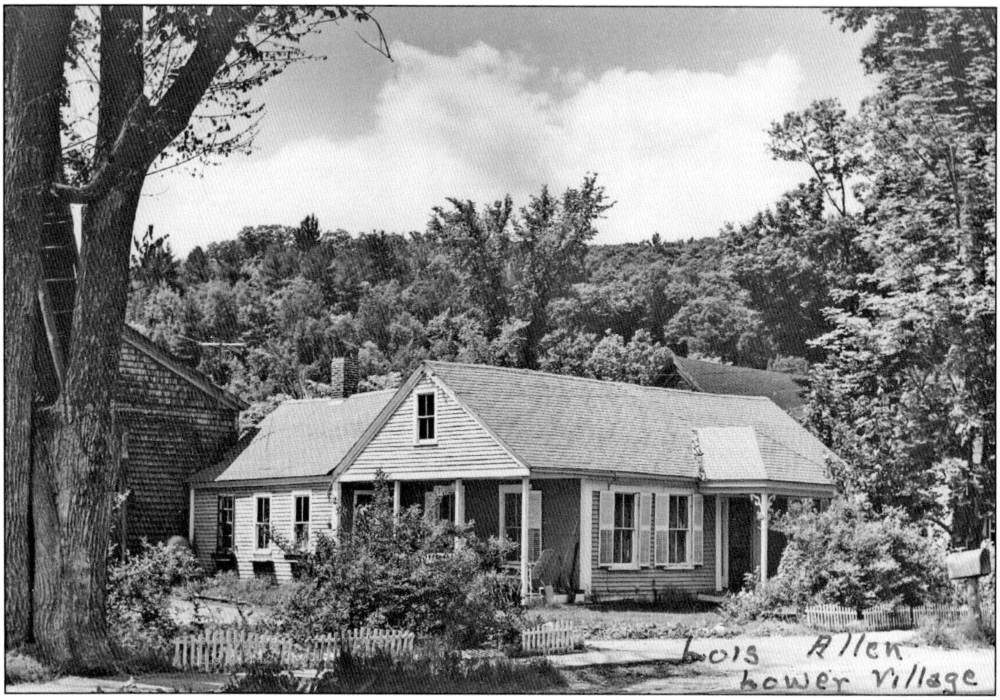

Believed to have been one of the oldest houses in town, the Herting House was on Route 175 in the Lower Village, near the old bridge that crossed the Mad River.

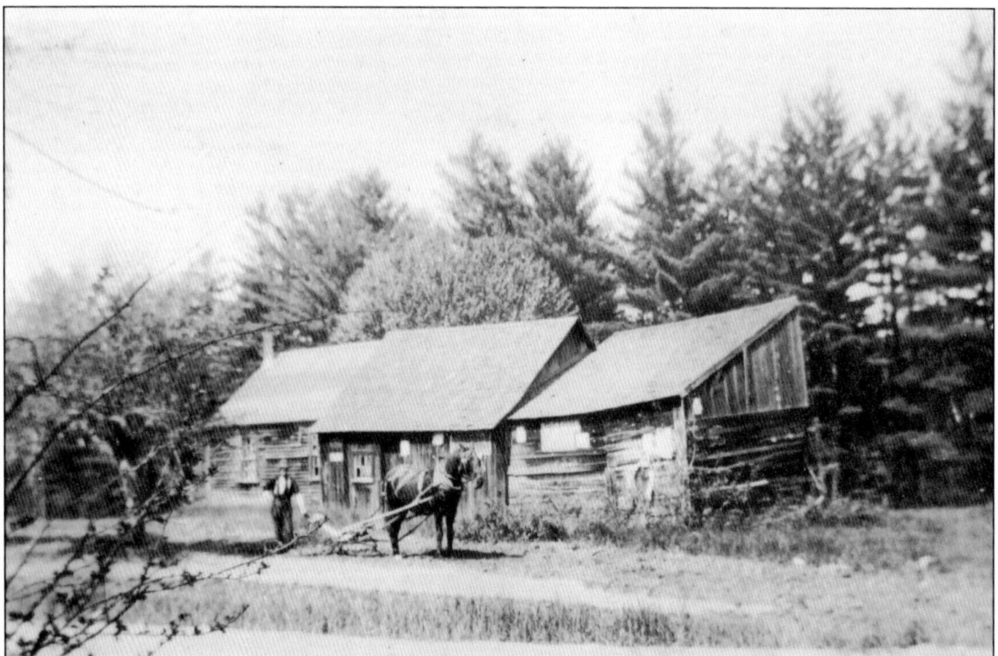

The Merrill-Cass House was on Route 3 in Blair, just south of Cook's Corner. Charles Merrill and his horse, Ned, are in the yard. The house was torn down in the early 21st century, and the barn was reconstructed on another nearby site.

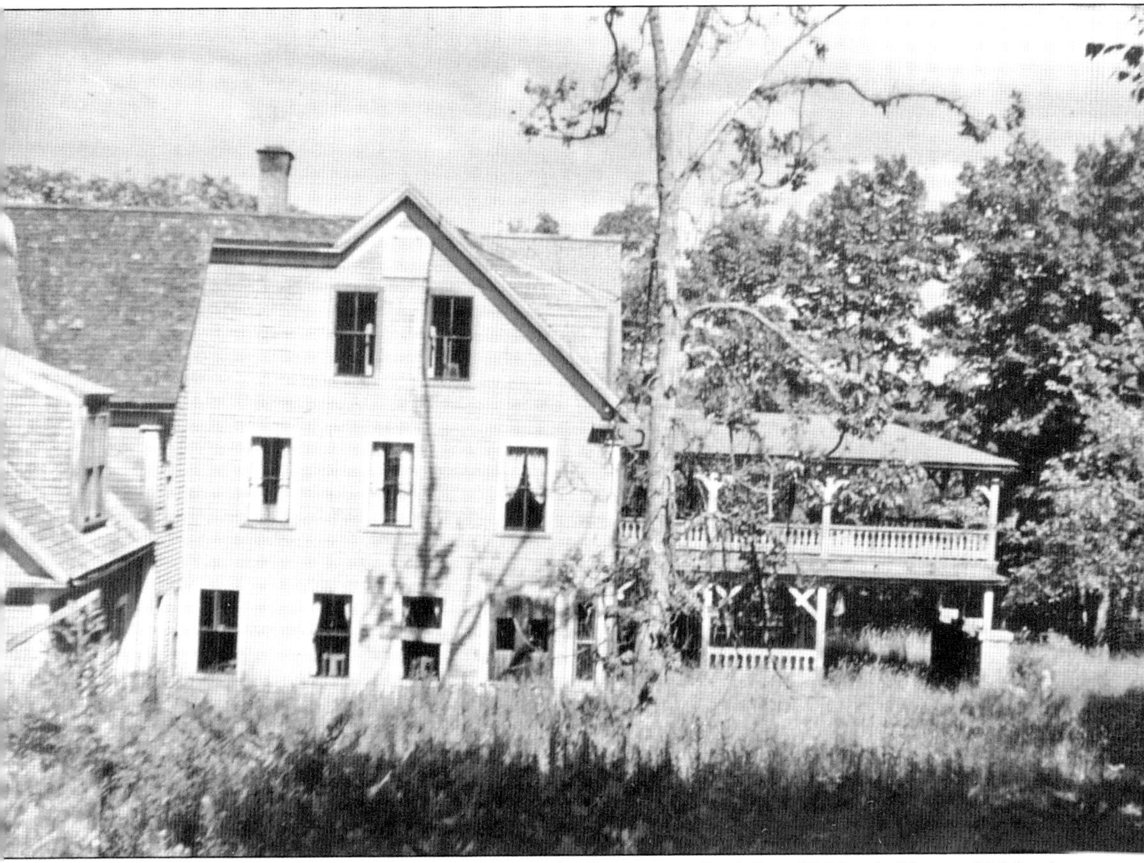

Butternut Farm, on Chandler Hill Road, was also known as the Mary Hildreth House. Hildreth adopted 11 children who were orphans or had come from broken homes and also provided foster care for many others. She held Christmas and birthday parties for her children, and well into the late 20th century, there were local people who fondly remembered being invited to these parties (see page 53).

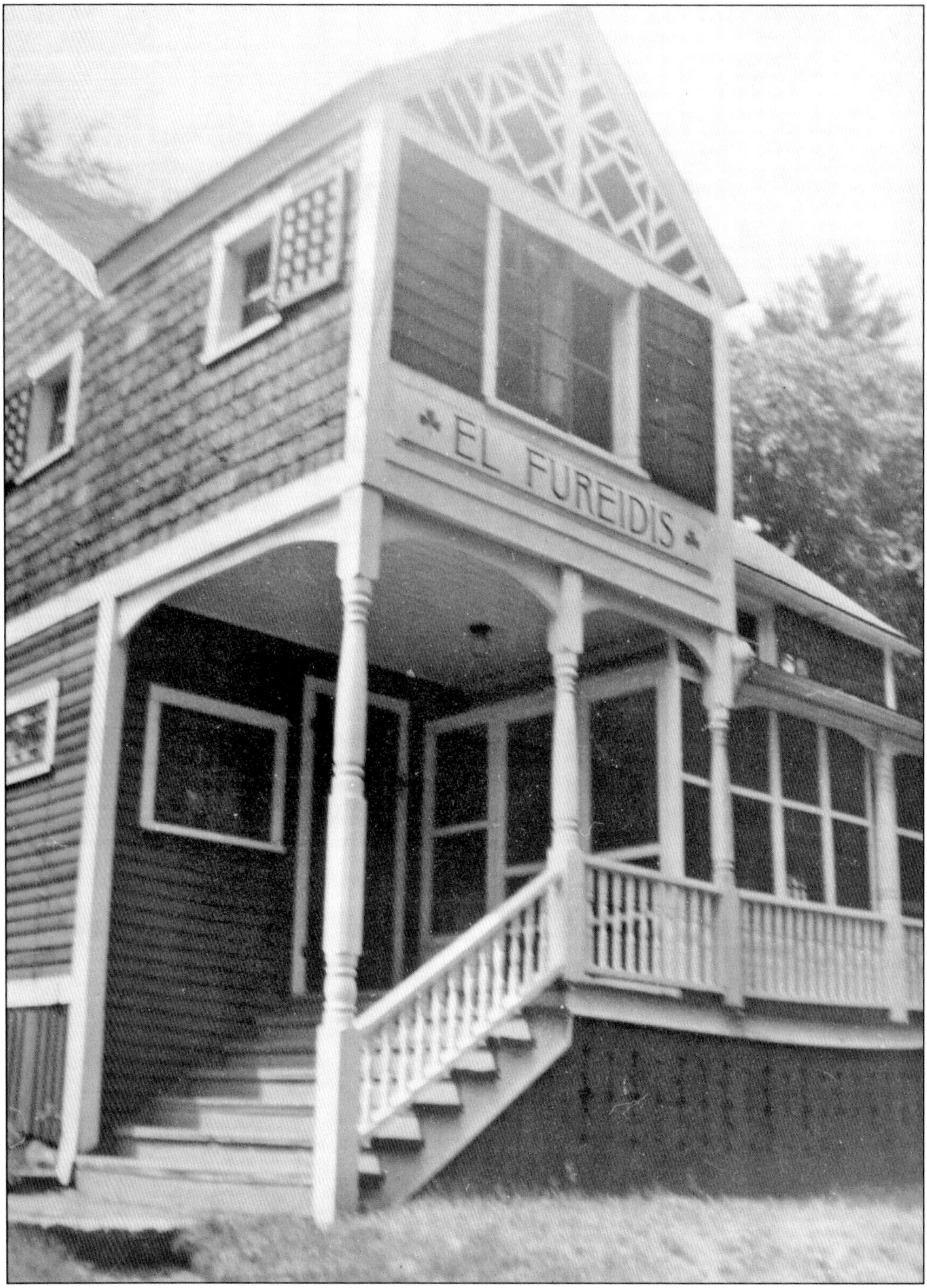

El Fureidis (meaning "Little Paradise" in Arabic) was one of three houses designed by F. Schuyler Mathews, a well-known local artist and naturalist of the late 19th and early 20th centuries. The three houses were located just north of where the Days Inn is today. El Fureidis, the summer home of the Mathews family, and one other house were taken down when I-93 was built. The remaining house is still standing on the south, dead-end section of Town Pound Road.

Blair Railroad Station stood on the south side of Blair Road, near the covered bridge, between the tracks and the river. The cement foundation can still be seen beside the road and tracks. Area students as late as the 1920s took the train from Blair to Plymouth to attend high school. The building was torn down and the materials used to build a house on Route 175 in Campton.

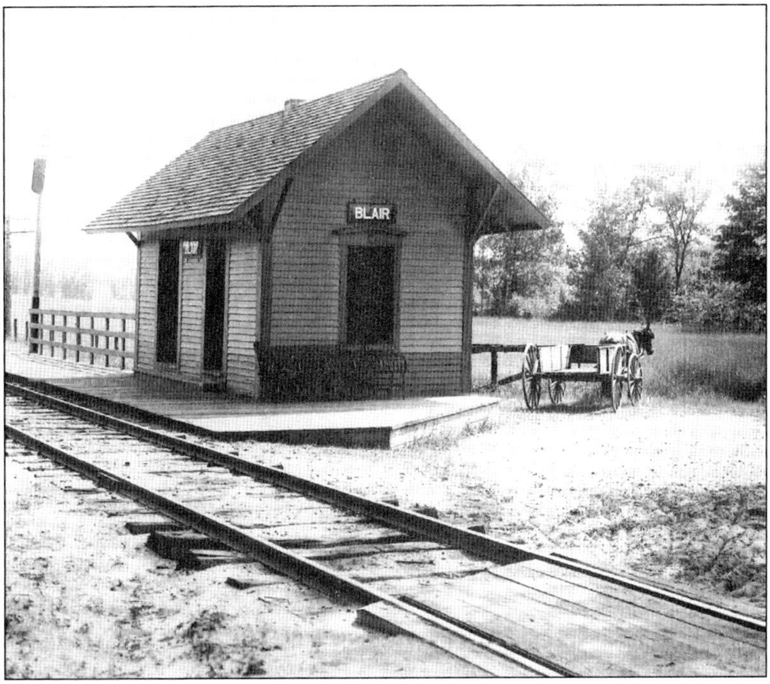

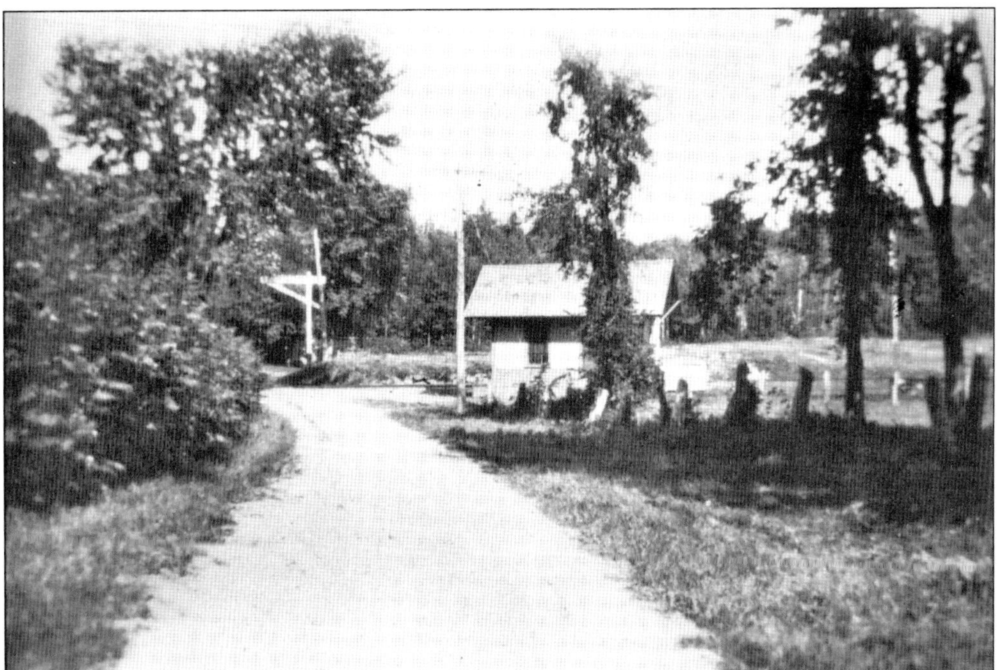

This picture of the Blair Railroad Station was taken from the Blair Covered Bridge. The station was on the east side of the Pemigewasset River.

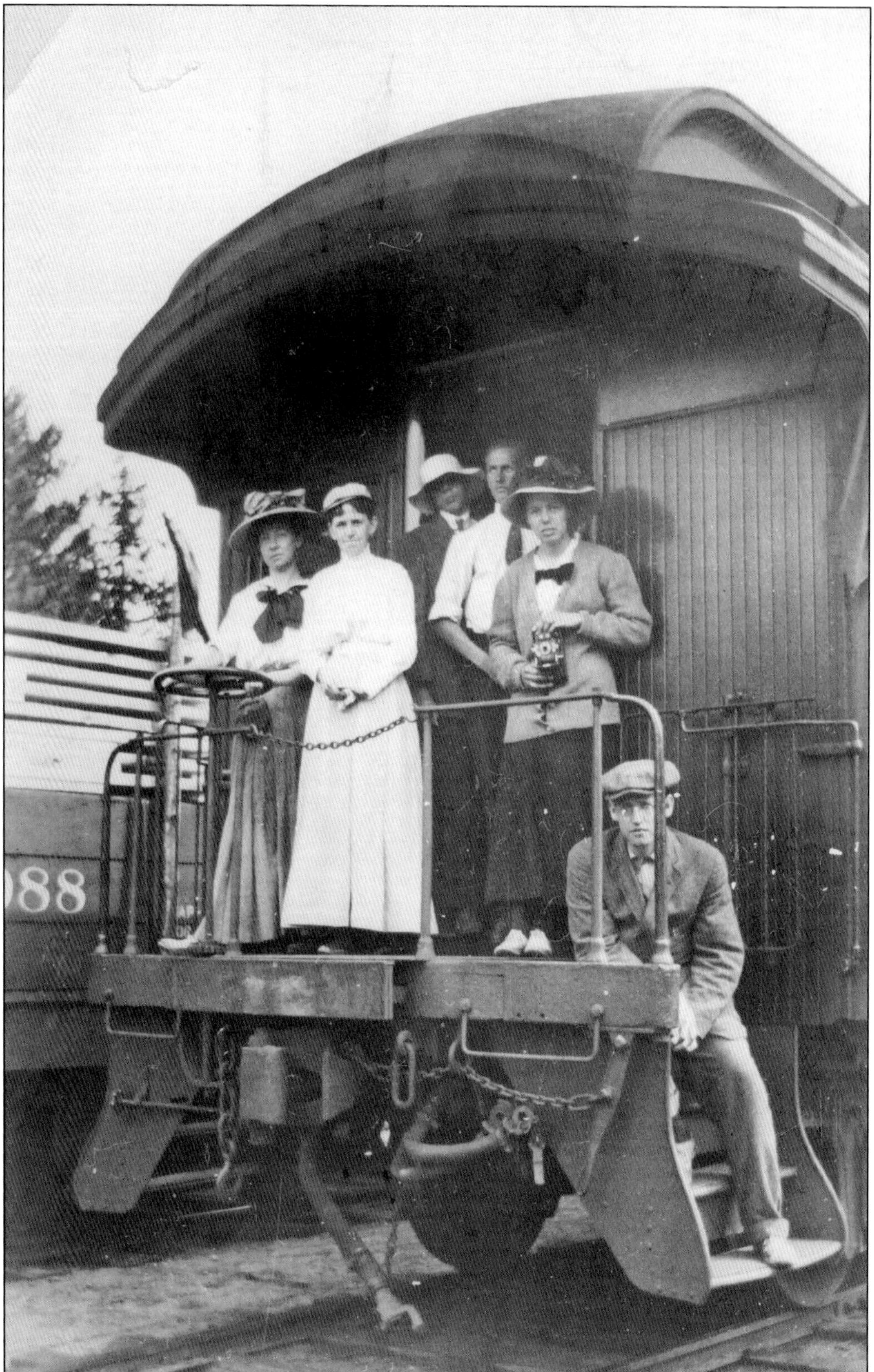

This 1890s picture shows passengers departing the Blair Station. More than likely, these passengers had been staying at Blair House. Several men living in this section of town would meet the train with wagons to take women and luggage to the hotels. The male guests frequently walked behind the wagons.

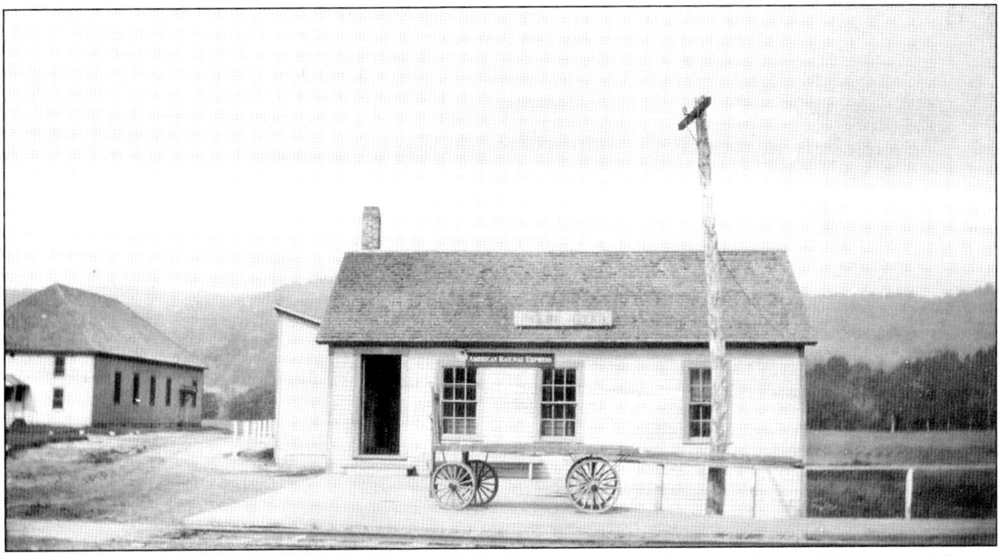

Beebe River Railroad Station would have been a busy station when the Parker Young and, later, Draper Corporation manufacturers were in full operation. In those years, the village of Beebe River housed approximately 250 people.

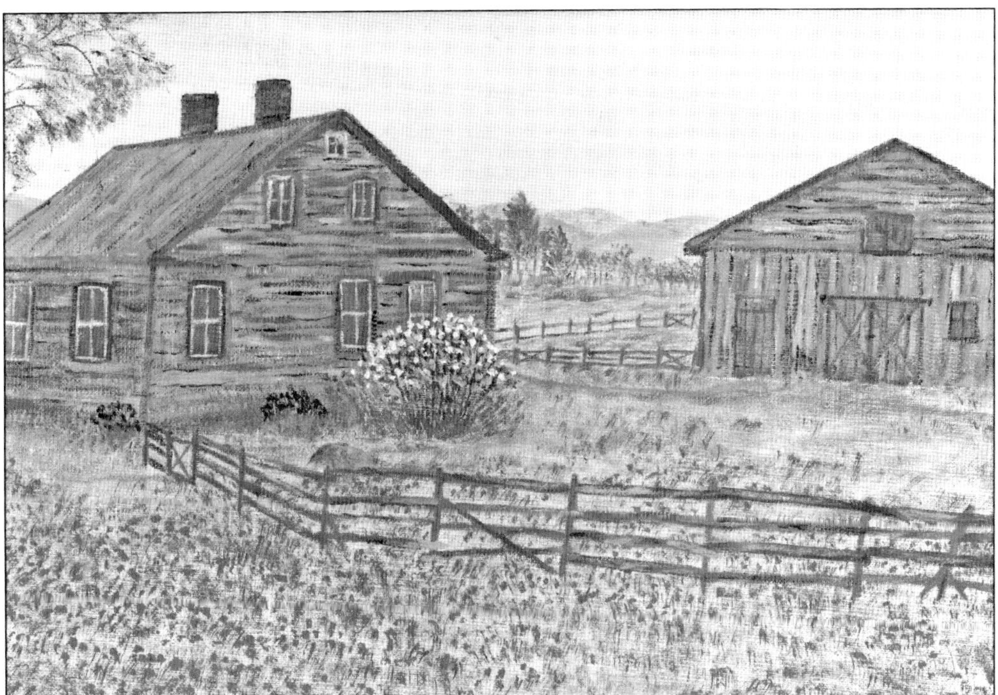

The Herman Avery Farm stood on Armont Hill on the Ellsworth Road, at the height of land. Hermie was the last of the family to occupy the old house. This painting, by local artist and selectman Max Haley, hangs in the Campton Historical Society building.

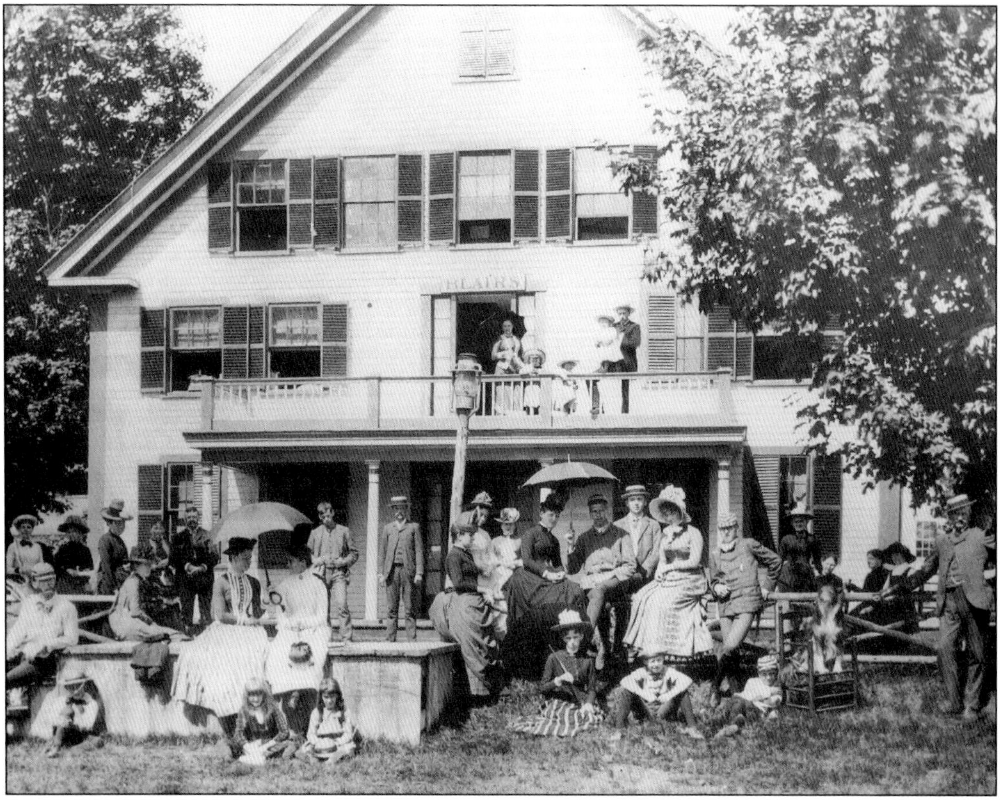

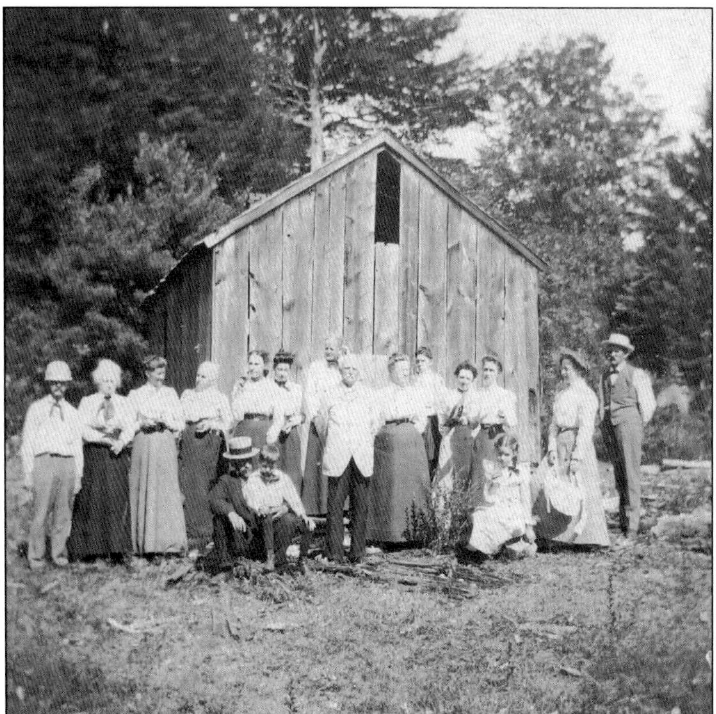

Blair House is shown as it looked in the late 1890s. Artist F. Schuyler Mathews is seated on the far left, and Joseph Coleman Blair, the proprietor of the hotel, is leaning on the fence on the far right. Notice the carriage block on which the two women are sitting; it was used to help women disembark from coaches.

The Blair Sugar House was located behind the hotel at the base of Round Mountain in the maple grove. During sugaring season, it was the scene of many sugaring-off parties. This party was hosted by F. Schuyler Mathews.

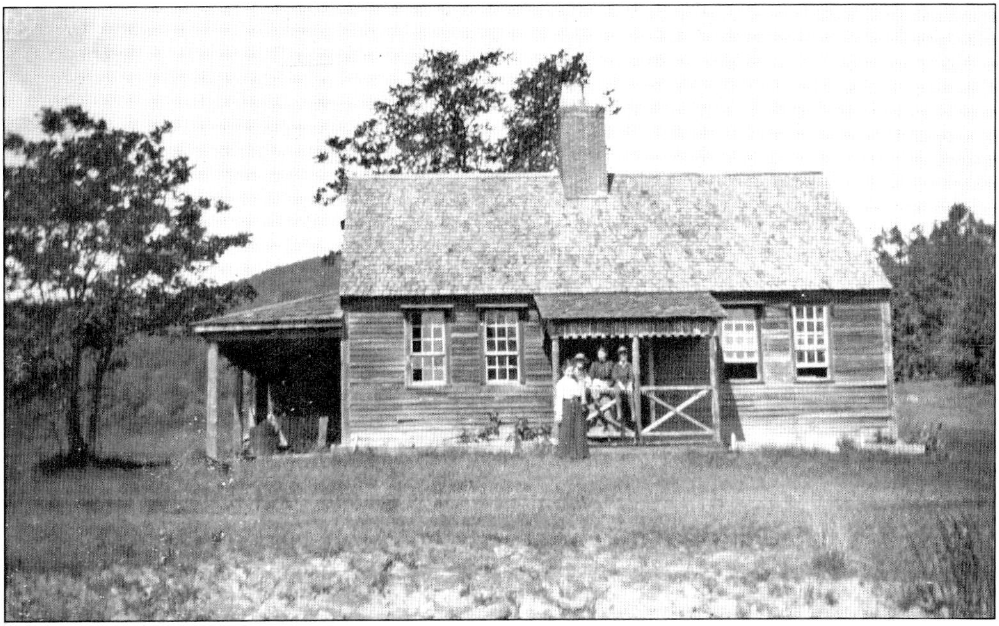

The Pelican was originally on the Judge Livermore Trail, which ran to the west of today's US Forest Service parking lot. The house was moved to the Blair property on Route 3 in the 1840s. A pelican was painted on one side of the kitchen mantel and an owl on the other side. This house was taken down by Robert Brayman, a member of the Blair family, in the early 1960s to make way for I-93.

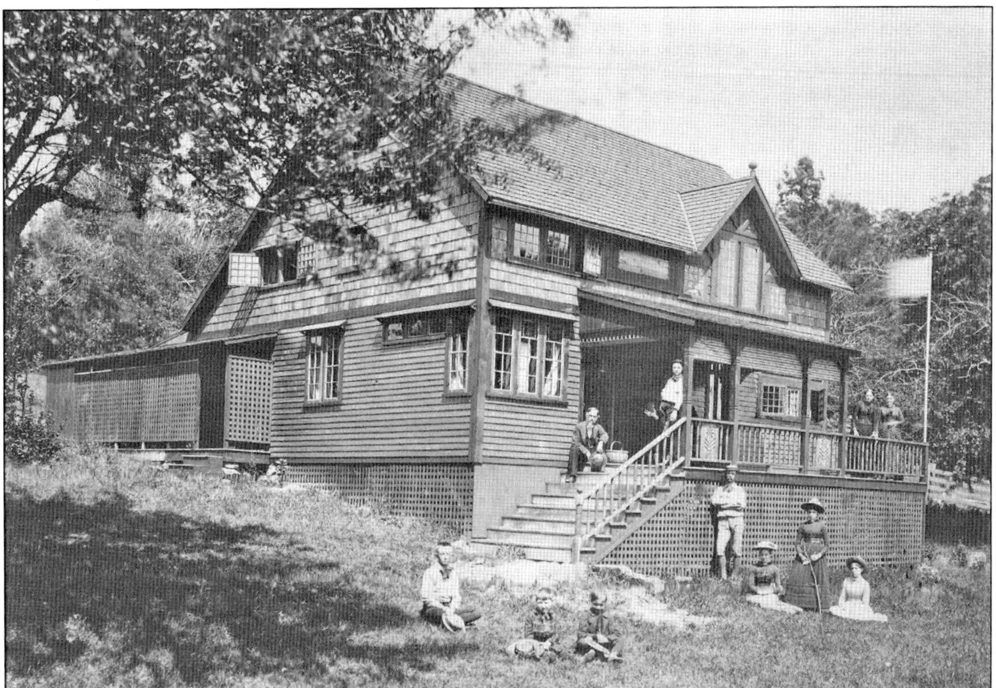

Built in 1884, the Victorian Cottage was the first of three cottages designed by F. Schuyler Mathews. It burned in 1893, and a second cottage was built the same year.

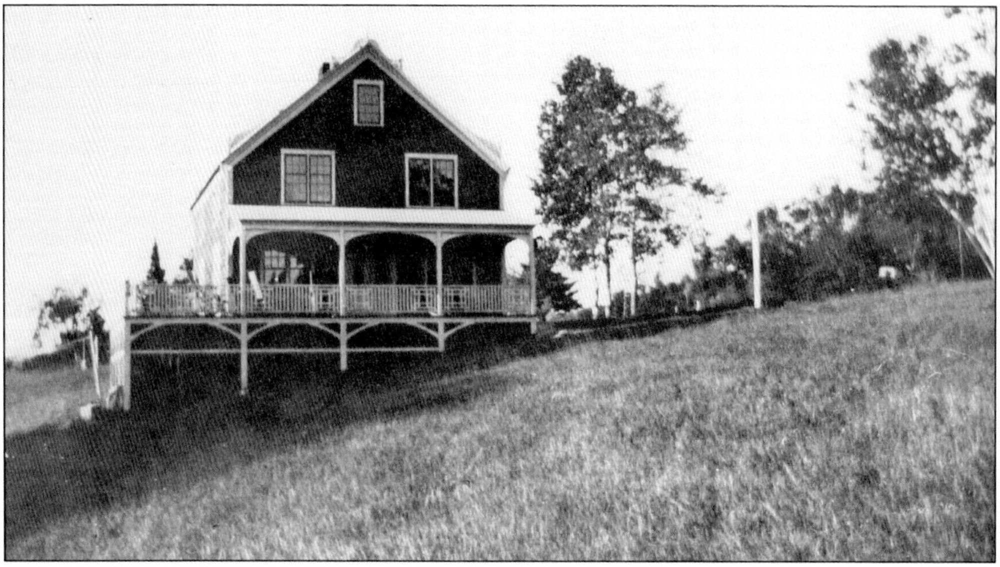

Gladstone Cottage stood on the east side of Route 3 near the Pemigewasset River. It was designed by F. Schuyler Mathews and was across the road from Blair House. The cottage was torn down in the 1960s when I-93 went through Campton.

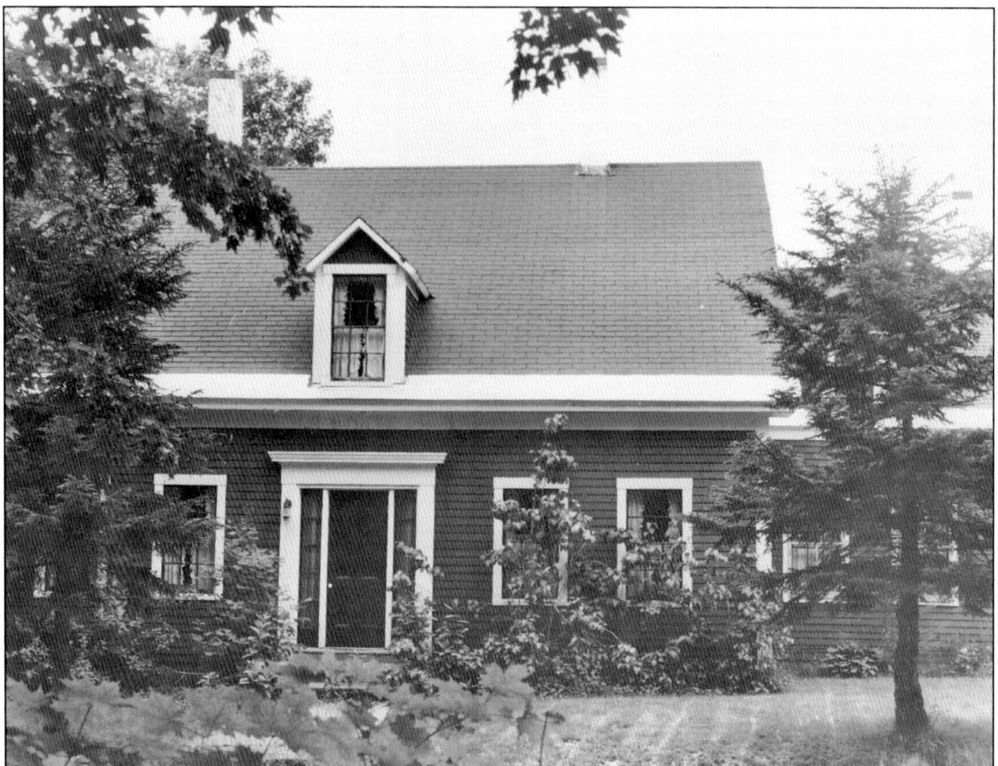

The Morgan House stood on Pulsifer Hill Road before it burned in the 1980s. A fire truck from a neighboring town, responding to the fire, parked so close to the burning building that the paint blistered on the front of the truck.

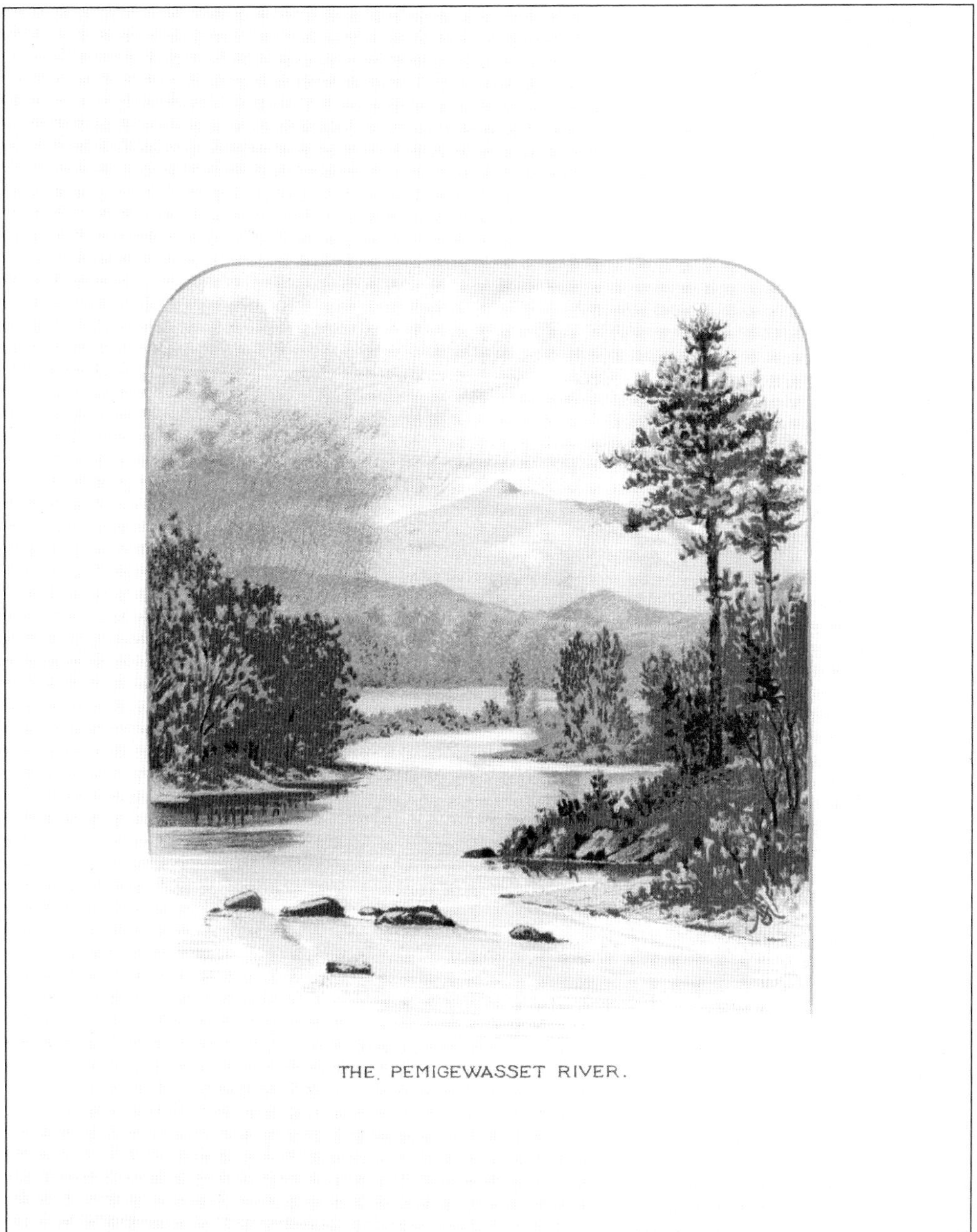

The Pemigewasset River was painted by local artist F. Schuyler Mathews in the 1890s.

Consistent with our mission to preserve history on a local level, this book was printed in South Carolina on American-made paper and manufactured entirely in the United States. Products carrying the accredited Forest Stewardship Council (FSC) label are printed on 100 percent FSC-certified paper.

MADE IN THE USA